With best wishes
for many years
of quality living

William Shepherd

Quality Living

in the

Semicircle of Life

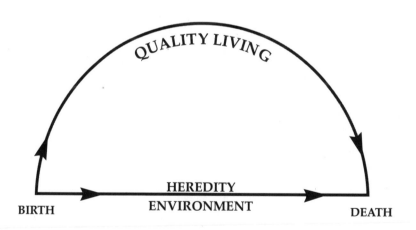

THE PERFECT SEMICIRCLE OF LIFE

Quality Living

in the

Semicircle of Life

William Gefter, M.D.

Rutledge Books, Inc.

Danbury, CT

Front cover photos provided by PhotoDisc

Cover design by John Laub

Interior design by Elena Hartz

Rutledge Books, Inc.
107 Mill Plain Road, Danbury, CT 06811
1-800-278-8533
www.rutledgebooks.com

Manufactured in the United States of America
Quality Living in the Semicircle of Life
    Gefter, M.D. William

    ISBN: 1-58244-155-3

    1. Ethics. 2. Medicine. 3. Life Expectancy. 4. Philosophy.
5. Healthy Living.

Library of Congress Control Number: 2001090790

Dedicated

To the Memory of

Sharon Greene

whose special qualities

will always be remembered

Also by William Gefter, M.D.

Synopsis of Cardiology

FOREWORD

Dr. William Gefter, the ethicist, is an experienced cardiologist, medical writer and hospital executive. He is a teacher of students, a friend to his colleagues and a healer of his patients' minds and bodies. In this book, he has drawn upon a wide variety of scientific facts accumulated in his lifetime of medical practice, reading and reflection. For his reader to use as a guide, he has painted a clear picture of the journey in pursuit of truth and wisdom. Dr. Gefter's scientifically trained mind has analyzed the facts of his personal life experience and then synthesized a coherent theory of the ideal "quality living in the semi-circle of life."

This insightful book will serve as a useful guide to all readers who have taken to heart the words of Socrates to the Athenians: ". . .I say again that the greatest good of man is daily to converse about virtue, and all that concerning which you hear me examining myself and others, and that the life which is unexamined is not worth living. . ." William Gefter's book helps all of us who read it to know that the examined life is worth living!

— Francis Coughlin, M.D., J.D.
President, Association of Yale Alumni in Medicine and
Vice-Chairman, Connecticut Commission on
Medicolegal Investigations

CONTENTS

PREFACE

I have devoted my entire career as a physician for more than sixty years to the improvement of the health of my fellow man in connection with a full-time teaching career in medical schools and in affiliated teaching hospitals.

In recent years, I have turned my attention to lecturing on my life-long and enthusiastic interest in quality living. It is based mainly on the need for everyone's compliance with the altruistic ethical principles that define and govern the ideal behavior of man in society in order to achieve mutual respect and compatible living.

My audiences have been attendees at Learning In Retirement Programs and Elderhostels. At the various presentations, I have been urged repeatedly to record my material in text-form, and I have finally relented. Accordingly, I have sorted out all my data, rearranged it, and herewith offer it as an inherent part of quality living, which, together with recommended corrections of hereditary and environmental adversities in pursuit of a natural life span, formulates a semicircle of life modeled after a perfect mathematical semicircle.

Throughout the writing, I am firmly obedient to the same ethical principles, which are proposed as the building blocks of the highest level of quality living.

Inasmuch as the material is predominantly directed at ethical issues, which by definition are controversial, I endeavor to maintain my role as an unbiased, scientifically oriented ethicist. The reader, however, has the luxury of offering any personal opinion in any of the controversial subjects.

The final copy of the text and its appearance on the market could not have been accomplished without the splendid assistance of Winnie Gefter for her inspiration and common sense; Dr. Warren Gefter for his wisdom; Rev. Kenneth Tenckinck and his staff for the privilege of making many presentations on a variety of ethical issues in health care, all of which comprise a substantial portion of the text; Jack Steinberg for his expertise in the publishing industry; Dolores and Tom Jennings for contributing their technical skill; Dr. Jesus Yap, Dr. David Widrow, and Dr. Paul Goldberg for their enhancement of our quality of living in a more perfect semicircle of life; John Laub, Marilyn Smith and Kim Phipps of Rutledge Books, Inc. for their fine contributions to the conversion of the raw manuscript to the finished product now in the hands of the reader.

William Gefter, M.D.

INTRODUCTION

MODEL: Perfect Mathematical Semicircle

GOAL: Emulation of Model with Quality Living in the Semicircle of Life

It was not so much by the knowledge of words that I came to the understanding of things, as by my experience of things I was enabled to follow the meaning of words.

—Plutarch,, 1st Century

INTRODUCTION

In order for man to achieve his *natural life span*, he must overcome all his life-threatening *1) hereditary* or *genetic* imperfections present at birth and acquired during his lifetime and *2)* ever-present *environmental* adversities which may beset him.

Mere survival, however, is insufficient and incomplete without man's fulfillment of quality living, which man develops progressively from birth to maturity. It tends to reach its summit at approximately midlife in *categories or tiers*, after which some of its elements gradually descend in varying degrees of intensity in the late years of life in accordance with man's natural declination. At its height, man's quality of living is distinctive and provides him with uniqueness of character. It is self-designed and molded in accordance with man's will. The components of man's quality of living are numerous but they may fall readily into *three tiers:*

The *first tier* is basic, egoistic, and inherent in all human beings because it is driven by the same *instinctual* self-preservation present in everyone. Its main constituents are happiness, well-being, independence, and security. Their origin dates to the ancient philosophical schools of thought that prevailed over the past 2,500 years. At this earliest level of quality, all men tend to seem alike in their behavior and desires.

The *second tier* in quality living is also egoistic and has the added special components of zeal and further self-interest that may then separate man from his neighbor because of their elements of greed and arousal of controversy. These include the drive for success, the accumulation of wealth, and the acquisition of power. At this point in man's pursuit of the highest quality of living, he can be readily identified because of the distinctive elements of the second tier.

There may be some evidence of altruism in man's ordinary, self-designed character, but for sure it is relatively insignificant at best in most people. The motive of self-interest is a dominant force in man's make-up. The feature of an aim for *compatibility* among neighbors may be satisfactory but is minimally adequate. Such is the status also among community and national interrelations.

The *third* and *highest tier* of quality living is distinctive in that it is exclusively *altruistic* in all its ingredients. Although some features of its make-up may begin early in life, they tend not to mature fully for a number of years, perhaps not before mid-life. Man comes to understand that, in the absence of the elements of this tier, he could be comfortable only if he lived in a vacuum or as a hermit, but could not exist compatibly with neighbors because of their diversity. Similarly, on an international level, one country could not exist apart from all others unless there was an altruistic relationship with other nations, based upon the third tier of quality living. It takes all the effort one can muster for man to appreciate and then actually perform all the requirements inherent in a conduct based upon the best interest of one's fellow man.

The constituents of the third tier may be grouped into four categories which together constitute the modern essential *ethical principles*. These principles define and govern the ideal behavior of man in society and represent the ultimate achievement for man in his effort to interrelate successfully with his fellow man, and thereby attain the highest quality of living in a pluralistic, sophisticated society. These principles are all derived from the philosophical schools of thought that date back to Socrates, Plato, and Aristotle over the past 2,500 years.

Category 1) is headed by man's *character* and includes honesty, sincerity, integrity, trustworthiness, and a general respect for the law. Category 2) concerns man's *conduct*, mainly that of non-maleficence, i.e., not doing anyone any harm. In the practice of medicine, it is a prime principle for the physician's "primum non nocere." Kindness and compassion are traits of behavior that are associated with non-malevolence. Category 3) is concerned with the utilitarian principle of *beneficence*, "doing the greatest good to the greatest number," practicing The Golden Rule in both its positive and negative forms. The practice of equality and justice are aligned with doing the most good. Category 4) pertains to the principle of *respect for the rights of all others* and the expectation of having one's own rights equally respected. Included are civil and human rights, respect for the right of freedom of worship, the right of privacy, autonomy, and self-determination, and the right to life, liberty and the pursuit of happiness.

The only conditional requirement is that with the expectation of rights go *responsibility*, as enunciated by St. Thomas Aquinas in the thirteen century.

Assuming everyone's recognition of his own responsibility in respecting the rights of others, and in complying with all the altruistic principles expressed in the third tier, it is possible to envision the achievement of quality living together with the successful attainment of one's natural span of life. Thus a semicircle of life would be completed that could be super imposed on the perfect mathematical structure of a semicircle.

The closer one is able to approach the goal of the perfect mathematical circle, the nearer one approximates a utopian existence with "peace on earth and good will to all men," reminiscent of Sir Thomas More's *Utopia*. In his representation five hundred years ago, an imaginary island was a place of ideal perfection. In his day, he too may have been contemplating a perfect semicircle of life.

It is the author's guarded belief that the solution to all the problems of heredity, the environment, and quality living (certainly insofar as all three are concerned collectively), could probably never be realized to its fullest extent of superimposing the semicircle of life on the perfect mathematical model.

The accompanying figure (page xxi) illustrates the author's attempt to demonstrate the relationship between man's best effort to develop quality living, which, together with the elimination of man's hereditary and environmental adversities, would depict a semicircle of life that could be superimposed upon a perfect structural semicircle.

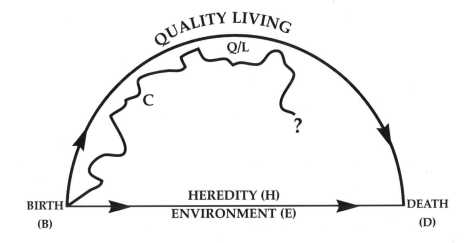

THE PERFECT SEMICIRCLE OF LIFE

DESCRIPTION OF FIGURE

Arrows on the linear and semicircular curves give direction in years from left to right (birth to death).

B) Birth or point of origin on semicircle of life; beginning of independent living, endowed with a unique composition of genes in a genome, fifty percent of which are inherited from the father, and fifty percent from the mother; also the beginning of quality living.

D) Death or point of departure from semicircle of life; end of independent living; end of quality living.

B-D) Natural span of life varying in homo sapiens from 85-115 years; an ideal, uninterrupted, encoded length, presuming that all of man's genetic mutations and environmental adversities are eradicated along the way; the natural span occurs in less than one percent of all life spans, and is determined by the absence of any hereditary (H) or environmental (E) causes of death. In the remaining ninety-nine-plus percent of life spans, death is not natural, and there is evidence of death-causing illnesses or disabilities. Thus, real life is shorter than the encoded life span. This, however, does not preclude the fact that many persons may live well past the minimal natural life span of eighty-five years and still die of disease.

Q/L) Perfect circumference of the mathematical semicircle as well as the imagined curve to be emulated by completion of a three-tiered quality of living in pursuit of a more perfect semicircle of life.

C) The *actual* or true course of life is a serpentine curve, unique and distinctive in its pattern for each and every person. It is the *real* upper limit of everyone's quality living. Its hills and dales represent episodes of improvement and decline, respectively, as a result of the impact of genetic and environmental (both earthly and cosmic) influences upon one's daily living. When circumstances in one's living are more favorable, the curve tends to approach the perfect semicircle more closely than when circumstances are less favorable and the curve is lower and farther from the perfect semicircle.

It should be everyone's aim to abolish the space between the real curve of living **(C)** and the perfect goal of curve **(Q/L),** because the space represents the unfulfilled and unaccomplished portion of one's quality of living. By superimposing **C** on **Q/L,** one would be achieving a perfect semicircle of life with optimal quality living.

Failure to correct the potentially harmful elements of heredity and the environment combine to make a bizarre-shaped hanging curve, distinctive for every person and without a determinable end.

The *question mark* at the hanging end of the real course of life **(C)** represents an unknown and unpredictable end of life, except possibly in terminal chronic disease when death can be approximated.

FORMAT OF THE TEXT

The text is in *four sections:*

Section A Heredity, Chapters 1-4

Section B The Environment, Chapters 5 and 6

Section C Quality Living, Chapters 7-10

Section D Seven Major Subjects in Health Care, *abounding in ethical issues* that relate to Quality Living:

Subject I: The Patient and the Doctor, Chapters 11 and 12

Subject II: Diet and Nutrition, Chapters 13 and 14

Subject III: Medication, Chapters 15-17

Subject IV: Advances in Biotechnology, Chapters 18-22

Subject V: Medical Research, Chapters 23 and 24

Subject VI: Decision-making in the Mature Years, Chapter 25

Subject VII: Health Care Reform, Chapter 26 and 27

SECTION A:

HEREDITY AND THE COURSE OF LIFE

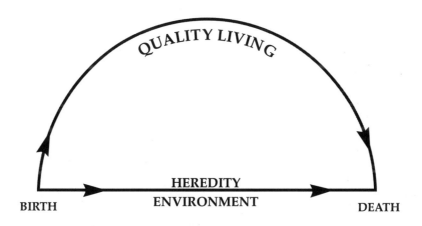

THE PERFECT SEMICIRCLE OF LIFE

CHAPTER 1

BIRTH AND THE GENOME

It is highly dishonorable for a reasonable soul to live in so divinely built a mansion as his body and yet be altogether unacquainted with the exquisite structure of it.

— Robert Boyle, 1627-1691

The basis for heredity, stated most simply, is in the science of genetics, which is an outgrowth of evolution.

Theories of Evolution (in chronological order):

Lamarck, 1801. Theory of Use and Disuse: The environment is the occasion for evolutionary change by its presentation of new needs of the organism. The newly acquired characteristics are inherited.

Darwin, 1858, Origin of Species and The Descent of Man: concerns natural selection and survival of the fittest. The theory is based on the Doctrine of Malthus, that a population increases more rapidly than its means of subsistence. The fittest, or those best adapted to coping with the environment, will survive.

DeVries, 1900, theorized that the basis of evolution lay in the phenomenon of mutation.

Other theories include Weismann's evolution through hybridization and the Theory of Intelligenent Design, a new challenge to evolution.

Genetics: The basis of genetics is Mendel's Law, 1865. He showed, through plant experimentation, that each parent contributes to the progeny.

Heredity: Predetermined by animal studies that chromosomes from each parent are endowed to the offspring. Sex is predetermined by one sex chromosome from each parent, as now described.

The birth of a human being is a biological event of enormous complexity and magnitude beginning with the entrance of a male sperm, known as a gamete, derived from the testis, into an ovum, also known as a gamete, derived from the female ovary. The male gamete contains twenty-two autosomal chromosomes and two sex chromosomes, one X and one Y. The female gamete contains twenty-two autosomal chromosomes and two sex chromosomes, one X and the other X as well. The end-product of the union is a fertilized egg known as a zygote, containing forty-four autosomal chromosomes and two sex chromosomes, one X from the egg of the mother, and one X or Y from the sperm of the father. The X chromosome from the father determines the sex of the newborn infant as female. The Y chromosome from the father determines the sex of the newborn infant as a male. The chromosomes contain less than 100,000 genes collectively called a genome. The genes are in the structural form of a double helix (Watson-Crick), and are comprised of deoxynucleic acid or DNA with billions of bases of nucleic acids, arranged differently in every human being. Ribonucleic acid or RNA transfers information from DNA to the protein-forming system of the cell. No two persons are alike as far as genes are concerned, yet all persons are like each other as a species (homo sapiens) as far as chromosomes are concerned. It is of great interest that the chimpanzee has almost the identical chromosome make-up as that of the human being.

The fertilized egg or zygote proceeds to divide, each daughter cell and eventually each organ having the identical genetic map as the fertilized egg. After one week of division, the zygote is known as an embryo, and after eight weeks the embryo is known as a fetus until birth, when it is called a newborn infant.

The reader is reminded that chromosomal abnormalities in structure, number, and arrangement cause a variety of congenital disorders that may have a devastating influence upon the life of the afflicted fetus. To be sure, the aberrations have great impact upon the quality of living of the entire family.

Everyone in health care with an abiding interest in the prevention and eradication of all diseases has eagerly been awaiting the mapping of the fewer than 100,000 genes in the form of a genome, unique for every person. Health care will then be revolutionized. Genetic mutations, the cause of abnormalities in the health of the newborn, are all products of heredity, inherent in the genome. They can then be identified at birth, or even in the fetus prior to birth, and any abnormality can be considered for correction or replacement with a normal gene.

CHAPTER 2

NATURAL LIFE SPAN

Life is the childhood of our immortality
— J.W. von Goethe, 1749–1832

Rapid advances in genetic engineering, biotechnology, public health, environmental protection, and quality living make it easy to imagine that the normal life span of man can advance readily to every human being's natural life span of 85 to 115 years (among the longest living in the animal kingdom). The exact number of years is encoded at birth in the genome of each person. Achievement of one's natural life span will require repair of all inherited genetic mutations prior to birth (in the fetus) and after birth by means of gene therapy. Throughout life, the genome can be surveyed for acquired mutations and corrections made accordingly. Unless an environmental mishap such as smoking, auto accident, or malaria, occurs, that shortens the life of the person, the natural life span can be reached. One may have confidence in this happenstance when one considers that the number of people living into their eighties (ninth decade of life) are increasing more rapidly than in any other decade. The survival rate among centenarians is also increasing rapidly, and may be approaching 100,000 in the United States. People are moving steadily from the lower levels of the natural life span upward as a result of remarkable advances in health care in recent years. In addition, let us not overlook the importance of man's immunologic armor in his inherent ability to cope with disease. It seems unlikely, however, that man will exceed the natural life span for the human species. At least, there is no evidence of such likelihood.

The most common causes of death that shorten the natural life span are: cardiovascular disease, stroke, cancer, trauma, infection, diabetes, pulmonary disease, drugs, war, and famine. They are all due to unnatural or organic pathological causes in more than ninety-nine percent of deaths. Natural causes of death occur in less than one percent, a rare event, requiring a person's survival for his encoded 85 – 115 years in the absence of intervening organic pathologic causes. In other words, the person dies at the end of his encoded life span without interference from hereditary or environmental abnormalities.

Survival to the natural life span by the elimination of all hereditary aberrations is the first step in emulating the perfect mathematical semicircle. The next step would require elimination of all environmental adversities—no easy task. The final step would be the successful attainment of quality living with the 1) basic instinctive, egoistic requirements of life-long happiness, well-being, independence, and security, 2) acquired egoistic, personal values of a successful career, wealth, power, and other zealous aims of importance to each person, and 3) commitment to an altruistic philosophy including all of the ethical principles governing man's ideal behavior in society, so that there can be an ideal interrelationship among men, communities, and countries.

CHAPTER 3

AGING

The wise man mourns less for what age takes away than what age leaves behind.

— William Wordsworth, 1780-1850

Definition: If one were to define aging, one could very easily age before running out of synonyms. A few of the more common definitions include: getting older, past 65 years, elderly, senile, at old age, graying, past youth, past middle life, reaching longevity, geriatric, over the hill, mature, on Medicare, and best of all, anyone older than I am.

Aging has also been known as the seventh stage of man on a scale of stages including: 1) the newborn, 2) infancy, 3) childhood, 4) teenage, 5) young adulthood, 6) maturity or middle age, and 7) old age or seventh stage. The first six stages have relatively fixed concepts and ages in identifiable ranges and numbers, whereas the seventh stage has varying numbers and an ill-defined range in years.

STATISTICS

In 1900, four percent of the population, and in 1990, twelve percent of the population, lived longer than sixty-five years. The fastest growing age group is the eighties. It is estimated that in 2030, 2.4 percent of the population will live longer than eighty-five years. The natural life span of the human species has remained at 85 to 115 years. The lower number has been climbing steadily, but there is a rare authentic record of anyone living beyond 115 years.

CENTENARIANS

The number of centenarians living in the United States exceeds 50,000, and the number is steadily increasing toward 100,000. The perennial question always asked of centenarians, "To what do you attribute your long life?," has surprising replies in that they lack a common denominator and are unexpected. For example, one attributed her success to wine and two cigarettes a day. A former Indian Prime Minister drank his own urine daily (a practice in Ayurvedic medicine). A Water of Life foundation in Bombay, India, recommends drinking one's own urine as a universal cure-all.

INCREASE IN LONGEVITY

A number of factors are responsible for the increase in longevity in recent years. These include:

    1) Improved prevention and treatment of disease—

        a) Advances in medical knowledge and biotechnology

        b) Improved infant care, including immunizations

        c) Control of risk factors that lead to an increase in vascular disease: hypertension, smoking, sedentary life style, saturated fats in diet, obesity, diabetes mellitus

        d) Control of infections: tuberculosis, sexually transmitted diseases, pneumonia, rheumatic fever, etc.

        e) Early detection of cancer and improved treatment with surgery, chemotherapy, and irradiation

    2) Improved social problems—

a) Better housing, education, nutrition, health care
b) Improved hygiene and public health measures
c) Better industrial conditions, e.g., seat belts in cars,
    elimination of lead and asbestos in the environment
d) Social security, Medicare, Medicaid
e) Improved institutional care, hospice care
3) Advances in medical research:
a) Molecular biology
b) Genetics
c) Biotechnology

PHYSIOPATHOLOGY OF AGING

There is some evidence that aging may actually begin at birth. Technically, however, it is more realistic to consider that aging continues through growth and development in youth, and then later at the middle of life. Although cell division continues in all body cells from birth for a total of 50-60 divisions (except in the central nervous system and in skeletal muscle, where none occurs), not until well after middle age does the process of cell division begin to slow in rate, progressively more and more, until cell division ceases at death. (Some division of cells may even continue for a brief period after death.)

CLINICAL ASPECTS OF AGING

The normal process of aging continues upward on the semicircular curve through growth and development to maturity at the height of the curve. As physiologic and physical attributes begin to decline thereafter, the curve descends to its natural end. To a lesser extent, one's mental prowess follows a similar curve.

The accumulated benefits comprising quality living follow the same path upward to a peak at about mid-life. Then they progress downward as a result of the invasion of chronic ailments, multiple disabilities, a variety of socio-economic problems such as need for long-term care, etc.

EXPERIMENTAL EVIDENCE FOR A POSSIBLE
DELAY OF AGING

It has never been appreciated that aging could ever be delayed. Experimental data in rats, however, suggest that such may be the case.

Background

The pineal gland, a pea-sized body in the brain of man, calcifies early in life. In 1958 a hormone, melatonin, was discovered to be secreted cyclically (especially at night) in childhood. Its activity declines sharply at puberty, and at least fifty percent drops off by middle age. In elderly people, the secretion is negligible. (Its virtual absence in old age is regarded as a possible reason for difficulty in falling asleep in old age. By the same token, melatonin has been found to have value in the treatment of jet lag.)

The experimental use of melatonin in rats shows a delay in aging by protecting cells from oxidation's free-radical damage and by boosting the immune system (considered also to be of suggestive value in the prevention of cancer). A concerning factor is that the side effects, particularly long-term, are unknown.

Experiments with human beings having the apolipoprotein E-2 gene showed them to be more likely to live 100 years than those with the apolipoprotein E-4 gene.

Two views are held currently regarding the aging process, I) spiritual and religious, and II) scientific. Each view has three phases: a) birth, b) growth and development, c) dying and death.

I) Spiritual and religious view:

      a) Birth is a miraculous event

      b) Growth and development are gifts of nature, and are spiritual milestones during life

c) Dying and death are a prescribed part of life, natural and expected, the ultimate event in life, a divine decree (God's will); the emergence of the soul and the immortal spirit are a prelude to life hereafter. Approximately fifty percent of the people who hold the spiritual and religious view are also adherents to the validity of the concept, "the will to live," a frequently heard expression among chronically and terminally ill patients. As its words indicate, there is an enthusiasm for living. It is regarded as a significant psychologic factor, and it has a probable correlation with longer living. In surveys regarding "the will to live," it is a considered factor in only about ten percent of those with a scientific view of dying and death.

II) Scientific view

a) Birth is a genetic event. Each cell in the body has 46 chromosomes (23 from each parent) and less than 100,000 genes, each with thousands of nucleotides, the building blocks of DNA and RNA.

b) Growth and development are biologically determined. Each cell undergoes a genetic doubling process (none in the nerve cells or skeletal muscle cells). With added hormonal influences, the natural life span evolves to approximately 85 to 115 years. During the process of division of the cells, the genes are replicated accurately in the normal daughter cells via a net balance between 1) *oncogenes*, which accelerate growth, division and proliferation, and 2) *tumor suppressor genes*, which slow or prevent, cell proliferation. Although the timing is genetically determined, the process is modified and influenced at any time by environmental adversities (in addition to acquired genetic mutations during cell division).

In aging, late in life, the doubling process undergoes progressive slowing and decline, resulting in a decrease in body system activities as follows:

1) Endocrine activity decreases with reduction in ovarian function leading to menopause; reduced pancreatic function

leading to non-insulin dependent diabetes mellitus (adult-onset or type II diabetes).

2) Immunologic functions decrease in activity, resulting in an increased tendency to cancer and an increased tendency to infection.

3) Physical and intellectual functions decline, resulting in decrease in strength and memory respectively. Quality living is then reduced as well on the semicircular curve of life.

c) Dying and death, according to the scientific view, are reserved for a further antemortem slowing of the doubling process en route to complete cessation. Death is the end-stage. The biologic life span is reached provided that there are no genetic or environmental interferences—a rare circumstance, occurring in less than one percent of deaths. In more than ninety-nine percent of deaths, it is more likely that the expected 85 to 115 years of genetically encoded natural life span will be shortened by a) inherited or acquired genetic defects and/or b) environmental adverse interventions.

PREVENTION AND TREATMENT

Except for meager experimental evidence of slowing of the aging process in rats, the current position regarding aging is that it is a normal uninterrupted component of the path along the curve from birth to death. Anti-aging measures are a misconception and non-existent, there being no scientific means available to slow the process in man. Aging may be shortened by early death due to disease, or lengthened to the natural life span as a result of correcting hereditary and environmental adversities.

In a passion for finding the fountain of youth in our society, superficial measures, mostly cosmetic, are in vogue. Hair transplants and elimination of wrinkles are among the popular enhancements, which are psychologically uplifting, but are not anti-aging. In Chapter 15 there is a discussion of off-label drugs and a disparaging reference to the unethical practice of using certain potent hormones inappropriately and dangerously as anti-aging therapy and preservers of youth.

Growth hormones have an important therapeutic role in hormonal deficiencies, but not as youth enhancers or as body builders. Attention to the survival of infants and children with periodic examinations and proper immunizations are among the best health measures that assure children's entry into the stage of life known as youth. The naive concept of aging that promotes spending time and wasting resources in search of ways to prevent or combat aging would be better spent in devoting more time and money in research regarding the detrimental diseases of the mature years, as well as education in the altruistic measures to improve quality living within a community. The path on the semicircular curve of life could then be made to appear more like the mathematical curve. Let the reader be assured that there is no anti-aging medicine that prevents or reverses the process of aging.

Finally, anti-aging should not be confused with geriatric medicine, which addresses the health problems of the elderly, in a manner not unlike the care of children by pediatricians. As a matter of fact, most specialists in medicine are geriatric specialists in that their respective specialties are concerned more often with the elderly than with young patients.

Does not the reference to anti-aging suggest working against aging? It would seem more appropriate to favor aging by opposing the many health factors that interfere with one's achievement of aging. Pro-aging is a more positive way of eliminating all factors that interfere with a person's achievement of aging and arriving at one's natural life span.

Is there not something inherently wrong with the contradictory thoughts that everyone desires to age and live long, but no one would be aged and old?

CHAPTER 4

THE END OF LIFE AND
START OF THE HEREAFTER

Death is not a foe but an inevitable adventure

— Sir Oliver Lodge, 1851-1940)

INTRODUCTION

An important role of the physician in the care of a terminally ill patient is to ascertain that the patient has prepared an *advance directive*. The physician must be sure that the patient has expressed his wishes *in writing* regarding his end-of-life care—and that he has chosen to pursue a *sanctity of life* ethic or a *quality of life* ethic, as a part of his decision-making process (see Chapter 24). If not, has a surrogate been appointed to act on behalf of or in the best interest of the patient? The physician must be competent in this role.

The physician is responsible for making the institutional authorities aware of the patient's wishes, for example, by noting DNR and NO CPR orders on the hospital chart, if the patient has stated such preference. Otherwise, a sensitive ethical issue may arise if an enthusiastic hospital staff proceeds to apply complex, advanced biotechnological life-saving measures in violation of the patient's expressed written wishes. Of course, if there are no such orders, the medical staff is expected to apply life-saving measures upon the patient unless or until withdrawal of life support is on order by the attending physician.

A further responsibility of the physician is to be aware (by the patient's written directive) of the patient's wishes regarding a pre-arranged organ donation for transplantation and whether or not an autopsy may be performed (unless decided in its favor by law, or opposed on a religious basis).

Sadly, only ten percent of the population actually make their organs available, although ninety percent express their willingness to be donors, when asked.

THE END POINT

The point of death (D, figure in Introduction) is the end of the horizontal line (the diameter of the mathematical circle) from point B (birth) and represents the natural life span, encoded genetically in the person's genome, somewhere between 85 and 115 years. In recent years the span has been moving closer and closer to the median of 100 years, as the population overcomes more and more of the hereditary and environmental adversities they encounter.

The point of death (D) is also the endpoint on the mathematical circumference of the semicircle. This curve is the ideal goal that man tries to emulate 1) by eliminating all harmful factors in his heredity and his environment and 2) by embracing all of the altruistic ethical principles necessary to provide him with the highest quality of living to share with his fellow men. He may then simulate the perfect mathematical semicircle with his own ideal semicircle of life.

In reality, however, man's actual course in life (C in the figure) is a vague semblance of a semicircle. Although it starts at birth (B), it moves in a sinuous path with mounds and depressions resulting from improvements and sufferings from adversities, respectively. Its course runs below the ideal semicircle because quality living, besides barely meeting its basic content of egoistic pursuits (happiness, well-being, independence, and security), is in a constant turmoil in failing to comply with all the altruistic ethical principles expected of everyone in his societal encounters.

The curve (C) in the figure ends with a question mark, mainly because the end point of life is unknown, unpredictable, and usually occurs sooner than the natural life span.

DIAGNOSIS OF DEATH
In defining death, the author is herewith making no attempt to be facetious. In the past, death was easily determined, or at least presumed, when the person stopped breathing and the heart stopped beating. Everyone can remember the diagnostic advice given to place a mirror before a prostrate person's mouth and nose. If the mirror did not become misty (from an exhaled breath), the person was diagnosed as deceased.

In recent years, however, as a result of advanced technology, beginning with cardio-pulmonary resuscitation and mechanical pulmonary ventilation, the lungs and the heart in tandem can be restored to function, and life can be sustained.

A new definition of death is now required, based officially upon the *UNIFORM DETERMINATION OF DEATH ACT* which followed the *PRESIDENTIAL COMMISSION TO STUDY DEATH, 1981* (see Chapter 24). The new criteria include permanent unconsciousness, irreversible cessation of circulatory and respiratory function, irreversible cessation of all brain function (includes higher cortical, subcortical, and lower brain stem activity), absence of all signs of receptivity and responsivity, and an isoelectric electroencephalogram (if available).

In view of the fact that a licensed physician is required by law to complete a death certificate, it may be stated jocularly that only a physician may state that "no one is dead unless I say that one is dead."

THE HEREAFTER

The author will deliberately make this discussion brief for fear of speculating with his ignorance in the mystique of the hereafter. As part of the definition of death, however, beyond the legal criteria, a spiritual consideration may also be invoked. When last rites are given and prayers at death are rendered by representatives of the clergy, most, if not all, are agreed that the spirit or soul of the deceased person is presumed to leave the body as a divine intervention. Since there is no unanimous belief in the role of the spirit, the author will venture into the thought, purely on the temptation to complete the semicircle into a full circle, that the spirit may reenter the body of a newborn child (a popular ancient concept known as metempsychosis). The concept is especially comforting and applicable in contemplating a role for the spirit of Mother Theresa. As stated previously, the author, out of personal ignorance, and in deep respect for the ministry, defers to biblical scholars for guidance regarding the role of the spirit after death.

SECTION B:

THE ENVIRONMENT

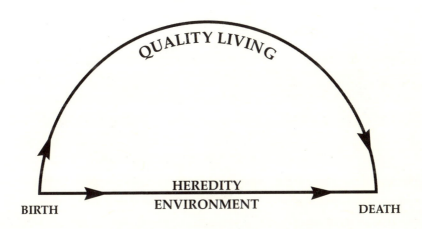

QUALITY LIVING

HEREDITY
ENVIRONMENT

BIRTH

DEATH

THE PERFECT SEMICIRCLE OF LIFE

CHAPTER 5

GENERAL CONSIDERATIONS

He who knows only his own side of the case knows little of that.
— John Stuart Mill, 1806-1873

When a fetus emerges from the uterus as a newborn infant, he is fully endowed with all of his inherited components in a genome, as part of heredity, fifty percent of which is inherited from his mother and fifty percent from his father.

Beginning with his first inhaled breath, the infant is immediately exposed to the evils of the environment, despite the sterile condition of the delivery room. He will then remain exposed for the rest of his life to the environment, which offers a multitude of adverse effects in addition to the essential life-preserving oxygen in the air and water to drink (required to make up the average seventy percent of a human being's body weight). The body, especially the brain, is also in need of sugar in order to survive. In addition, the body will soon be dependent upon dietary sources of carbohydrate, protein, fat, vitamins, minerals, and trace elements for its survival and well-being.

The environment is an aggregate of all external conditions and influences, which we deliberately or inadvertently allow to touch us at all times, thereby establishing a constant effect upon our lives. The environment is generally unfriendly and we should be alert and on guard at every moment against its hazardous forces.

We should avoid being careless in our behavior in the unreliable assumption that our genetic makeup and its powerful immunologic constituents will protect us at all times against every environmental enemy, both the visible and invisible ones.

The age-old conundrum requesting to know which is more important, heredity or environment, is really not an unresolvable query and, in fact, has a simple answer. In every disorder of health, heredity may play no role, a minor role, a major role, or the total role. Similarly, and inversely correlatively, the environment may play the total role, a major role, a minor role, or no role. Various combinations of influential involvement in all illnesses may range from zero to one hundred percent for heredity and from one hundred percent to zero percent for the environment. Together, the percentages of involvement contributed by heredity and environment will always total one hundred percent

Another way of looking at the heredity versus environment issue is to appreciate that both factors are equally important parts of our lives, always with us. Both are potential contributors to our illnesses as well as to our well-being, either separately or in some combination.

In considering the elimination of all hereditary aberrations by way of genetic engineering and gene therapy, beginning with the fetus in-utero and throughout its life, the probability of eliminating all genetic diseases, both hereditary and acquired, can be imagined and may be within reach. The contemplation of correcting all adverse environmental influence (biological, physical, chemical, and behavioral), however, is remote and a much greater challenge. Hence, the achievement of reaching everyone's natural life span is akin to man's landing on another planet. The mere thought, for example, of over-coming such natural forces as an earthquake, volcanic eruption, and tsunami is beyond imagination, especially in the realization that the environment is limitless, sightless, and unpredictable. Perhaps we should remind ourselves of Albert Einstein's oft-quoted observation that "imagination is more important than knowledge."

Illnesses that are due to environmental hazards are difficult to identify, especially if there is an additional hereditary component involved in the cause. It is, therefore, pertinent, in seeking a correct diagnosis for the patient to provide a detailed environmental/occu-pational history including past work-related areas of exposure. Sources of information are available for guidance in diagnosis by consulting governmental departments of health, National Institute for Occupational Safety and Health, Environmental Protection Agency, Centers for Disease Control and Prevention, Consumer Product Safety Commission, The Food and Drug Administration, computerized databases maintained by the National Library of Medicine, university and private specialists, and many more.

In the practice of medicine, physicians are often confronted with the common environmental and occupational disorders, particularly affecting the lungs and skin. Their index of suspicion and their sensi-tivity to environmental causes of disease fortunately are generally high.

Physicians, as do all members of society, rely upon governmen-tal responsibility to safeguard the rights of its citizens in their pur-suit of environmental protection. The government (federal, state, and municipal) responds to the needs by a series of commitments as follows:

1.) Adequate and a decent level of health care despite one's inability to pay for the service

2.) A safe water supply, clean air, shelter, food and clothing (Ed: Is that not what taxes are for?)

3.) Public educational opportunities

4.) Protection against foreign aggression, crime, fire, and communicable diseases

5.) Building codes for sanitary living and working conditions, inspection of food supplies by our federal, state and municipal governments in full acknowledgement of their commitment to environmental protection

Hereditary changes may occur as a result of environmental changes. In addition to the genetic mutations that may occur as cells divide throughout the life of every human being, mutations of genes also occur as a result of everyone's exposure to the environment's ill effects. These include poisons and toxins, pollutants, venomous bites and stings, germs, hyperthermia, hypothermia, drowning, electrical injuries, ionizing radiation, dietary indiscretion, famine, war, accidents, natural phenomena, etc., etc., etc.

CHAPTER 6

ENVIRONMENTAL CLASSES

Man has three great foes—ignorance, which is sin; apathy, which is immorality; and vice, which is the devil.

— Anonymous

There are numerous real as well as potential adversities in the environment with which everyone must contend.

They may be categorized into *four classes:*

1) Biological
2) Physical
3) Chemical
4) Behavioral or Societal

1) BIOLOGICAL CLASS

Ever since the sulfonamides and then penicillin became generally available in the early 1940's, the progress in the control of infection has been extraordinary. Despite the advances, however, it is inconceivable that all pathogenic microorganisms will ever be eradicated from the earth, mainly because they have a remarkable self-protective propensity, by way of *mutation*, to become *resistant* to man's continuous therapeutic antibacterial discoveries. The result is a fierce battle between man and beast, in which the germs usually emerge victoriously.

To date, there is only one comforting precedent in man's war against germs, to wit, the elimination of the smallpox virus by vaccination, a procedure in itself a remarkable discovery by man. That precedent has now been duplicated by the application of vaccination in the prevention of many other illnesses, such as poliomyelitis, contagious diseases of childhood, influenza, and pneumonia. Nevertheless, the eradication of the causative viruses or bacteria has not been accomplished. A future consideration is the possible prevention of cancer by vaccination.

The myriad of saprophytic and disease-producing biological organisms exist around us in unimaginable and countless super-abundance in the air we breathe, the water we drink, the food we eat, the things we touch, and in the things that touch us. It is easy to predict that the incalculable exponential rate of production of germs and their ability to defy us and to outlive us will continue to be a major biologic factor in our struggle with the environment. We are also not overlooking the presence of a multitude of additional invisible enemies in the microcosm. Besides pathogenic bacteria and viruses and the mosquitoes and flies that serve as their transmitters are fungi, protozoa, parasites, and helminths.

Infection, despite the therapeutic advances, remains among our most common causes of death worldwide. The human immunodeficiency virus (HIV), a bacterium (M. tuberculosis), and a parasite (P. falciparum) cause five million deaths annually (AIDS, TB, and malaria respectively).

2) PHYSICAL CLASS
Accidental injuries rank high among the number of causes of disability and death. They are generally inclined to be sudden, unexpected, unpredictable and unforeseen. They may occur at home, on the highway, at work, at play, and during hostilities at war.

Statistics reveal that most accidents are due to *carelessness* and negligence and can be prevented.

Also included among physical factors are hyperthermia (excessive heat), hypothermia (excessive cold), ionizing radiation, including radon, and electrical injuries.

Lack of exercise and a sedentary life are serious physical factors that contribute to the evolution of coronary artery disease, and are a high risk for disability and death.

The causes of injury, disability, and death due to physical factors in the environment can be avoided to a great extent by paying more attention to preventive measures in our life-style, diet, avoidance of carelessness, obedience of laws, and in appropriate societal changes.

There is little to say at this time regarding the major natural catastrophes in the environment that cause death. Man is inclined to accept earthquakes, hurricanes, volcanic eruptions, and floods as angry expressions of nature, although scientists have explanations for their cause. Perhaps in the next few millennia, man will harness these and other disabling phenomena of nature.

3) CHEMICAL CLASS

Our exposure to harmful chemical substances is an ever-increasing health hazard as civilization becomes more and more complex. Thousands of *synthetic compounds* are used daily in industry with potential harm to our health. As the population grows in numbers and in sophistication, manufacturing will be correspondingly increased to sustain and advance our quality of living, which, after all, is our goal in completing a perfect semi-circle of life.

Despite the frightening specter of adverse chemical engulfment, however, we are paradoxically managing to become *centenarians* in increasing numbers, a sign of improved survival and better coping as we head toward our natural life span.

Also, in spite of constant and vigilant attention by public health and environmental monitoring, there are always new and serious contaminations of the water we drink, the air we breathe, and the food we eat. There is never-ending exposure to the hazards of nicotine, asbestos, silica, lead, arsenic, mercury, cobalt, tin, cadmium, thallium, and carbon monoxide. As offensive agents are brought under control, new offenders emerge, such as the discovery of the evils of saturated fats in the diet, or that Parkinson's disease may be caused by an environmental pollutant.

Of critical concern are *acute poisonings*, especially from contaminated foods and from drugs. Most reactions are accidental, although a few are intentional (suicidal). The organs they involve are mainly the gastro-intestinal tract in seventy-five percent of the cases, the skin in ten percent, the lungs in ten percent, and the eyes in five percent.

The side-effects of our medications cause death in significant numbers. (Medications are addressed in detail in Section D, Subject III, Chapter 15).

4) THE BEHAVIORAL OR SOCIETAL CLASS

The behavioral or societal class of environmental factors that contribute to our ill health and thereby impair our quality of living are many. The correction of the problem requires an *altruistic* philosophy. Man should be worried about the many *social ills* including poverty, hunger, lack of adequate housing, and ill health among the least fortunate people in our society. The evils of illicit drug abuse, nicotine, alcohol, crime, and faulty gun control are also behavioral issues that are inadequately addressed. A prominent societal concern of everyone is the prevention and control of *obesity*, which has serious effects upon health (see Chapter 14).

The war against the manufacture and sale of cigarettes, especially among young, new smokers, does not seem to eliminate the use of *nicotine*. It is difficult to comprehend and accept the persistent insistence by some of the spokespeople for the tobacco industry that nicotine is neither addictive nor carcinogenic. Overwhelming scientific evidence shows that lung cancer, the most common cause of death due to cancer, is caused by the nicotine in cigarettes and is the most preventable cause of cancer known to man. Smoking remains among our most common and most serious ethical issues (see Chapter 16).

The personal ill-effects of *alcohol* are discussed in Chapter 16. As a societal problem, it cannot be emphasized enough for all to be aware of, and vigilant against, the destructive features of excessive alcohol consumption in home life and in drunk-driving. A key factor in alcoholism is that alcohol, in a subtle way, has a diabolic effect upon the brain that causes the imbiber to imagine that he knows what he is doing (no matter how little or much he is consuming), when in fact, he is being irrational.

An important unresolved issue in our way of life is the emotionally-charged concern over *gun control*. Some actually insist that we have sufficient laws in place to resolve our problems. The majority of people, however, are indignant that we do not make drastic changes in our laws and in our behavior to prevent further losses of innocent lives, especially among children.

An astounding figure is that forty percent of the adult population is *obese* and all are subject to serious complications. Obesity rates along with cigarette smoking as the two most preventable causes of disability in our society. The problem with obesity as a behavioral disorder is that, in a sense, it is an addiction like smoking. A thought-provoking view regarding the possible control of obesity is the awareness that it is not as common a societal concern anywhere in the world as it is in the United States. If it can be managed everywhere else in the world, then why not here? The reader is referred to Chapter 14 for further discussion.

There are many additional social factors in our environment which are best described collectively under the heading of societal *decadence*, considering that most are worsening and only a few may be improving. In no order of importance, just to name a few as they readily come to mind, are the following:

1) absence of comprehensive and universal health care in a country with the best available health care in the world; 2) inadequate health care for millions because of lack of health insurance; 3) poverty; 4) homelessness; 5) broken family structures; 6) high divorce rate; 7) teenage pregnancy; 8) AIDS; 9) crime; 10) abuse of children and the elderly; 11) illicit use of addictive drugs; 12) absence of adequate gun control; 13) too few Mother Theresa-like personalities; 14) enormity of unethical practices in business and in politics; 15) ability to purchase political power; 16) lack of respect for civil and human rights; 17) ethnic and racial discrimination; 18) terrorism; etc., etc.

As long as these dark sides of our societal interrelations exist, we will never have a society with a high level of quality living and be able to achieve the perfect semicircle of life. In extending this view globally, we must appreciate the important social need for compatible existence and cooperation among our neighbors and countries.

Each person may be fulfilling his own quality of living with personal happiness and well being, but if he fails in his compliance with the ethical principle of respect for the rights of his fellow-man, especially civil and human rights, he may be at risk permanently for hostility and war, which are surely among the most egregious causes of destruction to our quality of living.

SECTION C:

QUALITY LIVING

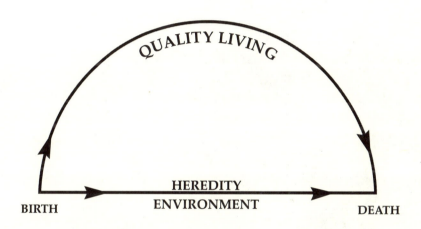

THE PERFECT SEMICIRCLE OF LIFE

SECTION C

QUALITY LIVING

Look humbly upon thy virtues; and though thou art rich in some, yet think thyself poor and naked without that crowning grace, which thinketh no evil, which envieth not, which beareth, hopeth, believeth, endureth all things.

— *Sir Thomas Browne, 1605-1682*

SECTION C

QUALITY LIVING

INTRODUCTION: BASIC ETHICAL VALUES

In the previous six chapters, an attempt was made to explain that *heredity* and *environment* together are the only fundamental factors concerned in the establishment of the length of one's life-span after birth. If neither heredity nor environment is influential in shortening one's life, one can achieve a full, natural, pre-coded life span of 85-115 years in a direct line from birth to death. This can be accomplished, however, in less than one percent of lives because such achievement requires that death occurs at the end of one's life span with no hereditary or environmental causative factor at blame. In more than ninety-nine percent of people as stated previously, life is shortened by some adverse condition in heredity and/or in the environment to which one is constantly exposed.

The factors that make quality living are at least as important as heredity and environment in man's accomplishment of a successful semicircle of life. Unlike heredity and environment, however, the factors are *entirely* conceived, produced, and controlled by man himself in his own egoistic best interest. At birth, quality living is non-existent at point zero. Man then raises it progressively with time and effort in his own behalf. The peak of achievement consisting of basic as well as supplemental factors (tiers 1, 2, and 3) is usually at about mid-life. The curve then gradually descends, as the basic and supplemental factors are eroded, and slowed essentially by aging and decline in health to point zero at death.

The *earliest basic* values that comprise the *first and lowest tier* in quality living are common in everyone and are based upon a hedonistic, egocentric, and instinctive biological drive for self-preservation. The values include: 1) happiness, 2) well-being, 3) independence and freedom of movement within the law, and 4) comfort and security for self and loved ones. *Egoism* or self-interest is the basis for man's early behavior.

Beyond these universal values that comprise everyone's quality of living, man proceeds to add a *second tier* of personal desires and interests based upon zeal or even greed, that give one a supplemental set of values that then comprise man's new quality of living in his best personal interest.

These supplemental factors vary extensively, even though they may be shared in common. Interest in financial success, achievement in vocation, and acquisition of power are the leading values. Everyone's quality of living, as it heads for its peak, is unique, but *egoism* still dominates all pursuits in everyone's aim toward a life of contentment and accomplishment.

Unfortunately, uniqueness implies the acquisition of new traits that make for *dissimilarities* that become greater and greater among neighbors. Differences invariably arouse biases, prejudices, discrimination, antagonism, confrontation, controversy, hostility, and other unfavorable displays in behavior. The direction of such dangerous concepts readily spreads and easily involves communities and countries. One may now readily recognize the character of the world in which we live.

The basic values in the first and second tiers of quality living would be sufficient as long as man live in a vacuum or as a hermit. Antisocial behavior, however, is incompatible with successful living, which demands an interdependent complexity of relationships in society. Living is not easy in a milieu overburdened with unattractive traits of intolerance, uncivility, xenopobia, and genocide in a multicultural, multiracial, multiethnic society. An egoistic quality of living cannot endure without the added introduction of a set of advanced, modern ethical principles, entirely new for the most part, based upon a philosphy of altruism with a high regard for, and devotion to, the interests of everyone else, in addition to one's self. That is of course said than done. The key is that everyone must agree to accept, comply with, and practice the altruistic principles which can govern the ideal behavior of everyone in society in the expectation of quality living for all. Everyone would then be utilitarian and practice the greatest good for the greatest number. All would then share in cooperative and negotiated responsibility leading to quality living ultimately approaching Sir Thomas More's Utopia, described five-hundred years ago. A semicircle of life would thereby be created, simulating the goal of the perfect mathematical semicircle. Compliance with the ethical principles represents the highest and noblest act of man.

What are these idealistic altruistic virtues that will advance our quality living to a state of perfection? They are in essence best enunciated in the *modern ethical principles* that are derived from two-thousand, five-hundred years of philosophical thought to be reviewed briefly in the forthcoming Chapter 7 and outlined in detail in Chapter 8. The ethical principles are universal and apply equally as well to health care as to business, politics and all other branches of society. Those pertaining to health care are discussed in detail in Chapters 9 and 10.

CHAPTER 7

EVOLUTION OF ETHICAL PRINCIPLES IN PHILOSOPHICAL SCHOOLS OF THOUGHT

One ought always to ask oneself what would happen if everyone did as one is doing.

— Jean Paul Sartre, 20th Cent

The basic principles concerned with quality living have been given considerable attention for 2500 years beginning with the Greek era of enlightenment when Socrates (470-399 BC), Plato (427-347 BC), and Aristotle (384-322 BC) reigned in their respective philosophical schools of thought. Since then, philosophical writings have formed the backbone and the fundamentals of modern ethical principles, which are discussed in Chapter 8.

This text is dependent upon these principles in its selection of seven major medical subjects (see section D). Each is saturated with ethical controversies requiring resolution and adjudication prior to anticipated societal acceptance.

Many philosophical schools of thought have prevailed since Socrates and have been concerned with the ethical branch of philosophy, collectively leading to the modern principles or standards that define and govern the ideal behavior of man in society.

Among the earliest recorded ethical concepts concerning quality living was the search for personal *happiness* or pleasure as the *sole good* and chief end. *Plato* modified the concept by propounding that pleasure of the body was subordinate to *pleasure of the mind*. *Happiness* was generally regarded, as it still is today, as consisting of physical, mental, emotional, moral, and financial well-being. Originally, freedom from all troubles was a concern of every individual, but in time it took two forms: 1) *Egoism* and 2) *Altruism*.

The advocates of *egoism* were originally the *hedonists* who believed that personal pleasure is the sole good in life. They were represented by the *Cyrenaics*, led by *Aristippus* of Cyrene (435-356 BC), a disciple of Socrates, and by the *Epicureans*, led by *Epicurus* (342-270 BC), who included in the aim for happiness a life of *intellectual pleasures*, honor, and justice. The *Eudaemonists*, followers of Aristotle, included a life governed by *reason* and *well-being* as ingredients in their desire for happiness.

The advocates of *altruism* were primarily the *Utilitarians*, who favored happiness as *the greatest good for the greatest number.* Their leading advocates were *Jeremy Bentham* (1748-1832) and *John S. Mill* (1806-1873). Their concept embraced *usefulness of purpose* in the provision of good. The principle of greatest good for all (benevolence, beneficence) implied lesser harm to all (non-malevolence, non-maleficence).

Four important philosophical schools which contributed to the modern ethical principles included: 1) Stoicism, 2) Scholasticism, 3) Rationalism, 4) Modernism.

1.) *Stoicism* was founded by *Zeno* (346-264 BC), who led a group that was *indifferent* to pleasure and taught that the world reveals itself as an embodiment of *divine or natural law*, that man should be free from passion, is governed by divine law and is submissive to it. A prominent advocate was *Epictetus*, a Roman stoic philosopher (60-120 BC), who taught that the greatest good lies in man's independence of external factors and in man's reliance upon one's *inner life* or character.

2.) *Scholasticism* was founded by *Scotus Erigena* (ninth century AD). *Thomas Aquinas* (1225-1274) was a strong advocate in his principle of divine law. He preached that all in nature is good and that man must find the highest good by way of *obedience to natural or divine law*. Furthermore, divine law was discernible to reason by *deduction*, the form of reasoning developed by Aristotle. (Socrates had proposed *inductive* reasoning.)

Additional factors in Scholasticism included the thought that man is deferential to authority and that *immoral* behavior relates to the *will* or intent of man.

3.) *Rationalism* is a form of natural or divine law that relates to *reason* as the source of knowledge arrived at by *deduction*. The process is superior to, and independent of, sense perception. It relies on reason as the basis for the establishment of religious truth. It holds that there are *natural rights* to life, liberty, and the pursuit of happiness, a concept which became a basis for Jefferson's famous insertion in the Declaration of Independence in 1776.

4.) *Modernism* held that the rules of nature are linked to society, but are apart from man-made laws. Its intention was to accommodate traditional religious teaching and contemporary thought, and especially to devalue traditional supernatural elements. An illustration of this form of natural or divine law is exemplified by the endeavor of Pope Pius X, early in the 20th Century to reconcile church doctrine with conclusions of science (as in the acceptance of Galileo's discovery that the earth revolves around the sun, a concept which the church had originally condemned). A philosophical school led by *Thomas Percival*, British physician, offered a doctrine of British medical ethics in 1803, which became the prototype for the American Medical Association's first *Medical Code of Ethics* in 1847. Its basic feature was that of *Primum Non Nocere (first do no harm)*. Non-maleficence and beneficence are the physician's primary obligations—concepts which are inherent in the *Oath of Hippocrates*..

A philosophical school of thought identified as one of *Perfectionism* declared that *self-realization* of one's moral character took precedence over one's happiness, that the perfection of moral character constitutes man's highest good and that a state of freedom from sin is attainable on earth.

Another school of thought held that *Theism*, in addition to the belief in the existence of one God as the creative source of man and the basis of man's relation to the universe, also included *awe of the deity* and fear of retribution in the hereafter. The bottom line was that faith was equivalent to morality. *Charles Darwin's* (1809-1882) ironclad *theory of evolutionism*, in his Origin of Species and The Descent of Man (1859), basing man's development on natural selection and survival of the fittest in contrast to *creationism*, was a staggering and humbling concept to the world, especially to the *fundamentalists*.

A group of philosophers led by *John Locke* (1632-1704) and *David Hume* (1711-1776), taught *Empiricism*, that knowledge of right and wrong was based upon *experience* or habit, and was disrespectful of scientific theory or proof. As a matter of fact, the concept, as expected, became the basis for *charlatanry*.

One of the outstanding contributors to philosophical thinking that influenced modern ethical principles was *Immanuel Kant* (1724-1804), who was a skeptic of empiricism. He was the father of the *Golden Rule*—to do unto others as you would have others do unto you. He promoted an individual's rights to *autonomy*, *equality* and *justice* (egalitarianism) and the elimination of inequalities among men. Kant had many followers, among them most prominently, F. Schelling, J. Fichte, and G. Hegel in the early 19th Century.

Another philosophical school of thought was known as *Intuitionism*, in which moral views were known by *innate* conception of right and wrong—a sixth sense, as it were. Truths were self-evident. A striking illustration is that of the Supreme Court jurist who stated that he could not define pornography but would know it when he saw it.

A long held view of many is *respect for the law* and to follow it with total compliance for fear of punishment. They believe that laws must be adhered to and not violated. If laws are undesirable, they can be changed. The net concept is that legality is equivalent to morality in the same sense that religious faith is equivalent to morality among the theists.

The last group to be considered among the philosophical schools that led to the modern principles governing the ideal moral behavior of society includes those who preach (to many deaf ears in society) the concept of *respect for the rights* of others. There are privileges to which all people are entitled on the basis of the general acceptance of ethical principles as a significant part of everyone's quality of living. The sine qua non of rights is the expectation of everyone to be *free from harm*, the bases of which include: 1) the biologic instinct of self-preservation, the spine of egoism, 2) the solemn oath of 'primum non nocere', and 3) the Golden Rule in its negative form: do not do unto others what you would not have others do unto you. The most passionate followers of respect for rights consider that *denial* and violation of rights lead to *dogmatism*, bias, unethical concepts, and immoral conduct, the extreme expression of which is fanaticism. *Fanaticism,* the most devastating opponent of respect for rights holds that all must believe and practice what the fanatic believes and practices or risk *persecution*—the ultimate concept of *man's inhumanity to man.* The most egregious violations of rights that readily come to mind are: *1) Slavery,* well-known since biblical times when Pharaoh, the tyrant of Egypt, ruled. It ultimately led to Lincoln's Gettysberg Address and the Emancipation Proclamation in 1863 during the Civil War; and *2) Hitler's Nazism* and its savagely brutal and outrageously cruel atrocities in World War II.

A close relative of fanaticism is the modern practice of *terrorism,* both locally and globally—a third example of flagrant violations of rights.

The foregoing historical ethical concepts have evolved into the modern ethical principles or standards that define and govern man's ideal societal behavior (see Chapter 8).

CHAPTER 8

MODERN ETHICAL PRINCIPLES

We should not judge of a man's merits by his great qualities, but by the use he makes of them.
> — Duke F. de La Rochefoucauld, 1747-1827

The philosophical schools of thought that have flourished for 2,500 years since the days of Socrates (see Chapter 7) are responsible for the modern ethical principles which the author regards as basic to the text and vital to the achievement of the goal, a perfect semicircle of life. These principles actually represent the third and highest tier in man's pursuit of quality living, which should be achieved by mid-life and then sustained until the decline due to aging sets in.

As long as everyone recognizes, respects and practices these principles, everyone can have meaningful, successful, interdependent relationships and quality living alongside his neighbor.

As a third tier, the principles differ from the first and second tiers in man's quality of living, both of which are egoistic and self-serving. The third tier, on the other hand, is entirely altruistic, designed only to relate to and serve others. Is it cynical, as some believe, that there is a hidden element of egoism in altruistic behavior? In complying with these principles, it is not suggested that one must love all neighbors, but rather that one be able to live symbiotically with them. In the mutual expectation of respecting rights, neighbors must be cognizant of the responsibilities that must accompany those rights.

We come finally to a description of the modern ethical principles that define and govern the ideal behavior of everyone in society. They may logically and conveniently be grouped into four main altruistic categories:

1.) *Character:* Display of virtues such as honesty, sincerity, integrity, trustworthiness, respect for the law

2.) *Conduct:* Essentially one of non-malevolence and non-maleficence, wishing and doing no harm to anyone (primum non nocere); also showing kindness and compassion (humanitas et misericordia)

3.) *Greatest Good:* Displaying only benevolence and beneficence, wishing and doing good to others (utilitarianism); practicing the Golden Rule: doing unto others what one would have others do unto you; obeying and practicing virtues of equality and justice

4.) Showing *respect for the rights* of all: civil rights; human rights; freedom of worship; respect for life, liberty and the pursuit of happiness; rights of privacy, autonomy, and self-determination. A sound theorem holds that, in devoting one's life to respecting all others, one must in return not covet anything from anyone other than respect

It is readily apparent that if all people practice all components of the cited ethical principles, the most ideal arrangement in human interrelations and the highest quality living among all in society would be created.

Violation of a single component of the ethical principles constitutes *unethical* conduct. Besides creating unwelcome ethical issues, it makes for an impossible expectation of a perfect semicircle of life. Two extremes readily come to mind: Consider first the ideal behavior of *Mother Theresa*, who was admired by all but followed by few. Hers is the best example of man's *humanity* to man.

Then consider the total failure of *Hitler's* a) concept of a 'master race', hence the irrationality of *eugenics* and b) *disrespect* for the rights of many, and its obvious consequences. In the history of the human race, there is no more egregious example of man's *inhumanity* to man.

The reader is reminded that the ethical principles are standards that form the basis for the composition of the third tier in building the highest level of quality living, which is the theme of this book. (Together with the replacement of a man's genetic mutations, both hereditary and acquired, and the elimination of his environmental adversities, attainment of the highest quality of living enables man to exist in a peaceful society and to approach the perfect semicircle of his life.)

The third and highest tier then has the following distinguishing characteristics:

1) Each of the elements comprising the ethical principles is purely altruistic in contrast to the egoism of tier one (consisting of personal happiness, well-being, independence, and security) and the egoism of tier two (consisting of personal success, wealth, and power).

2) Whereas tiers one and two serve to enrich a man personally, they fail to provide him with the qualities he needs to interrelate compatibly with his fellow-man in the achievement of a peaceful society. All men must incorporate the ethical principles into their behavior in order to communicate with each other on acceptable terms, achievable only by the adoption of tier three and its ethical principles.

3) Whereas tier two compounds and solidifies the personal egoistic quality of living when added to tier one, by its very nature,

tier two is antagonistic and hostile to the communal advantages of the essential addition of tier three.

The more successful is tier two for the individual, the more its owner would withdraw from the need for tier three. If man has it all, why would he need a favorable relationship with his neighbor?

A saving feature in the successful achievement of tier two is that wealth enables some men to become philanthropic and charitable in their societal behavior. If one examines the composition of the principles carefully, contributing to less fortunate persons and to needy causes, despite their commendable features, does not rise to the level of a community interrelationship defined in the ethical principles.

4) The use of the term, *tier*, should not be misinterpreted. It does not mean that tier three is built atop of tier two like a third level in a house. Tier three should come as early as possible in the life of man as soon after the instinctual features of tier one fall in place. Tier two historically is an inevitable goal in every man's aim for quality in his personal living, but tier three is vital to every man's highest quality of living, (i.e., his compatible existence in a multicultural society).

Tier three is independent of tier two, and is as important in its altruistic needs as is tier two in its egoistic needs.

CHAPTER 9

HISTORICAL MEDICAL ETHICAL LANDMARKS

Science cannot solve the ultimate mystery of nature, and that is because, in the analysis, we ourselves are part of nature and therefore part of the mystery that we are trying to solve.

— Max Planck, 1858-1947

In the evolution of modern medical ethics over the past 4000 years, a number of important contributions have been made toward steady progress, and are looked upon as landmarks. Some of these are, as follows:

2000 B.C.: Hammurabi, Babylonian King, issued his Judgments of Righteousness

1600 B.C.: Egyptian Papyri

1300 B.C.: Moses, Hebrew prophet, Old Testament, Judaism

500 B.C.: Confucius, Chinese Philosopher

5th Century B.C.: Buddha, Gautama Siddhartha, founder of Buddhism

460-377 B.C.: Hippocrates, Greek physician, Father of Medicine

B.C.-A.D.: Jesus, New Testament and Christianity

6th Century A.D.: Muhammad, Arabian prophet, received revelations from Allah through the angel, Gabriel, leading to the Koran, basis for Islam

900 A.D.: Rhazes, Arab Physician

1000 A.D.: Avicenna, Persian Physician

1200 A.D.: Frederick II, Sicilian Ruler

1520 A.D.: Rules of Conduct, Royal College of Physicians, London

1803 A.D.: British Doctrine of Medical Ethics

1847 A.D.: Code of Ethics, American Medical Association

1864 A.D.: Geneva Convention

1903 A.D.: Principles of Medical Ethics, AMA

1912 A.D.: Idem, revised

1947 A.D.: Nuremberg Code

1948 A.D.: Universal Declaration of Human Rights, Geneva
　　　Assembly, United Nations

1964 A.D.: Declaration of Helsinki, World Medical Association

1984 A.D.: Ethics Manual, American College of Physicians

1993,1998 A.D.: Idem, revised

CHAPTER 10

EVOLUTION OF ETHICAL ISSUES IN HEALTH CARE

Tell me and I will forget; teach me and I will remember; involve me and I will learn.

— Benjamin Franklin, 1706-1794

CONCEPT OF AN ETHICAL ISSUE

In the presentation to society of many diagnostic and therapeutic biotechnological advances which are made on a regular and ongoing basis, most innovations are accepted enthusiastically by society without disagreement, and there is no concern regarding the need of resolution. Thus, no ethical issues evolve.

In our pluralistic society, however, many instances of disagreement arise in connection with innovations, and the differences of opinion lead to controversy and to conflict without resolution. These become *ethical issues* requiring intervention by the law and *adjudication*. Acceptance by society then often follows, even reluctantly, and the issue may then be considered as resolved, although not necessarily permanently. At other times, however, despite the intervention of the law in support of the innovation, elements of society, often on a religious basis, refuse to accept the legal resolution, and the ethical issue, although resolved legally, persists as an ethical issue. An outstanding example is the pro-life, pro-choice issue regarding abortion. Failure of societal acceptance despite legal resolution of this or any other issue serves only to perpetuate an obstruction to man's achievement of a placid interrelational quality in living, thereby preventing the formation of the perfect semicircle of life. (The reader should note that disobedience of the law, besides being unlawful, is also unethical on the basis that obedience or at least respect for the law is an ethical principle under the heading of Character.) It would appear that, on a rational basis, by communication and *negotiation*, any issue could and should be settled as long as obstinacy can be forsaken. Such, however, is often not the case.

An ethical issue then is an unsettled ethical question that is in controversy or dispute between two or more elements of society and fails to receive unanimous acceptance by all members of society.It was succinctly expressed by the American poet, Robert Frost: *nature within her inmost self divides, to trouble men with having to take sides.*

WHAT IS UNETHICAL?

A matter is *unethical* when it is in violation of any of the components of the four major ethical groups of principles described in Chapter 8.

WHAT IS MORALITY?

It is pertinent here to discuss *morality*, a term often used synonymously with ethical behavior. Actually, morality is the *practice* of the principles of ethics. It refers to the capability of distinguishing right from wrong and *acting* appropriately.

Immorality would therefore be defined as the practice or act of violating an ethical principle.

The author chose also to distinguish between an *ethicist* and a *moralist*. The ethicist is a specialist in philosophy, who analyzes and explains all aspects of an ethical issue and opines whether any matter is of ethical question or concern. He does not advocate or propose a solution to any issue (unless requested to do so). He is not by definition endowed with wisdom superior to all men, as though he were Solomonic.

SHOULD AN ETHICIST BE A MORALIST?

If an ethicist chooses to volunteer a solution to an issue, he then assumes the role of moralist (who professes to know right from wrong, and to practice or render his opinion at will).

EVOLUTION OF MORALITY

It is pertinent at this point to give some thought to the *evolution of morality*, a basic requirement of which is living in groups

1) that depend upon themselves or their families and others for subsistence and defense. The object is the fulfillment of the instinct of *self-preservation* and freedom from harm.

2) that cooperate with family and others despite independent and differing beliefs, wishes and interests, the aim being the fulfillment of the instinct of *race preservation*.

MEDICAL SCIENCE AND THE LAW

In the interrelationship between *medical science and the law*, two basic principles must be invoked. All people are 1) equal under the law with equal rights and are 2) obligated to live within the law and obey established boundaries of conduct.

The law often fails to keep pace with dynamic, innovative, ever-changing biotechnology, resulting in ethical issues that insist on adjudication. In the absence of an appropriate law, any attempt to comply within ethical tenets may result in violation of existing law and demand adjudication.

A common example of an issue involving medical science and the law that required and received adjudication was in vitro fertilization, although it remains replete with ethical issues. Assisted suicide and fetal tissue transplantation, however, have not yet been resolved legally, and remain as subjects with issues (see Section D).

A point should be made concerning some recent tendency to a reversal of trends. For example, Congress has passed laws prior to organized medicine's resolution of a knotty medical problem: forcing health insurance plans to pay for 48-hour hospital stays after delivery; promoting mammography for women in their forties; outlawing abortion by intact dilation and extraction (so-called partial birth abortion). The action by Congress in such matters has been looked upon as practicing medicine without a license. Their attitude is often unscientific and medically unacceptable, and may be referred to as a one-size-fits-all mentality. Should complex medical decisions be made by politicians responding to the emotional appeal of voters in lieu of expert scientific judgments and decisions made by doctors and their patients at the highest levels of medical knowledge?

THE LAW AND SOCIETY

In the interrelationship between the law and society (mainly the religious element), religion reacts even more slowly to innovations in medical science than does the slow-moving law. As a result, there is further delay in acceptance of change. An outstanding example is the pro-life versus pro-choice issue (Roe versus Wade), wherein religion fails to accept the law's decision in the matter. Religion, as a part of society, then perpetuates the ethical question as an ongoing issue in violation of the law.

In the relationship between *MEDICAL SCIENCE AND RELIGION*, as previously noted, religion is generally very slow in accepting the rapid changes in science and human behavior, to the extent at times of even permanent non-acceptance. The result is controversy, conflict, dilemma and eventually an *issue*. Examples include the Galileo incident, evolution versus creationism, and the origin of the universe with respect to the Big Bang theory versus biblical Fundamentalism. A common medical concern is the refusal of a needed blood transfusion on religious grounds, causing much distress in hospital care. Organ transplantation is a frequent problem in the refusal by certain religious beliefs to accept organ donation even to save a life. A tragic area is the refusal by parents on a religious basis to allow a child with a serious, curable illness such as diabetic coma or bacterial meningitis to die rather than have life-saving medical care, which is opposed by the parents in favor of prayer.

The autopsy, an essential part of health care in 1) determining cause of death and 2) medical education, is forbidden on religious grounds in several forms of worship. This is not arguable, but is indeed unfortunate in its hindrance of medical progress in the best interest of well-being as an aim in life.

The Galileo incident is well worth recounting. The great Italian scientist, Galileo, was condemned in 1633 by the church as a heretic for teaching that the earth revolves about the sun, an important astrophysical observation. He was compelled to recant his belief before a body of assembled cardinals and to renounce his life work. He refused, but was allowed to escape the torture of burning at the stake. He won a sentence of house arrest for life. In 1993, 360 years later, Pope John Paul II proclaimed that the church erred and called the condemnation a tragic mutual incomprehension. Another example of conflict between the church and science is the literal interpretation of God's creation of man and the earth in six days, presumably some 10,000 years ago, despite scientific evidence of man's existence some four million years ago and the earth's age as perhaps some twelve billion years. Interestingly, the Supreme Court bars the teaching of creationism in public schools on constitutional ground. Regarding evolution, however,

Darwin's Origin of Species and The Descent of Man (1859) are a standard part of the curriculum in all schools. Recently, there has been some effort to negate the teaching of Evolution and revive the concept of Creationism in the schools' education. Fossil recordings by modern methods including radiometry reveal that hominids were the earliest upright walking primates four million years ago. According to the most accepted hypothesis, the lineages of human beings and chimpanzees split from a common ancestor 5-6 million years ago. Opponents of this concept have a very difficult time explaining why the human being and the chimpanzee have an almost identical chromosomal composition.

In 1996, Pope John Paul II announced that the *theory of evolution is more than just a hypothesis, but the spiritual soul was created by God.* Also with regard to the Big Bang theory, the Pope indicated that *God preceded the first second of the big bang.*

SCIENCE AND INDUSTRY

Innovations in medical science and biotechnology exert constant and enormous influences in business and industry, causing conflict and the creation of ethical issues as with science and the law and as with science and religion. In manufacturing, the duplication of drugs with minor alterations in chemical structure (to avoid infringement upon patent rights) may encourage the manufacturer to make important-sounding claims of superiority. In fact, what is often created is a glut of drugs and much confusion among doctors and patients because of the existence of many duplications with minor changes.

Another example is excessive advertising of drugs by a manufacturer directly to patients via television, for the treatment of certain symptoms without first emphasizing the need of a medical examination for proper diagnosis. This practice raises dangerous ethical issues.

There are reported instances of corporate suppression of the release of generic drugs by another manufacturer with claims that the studies were *flawed*. One wonders if the suppression effort might not be an ill-founded attempt to influence the price and sale of the accuser's own products.

In the stock market, new drugs and technologies are watched very closely from the standpoint of stock investments and sales. Should a fly-by-night new drug, that may have little if any durable value, have a serious effect upon an individual's hard earned income given to investment in an established pharmaceutical company?

PERPETUATION OF ETHICAL ISSUES

In the interrelationships between medical science and 1) the law, 2) religion, and 3) industry, ethical issues will continue to evolve and hopefully be resolved or eliminated. Unfortunately, however, they often fail to be adjudicated or to disappear. The reasons for their perpetuation are as follows:

1) A failing effort by society, including its religious component, to accept adjudicated medical innovations based upon the character principle of honesty, sincerity, integrity and respect for the law

2) A failing effort by society to enforce ethical principles rooted in non-malevolence, charity, kindness and compassion

3) A failing effort by society to prevent violation of ethical principles designed to protect and benefit all

4) A failing effort to teach and practice the ethical principle rooted in the concept of benevolence, justice, equality and altruism

5) A failing effort to abandon concepts of injustice, inequality, egoism, greed, and persecution (man's inhumanity to man)

6) A failing effort to adhere to the ethical principle of respect for everyone's rights

SECTION D:

SEVEN MAJOR MEDICAL SUBJECTS WITH ETHICAL ISSUES RELATING TO QUALITY LIVING

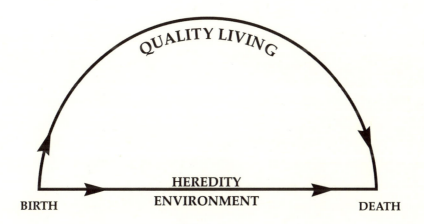

THE PERFECT SEMICIRCLE OF LIFE

SECTION D

SEVEN MAJOR MEDICAL SUBJECTS WITH ETHICAL ISSUES RELATING TO QUALITY LIVING

Perhaps no sin so easily besets us as a sense of self-satisfied superiority to others. It cannot always be called pride, but more often it is an attitude of mind which either leads to bigotry and prejudice or to such a vaunting conceit in the truth of one's own beliefs and positions, that there is no room for tolerance of ways and thoughts which are not as ours are.

— Anonymous

INTRODUCTION

The previous Section C was concerned with Quality Living, and its last Chapter (10) dealt with the evolution of ethical issues in health care. In the forthcoming Section D, seven major subjects in health care have been selected because they all are replete with ethical issues relating to quality living and requiring resolution for universal societal acceptance. They are: 1) The Patient and the Doctor, II) Diet and Nutrition, III) Medication, IV) Advances in Biotechnology, V) Medical Research, VI) Decision-making in the Mature Years, and VII) Health Care Reform.

RESOLUTION OF ISSUES

By deliberately avoiding the temptation to suggest means of resolution and by merely describing all aspects of the issues, the author remains as an unbiased medical ethicist. At times, however, recommendations may be offered, which are not the author's but rather are gleaned from intelligent opinions of experts in health care.

The readers on the other hand, do have the luxury of indulging in their own temptations and inclinations to resolve issues and render opinions. It is the reader's privilege to express and practice what he thinks is right or wrong, thereby functioning as a moralist (according to the author's definition).

The result is that the reader participates actively in the controversies emerging from the issues and also, by way of a common agreement among all of the readers, may then resolve an issue. After all, if all ethical issues are resolved, the highest level of quality living is thereby attained and man can come that much closer to the perfect semicircle of life that everyone seeks.

The author assumes that the readers are typically diverse representatives of societal culture and arrive at widely varying ethical considerations and opinions regarding biotechnological innovations. The effect, as expected, would be dissension and controversy among the readers themselves and also between the readers and the content of the ethical issues formulated by the author in the forthcoming Section D. New ethical issues would then emerge and more legal adjunction would be required before resolution and possible societal acceptance could follow. The likely reaction among a heterogeneous group of readers would be a balloon-like expansion of the issues, and further delay in their resolution. All issues must be expressed with candor, else resolution could never be realized.

SECTION D

SUBJECT I:
THE PATIENT AND THE DOCTOR

Knowledge is proud that he has learned so much; wisdom is humble that he knows no more.

— William Cowper, 1731-1800

CHAPTER 11

THE PATIENT'S RIGHTS, INFORMED CONSENT

The voice of the intellect is a soft one, but it does not rest until it has gained a hearing. Ultimately, after endless rebuffs, it succeeds. This is one of the few points in which one may be optimistic about the future of mankind.

— Sigmund Freud, 1856-1939

It is proper that the first of the seven major medical subjects should relate to the patient and the doctor, and that the first chapter (11) should pertain to the *patient's rights* and to *informed consent*. Historically, patients who are the intended recipients of health care have been denied rights for as many years as patients have been receiving health care. When the Israelites were slaves of the Pharaohs, they surely had no rights, and their slave physicians likewise had no rights. Man has made no greater progress in the advance of civilization than in human rights.

The rights of patients, as with all other human beings, are based on respect for human life, and are best expressed in the modern ethical principles (see Chapter 8), compliance with which forms the foundation for man's highest tier in his pursuit of quality in living.

The principles are well worth repeating here briefly: 1) displaying honesty and sincerity of character in all encounters between individuals; 2) doing no harm to anyone; being kind and compassionate to all; 3) doing only good and practicing the Golden Rule; treating everyone with justice and equality; 4) showing respect for everyone's rights and expecting the same in return; included are civil and human rights; right of privacy, autonomy, and self-determination (based upon informed consent); respect for everyone's cultural and religious observances; right to life, liberty, and the pursuit of happiness. In expecting rights, everyone must give assurance of taking responsibility for those rights.

HISTORICAL BASES FOR RIGHTS

The fourth modern ethical principle of respect for rights is embodied in the following important historical documents now revered as milestones in the evolution of the rights of patients regarding their health care:

1) Hippocratic Oath, 5th Century BC
2) Declaration of Independence, 1776
3) Geneva Convention, 1864
4) Nuremberg Code, 1947
5) Universal Declaration of Human Rights, 1948
6) Declaration of Helsinki, 1964
7) Patient's Bill of Rights, 1973, revised 2001

THE HIPPOCRATIC OATH

The Hippocratic Oath (early *fifth century, BC*) is among the oldest documents expressing the *rights* of patients, not stated in a positive way, but indirectly. For example, in referring to the sick, the physician swears that "I will keep them from harm and injustice." The principle of doing no harm or nonmaleficence (primum non nocere) is in the granting of a patient's right. Further, there is reference to a patient's right of privacy.

THE OATH OF HIPPOCRATES
(460-377 BC)

I swear by Apollo, physician Aesculapius, Hygieia and Panaceia and all the gods and goddesses, making them my witnesses, that I will fulfill according to my ability and judgment this oath and this covenant:

To hold him who has taught me this art as equal to my parents and to live my life in partnership with him, and if he is in need of money to give him a share of mine, and to regard his offspring as equal to my brothers in male lineage and to teach them this art—if they desire to learn it—without fee and covenant; to give a share of precepts and oral instruction and all the other learning to my sons and to the sons of him who has instructed me and to pupils who have signed the covenant and have taken an oath according to the medical law, but to no one else.

I will apply dietetic measures for the benefit of the sick according to my ability and judgment; I will keep them from harm and injustice.

I will neither give a deadly drug to anybody if asked for it, nor will I make a suggestion to this effect. Similarly, I will not give to a woman an abortive remedy. In purity and holiness I will guard my life and my art.

I will not use the knife, not even on sufferers from stone, but will withdraw in favor of such men who are engaged in this work.

Whatever houses I may visit, I will come for the benefit of the sick, remaining free of all intentional injustice, of all mischief, and in particular of sexual relations with both female and male persons, be they free or slaves.

What I may see or hear in the course of the treatment or even outside of the treatment in regard to the lives of men, which on no account one must spread abroad, I will keep to myself holding such things shameful to be spoken about.

If I fulfill this oath and do not violate it, may it be granted to me to enjoy life and art, being honored with fame among all men for all time to come; if I transgress it and swear falsely, may the opposite of all this be my lot.

DECLARATION OF INDEPENDENCE, 1776

In Thomas Jefferson's Declaration of Independence on July 4, 1776, rights are expressed succinctly and outstandingly well: "We hold these truths to be self-evident, that all men are created equal, that they are endowed by their creator with certain unalienable rights, that among these are life (Ed: Right to health care and freedom from harm), liberty (Ed: Freedom of worship, freedom of movement within the law, right of privacy, autonomy, and self-determination), and the pursuit of happiness (Ed: Equal opportunity, security, independence)."

THE FRENCH REVOLUTION, 1789

A striking and dramatic illustration of a people's demand for *rights* was the motto of the French Revolution expressed in 1789 during the storming of the Bastille: *liberte, egalite, fraternite,* It was an outstanding, dynamic and memorable announcement.

THE GENEVA CONVENTION, 1864

The Geneva Convention in 1864 represented an agreement by

European powers to offer *rights* to non-combatants of war and prisoners. There was general agreement that new and more humane regulations would be recognized with regard to the treatment of prisoners of war, sick and wounded, as well as to the treatment of those who minister to them. Chaplains, physicians, nurses, ambulance corps, ambulances, and military hospitals were all granted neutralization.

The agreement was a serious consideration, as it was revised in 1868 and reaffirmed by most nations.

It was a remarkable advance in the matter of rights, but quite ironic, if not oxymoronic, that war itself was not outlawed and combatants in war were given no special consideration (Ed: One must always be grateful for little favors.)

PASTOR MARTIN NIEMOELLER, a victim of the Nazis (see Chapter 23) made a touching statement that bears on *rights.*

"First they came for the Jews, and I did not speak out because I was not a Jew.

"Then they came for the communists, and I did not speak out because I was not a communist.

"Then they came for the trade unionists, and I did not speak out because I was not a trade unionist.

"And then they came for me, and there was no one left to speak for me."

NUREMBERG CODE OF 1947

It was inevitable following the defeat of Nazi Germany and the end of World War II that a trial would be held in which sixteen of twenty-three accused Nazi physicians were found guilty of committing torturous and lethal experiments on prisoners in concentration camps. One wonders about the mentality of these physicians, when one considers that they took the Oath of Hippocrates when they graduated from medical school, as did American medical school graduates. Some feeble justification for their behavior was offered on the basis that they were employees of the military and were carrying out orders. That argument is not tenable when the physician's code of ethics requires that he may never compromise his own professional code of ethics in favor of an opposing ethical code mandated by an employer.

Following the trial, the Nuremberg Code of 1947 was an expected aftermath, formed on the basis of *Global Human Rights Law*. It is extensive in its purview, and is applicable in the protection of the *rights* of human beings as subjects in modern medical research. For example, The Nuremberg Code requires the humanitarian conduct of safety and freedom from harm, the anticipation of beneficial effects, the scientific and moral integrity of the research investigators, the provision of disclosure to the voluntary participants, and their understanding to result in *informed* and *voluntary consent*. The participating subjects must not be victims of duress or bias, and must have the right of refusal. Above all, the experiment must be in the best interest of the subjects.

The readers are invited to recall a gruesome aftermath of the barbaric experiments done on concentration camp prisoners in World War II. One physician collected data from autopsy findings in order to publish a textbook of anatomy, which was then used in German-speaking medical schools, until it collapsed under the weight of its own notoriety, and the text was withdrawn.

THE UNIVERSAL DECLARATION OF HUMAN RIGHTS, adopted in *1948* by the General Assembly of the United Nations, may be the best-known *Global Defense of Rights*. It guaranteed security, well-being, and equality of dignity to all people of the world. It laid the foundation for laws and treaties in the protection of *human rights* with regard to:

a) Health, food, shelter, clothing, education
b) Environmental protection
c) Freedom of expression

d) Freedom of movement within one's country

e) Just and favorable working conditions

f) An adequate living standard

g) Safety from persecution and torture; discrimination against religious and racial minorities, free expression of political opinions

h) Immigration status

i) Oppression of women

The aim of the General Assembly was for the teaching of *human rights* at every level of education and for its practice at every institution throughout the world.

In celebration of its fiftieth anniversary in 1998, the General Assembly proclaimed December 10 as *Human Rights Day*. The problem is that the declaration is not binding in accordance with international law.

THE DECLARATION OF HELSINKI was developed in *1964* by The Committee on Medical Ethics of the World Medical Association. It is among the most quoted references to a patient's rights. Among its outstanding requirements are that there be:

a) Established guidelines and standards for ethical conduct in research involving human subjects

b) Included informed consent, minimizing risks, and protecting the welfare of the subjects

c) A clear formulation of design and performance

d) A transmittal of the protocol to an independent committee, such as an Institutional Review Board, for consideration, comments, and guidance

THE PATIENT'S BILL OF RIGHTS, established in *1973*, is the product of the labors of a national welfare and rights organization. It has the approval of the American Hospital Association and serves as the preamble to the official statement of The Joint Commission on the Accreditation of Health Care Organizations. There is mandatory compliance in all health care facilities.

    Twelve rights of the patients are listed (not verbatim), as follows:
        1) To considerate and respectful care
        2) To obtain information regarding one's diagnosis, treatment, and prognosis
        3) To information needed to give informed consent regarding a procedure or treatment
        4) To refusal of treatment and its consequences (based on the right of self- determination)
        5) To privacy
        6) To confidentiality
        7) To a response to a request for services
        8) To information regarding the hospital's relation to other health care institutions
        9) To advice regarding human experimentation and the right of refusal
        10) To continuity of care
        11) To explanation of the bill
        12) To hospital rules and regulations regarding the patient's conduct

    In the new millenium, our Congress is expected to consider modifications and updating that have been recommended because of reforms; for example, whether or not a patient has the right to bring suit against a health maintenance organization under appropriate circumstances. This and other issues are points of contention in our two-party Congress.

SELECTIVE RIGHTS OF PATIENTS TO THE REQUIREMENTS OF PHYSICIANS

In the performance of their duties, physicians have certain

requirements as expressed in the Code of Ethics of the American College of Physicians (referred to in Chapter 12, the Doctor-Patient Relationship). Patients have rights to the expectation of these requirements by their physicians:

1) The doctor must be competent, compassionate, do no harm, relieve pain and suffering, provide adequate and on-going care, maintain confidentiality, especially in sensitive areas such as sexually transmitted diseases, acquired immunodeficiency syndrome, psychiatric disorders, and pregnancy.

2) The physician must avoid bias and paternalism in his presentation.

3) He must resort at least to *reasonable disclosure* of his recommendations to enable a patient to respond with *informed consent.*

4) The doctor must provide *full disclosure* as to the diagnosis, treatment, and prognosis to enable patients in decision making regarding their *end-of-life* care (see Chapter 25).

5) The physician must respect the patient's rights of: a) autonomy and of self determination, concepts based upon the principle of *informed consent*, and b) best interest, as determined by the physician, with input from the close family relatives of the patient or designated surrogate.

Following the physician's disclosure, the patient, having been informed, may take action and give his consent on the basis of his right to autonomy or he may refuse the physician's recommendation on the basis of the patient's right of self-determination. Refusal implies that the patient may be compelled to resort to his right of dissolution of his relationship with his physician, unless the physician chooses to abide by the patient's refusal or recommend alternatives.

ACCESS TO MEDICAL RECORDS
Patients have a right to the access of their medical records and X-rays, although medical records and X-rays do not belong to the patient. They are the property of the health care provider.

REQUEST FOR DISCLOSURE

Upon *written request* by the patient, he is entitled to a full disclosure of the information in his record as well as the record itself (or a copy thereof). The information may also be available to any authorized representative, such as an attorney or a third party payer, provided the patient has given his *approval*. In a court subpoena, the patient's approval is not necessary.

The regulations governing the medical record are mandated by the *Privacy Act of 1976*.

OPPOSITION BY PHYSICIAN

Under a variety of circumstances, the patient's physician may oppose release of records to a patient, thereby raising ethical issues, if in the opinion of the physician

1) the patient may misinterpret technical data and reports;

2) the information may be emotionally harmful to the patient;

3) the information may have been submitted in confidence from another source that expected its own right of privacy;

4) the information may reveal errors needing clarification before the patient becomes aware of them.

CONDITION OF THE RECORD

In view of the availability of records at any time, the record should be complete, legible, accurate, and up to date at all times.

If any errors are detected in the record, they may never be erased or whited out. Instead, a line is expected to be drawn through the error, and initialed by the one making the correction.

LIFE OF THE MEDICAL RECORD

Records must be kept for at least *seven years* from the date of the last treatment (and for three years after the death of a patient).

Included are pertinent pathology slides, electrocardiograms, electroencephalograms, etc. X-ray films must be kept for a minimum of three years. In the event of litigation, records must be retained until the case is settled.

Outdated records must be destroyed by *shredding*. A charge for copies of records is expected and valid. If the claim involves Social Security, there is no fee for copies.

RIGHTS OF A MINOR

A minor is generally regarded as a person under age 18, or age 21, depending on circumstances and states. In either case, the minor seeking the aid of a physician, should expect the same rights as an adult. Of particular concern to the minor is the right of confidentiality, which may be threatened by the physician's decision or at least the desire to involve the patient's parents in a discussion regarding consent, procedure, planning, payment of fee, etc.

Should the physician assume his right of involvement of parents without approval by the patient? Under certain circumstances, the physician may have a conflict between his ethical duty to confidentiality and his responsibility to the patient's parents or to the law. To resolve the issue, the physician must understand the state laws and he may need the aid of legal counsel.

RIGHTS TO A SMOKE FREE ENVIRONMENT

A person's right to smoke cigarettes has always been a privilege respected on both moral and legal grounds.

When the evils of nicotine became manifest in recent years, smoking remained a privilege legally, except as institutions began to forbid smoking in some public as well as in some private places.

PASSIVE SMOKE

Not until it was clearly demonstrated that exposure to passive smoke may be hazardous to one's health, did the right of smoking become an ethical issue between the smoker's legal privilege and its conflict with the hazard to the nearby non-smoker.

The basis for the dispute and the issue involved is that non-smokers exposed to cigarette smoking have been shown to have metabolic end-products of nicotine in their urine, thereby clearly indicating that the exposure of the non-smoker to the smoker may be harmful to the non-smoker. (At least five thousand deaths occur annually among non-smokers as a result of exposure to the smokers.) The non-smoker and smoker can avoid each other, thereby giving them both independent rights, but does the smoker still have the right to smoke when the presence of the non-smoker cannot be avoided, or when the non-smoker chooses to be free of exposure to cigarette smoke that can be very harmful to his health?

INFORMED CONSENT

In the initiation of an encounter between a physician and the patient, it is incumbent upon the physician to provide the patient with the essential information necessary for the patient to be able to make a decision regarding the physician's recommendation. The process is known as informed consent. It originated in England as a part of common British law in the late 1950's, and has been adopted legally in the United States as an expected component of all physician-patient encounters pertaining to the care of the patient.

Prior to the 1940's, patients in the United States were usually subjected to procedures and to research investigations without the benefit of the formal process of appropriate presentation of information with a corresponding request for consent. In the early 1940's, the presentations were made sketchily and without formal approval. Since then, however, the patient's *rights* began to crystallize and to be respected. Since its legalization in the 1950's, informed consent has become the basic ingredient, in fact the cement, of the doctor-patient relationship. it is currently in the forefront of every recommendation made by a physician to a patient, and is always, at the very least, *implied* when any routine suggestion or plan is offered without consent even discussed. Such circumstances arise, for example, in the commonplace requests that a patient have a routine blood test, or a routine chest x-ray, or an electrocardiogram, or even undress for a physical examination.

The *basic elements* in the process of informed consent are:

1) disclosure by the physician and 2) competence, comprehension, voluntarism, and consent by the patient.

Disclosure refers to the *essential* information presented by the physician. It includes the diagnosis and nature of the patient's condition, the proposed treatment or procedure, the possible outcomes and risks, alternative choices, and right of refusal. The extent of the disclosure must be reasonable in expecting informed consent, but it must be full and *complete* when the patient is expected to make a decision in connection with end-of-life care (see discussions of disclosure earlier in this chapter and in greater detail in Chapter 25). In fact, informed consent does not require full disclosure because the term implies that the disclosure can always be challenged as incomplete. Instead, it should consist of sufficient information given to a *competent* patient (unless legally declared incompetent) who must be able to *comprehend* the physician's recommendations and is able to make an informed medical *decision voluntarily*. The patient is then prepared to offer or refuse to give his *informed consent*, based on his rights of autonomy and self-determination.

THE PATIENT'S RIGHTS

The physician is obligated to respect the patient's right 1) to request a second opinion, or 2) to either agree or 3) refuse to agree to the recommendations. In the event of the patient's refusal, the patient should understand the alternatives, if any, before making a final decision.

THE PATIENT'S RESPONSIBILITY

At this juncture in the discussion, the patient is assuming *responsibility* for his actions, including the possibility that his relationship with his doctor may be at the point of termination.

HISTORICAL INFLUENCES

Key considerations that surely played a role in the solidification and legalization of the modern concept of informed consent in the early 1950's must have arisen in the shameful *notoriety* of 1) the infamous Tuskegee experiments by our government in the 1920's and 2) the concentration camp experiments by German Nazi physicians in the 1940's. In both, human beings were abused in the most egregious and inhumane manner imaginable as experimental subjects (see Chapter 23).

MODIFICATIONS OF INFORMED CONSENT

The principle of informed consent is not carved in stone. Modifications of the standard operating procedure of informed consent have been made that are based upon the policies and regulations of the institution with which the physician is associated in conducting tests and procedures on the patient.

CAN A PHYSICIAN FORSAKE INFORMED CONSENT?

Circumstances justifying a physician's decision to *forsake* the process of informed consent altogether are recognized by law. These include: a) a medical emergency demanding prompt and immediate action, b) incompetence of the patient, as a result of which the patient's surrogate acts in place of the patient, or in the best interest of the patient, depending upon, respectively, whether the patient's wishes are known or are not known, and c) the physician elects to utilize his therapeutic privilege to withhold the divulgence of information, which the physician believes would be potentially harmful to the patient psychologically.

THREAT TO THE RIGHT OF PRIVACY

Care must be exercised in the maintenance of a constant vigil over hard fought benefits in the achievements of *rights* for patients. There are always *threats* that tend, deliberately or inadvertently, to weaken accomplishments, which are never carved in stone like The Ten Commandments.

An example is based upon the rapidity with which the industrial aspect of medicine is *going online*. As a result, there is an increasingly more frequent availability of the *internet* and *e-mail* to search for and find highly personal medical information.

Those who *favor* the use of the internet include insurance companies in general, public health research scientists, doctors, and hospitals that monitor the health of patients, and patients who are concerned with their ease in obtaining their old records.

In *opposition* to the use of the internet are those who have deep concern over the following:

1) The centralization of information into a *centralizing power*. They regard this as a frightening potential.

2) The lack of federal laws to protect a patient's medical privacy (as, for example, the presence of federal laws that protect the privacy of titles of rented video tapes).

3) Office visits of patients to their physicians. These result in the creation of permanent records that could be available for anyone to follow a patient on the internet for the life of the patient.

4) Medical treatments, results of laboratory tests.

5) Payments by use of a credit card. In this regard, The Department of Health and Human Services has held hearings

pertaining to the National Identification System.

6) Health insurance data.

There are still further examples of threats to the loss of privacy via the impetus given by circulating confidential information in the digital world.

Will resolution of the ethical issues regarding a patient's privacy be achieved by determining whether the benefits outweigh the losses?

LIMIT TO A PATIENT'S RIGHTS

In considering the broadness and fairness to patients in the provision of granting rights, it is not unreasonable to assume that a patient's rights should be *balanced* against *fairness* to all members of a patient's family. In other words, no patient deserves more than a) a fair and equitable consideration, or b) an undue consideration of his interest.

RESPONSIBILITY AND RIGHTS

Reference has been made previously to the importance of the patient's assumption of responsibility with the exercise of every right. No one should expect any right without agreeing to take responsibility with that right. By responsibility, the author intends it to be understood that the patient show appropriate awareness and accountability for assuming his rights. Rights and responsibilities for them are as inseparable as conjoined twins, or like Tweedledum and Tweedledee. The earliest reference to responsibility appears in the Summa Theologica of St. Thomas Aquinas in the thirteenth century.

THE PATIENT'S RIGHTS AND SOCIETAL RESPONSIBILITIES

All patients, in appreciation of their rights and recognition of their responsibility for those rights, should agree to participate as a part of their *societal* responsibilities:

1) To share in the burgeoning costs of health care

2) To play a role in the equitable distribution of monetary resources

3) To help solve the complex problems in health care delivery systems, e.g., in health maintenance organizations, private health insurance, etc.

4) To show benevolence in providing health care to the poor, disabled, and elderly

5) To share in restoring the currently strained doctor-patient relationship

CHAPTER 12

THE DOCTOR-PATIENT RELATIONSHIP

The good physician treats the disease, but the great physician treats the patient.

— Sir William Osler, 1849-1919

INTRODUCTION

Except for the relationship between a man and his maker or a man and his family, there is no other human relationship, certainly not one pertaining to a man's well-being, that is more meaningful, more important, more private and more binding than the *ideal* relationship between a patient and his physician.

In addition, there is no subject with a greater impact upon one's quality living than is one's relationship with his physician. In spite of or because of its importance, however, the relationship presents one of the largest health care locales that is embedded with numerous *ethical issues* needing resolution and community acceptance in order to achieve a *societal* quality of living.

Historically, the doctor-patient relationship can be traced to *Hippocrates*, the Father of Medicine. In the fifth century B.C., he established an oath, known by his name, which has served for 2500 years as a covenant between patients and their physicians in a durable kinship. Hippocrates conducted a school in Cos, Greece, in which medical ethics was taught primarily about the physician's care of his patients. As a matter of fact, as a tribute to the importance of the oath, and despite its antiquity, the Oath of Hippocrates has been recited as a pledge in its original form by all medical school graduates for many years until recently. The Oath is now taken ceremonially by all medical students prior to their graduation, in a *modified* form, primarily to abandon the outdated reference in the original oath to the avoidance of abortion and to the oath's failure to include women as physicians. Otherwise, the Oath is as timely and pertinent today as it was originally formulated (see Oath of Hippocrates in Chapter 11).

WEAKENING OF THE BOND

In recent years, many factors have evolved that serve to weaken the traditional bond between physician and patient. For the most part, they are not caused by either the doctor or the patient, but are mostly due to the general circumstances of our times. As a result, the ethical principles that govern the ideal behavior of all men in society, although more applicable than ever previously, are more in jeopardy of violation.

A few of the *factors* responsible for the weakened bond in the doctor-patient relationship are readily apparent as follows:

1) The new approach to health care that features group practices with multi-specialty representations in addition to family physicians and general internists. The preservation of one physician as the monitor and guide for a patient's and his family's total health care is difficult to maintain under these new circumstances and is a definite threat to privacy, confidentiality, and to continuity of care. The problems arising in such settings are more manifest in the new managed care arrangements when compared with traditional private fee-for-service care.

2) There tends to be a loss of one-on-one history-taking because of elaborate forms to be filled out by patients even at home away from the usual office settings. In addition to the loss of valuable time spent in intimate discussion, important details are omitted that could provide valuable diagnostic clues.

3) Time spent during detailed physical examinations is reduced by use of technical devices such as blood pressure gauges by office personnel, ultrasonography in lieu of the stethoscope, replacement of physical examinations of body parts relating to symptoms by use of radiography, replacement of physicians by physician assistants, etc. Magnetic resonance imaging, one of the greatest modern technologic advances in diagnostic medicine, is too often abused at great expense by its replacement of the patient's history and examination.

4) The personal factor in the relationship is replaced by an impersonal, detached, and hurried manner.

5) Numerous problems saused by non-medical personnel in the insurance industry who deny reimbursement for proper patient care by the physician.

6) Frequent specialists are chosen by specialty-oriented patients in the care of problems properly manageable by the family physician or general internist.

7) Hospital emergency facilities are used in place of the family physician's office during nights and weekends when the physician may not be available personally.

8) Patients fail to appreciate the need of a single physician to supervise total care, including medications obtained from multiple physicians, and by way of self-service with over-the-counter drugs and medications obtained in herbal stores, etc.

9) The enormous increase in health care costs are not the fault of the physician as many patients believe, but are due to the high prices of drugs (for which there is little if any insurance coverage), laboratory tests, radiological procedures, surgery, hospitalization, inadequate insurance, out-of-pocket costs beyond insurance coverage, dental care, eyeglasses and hearing aids, home

care, long-term care, nursing home care, mental health, etc. As a result, the patient is often driven to self-diagnosis and *self-treatment* with over-the-counter medications, home-testing devices, herbal medicine, and alternative medical care, often by unqualified practitioners of health care.

In considering that the best available care in the world should be everyone's right, but really does not exist as such, the discouraged patient blames the physician. The physician, however, is really unable to resolve most of the problems, especially since he too is more the victim than the cause of the high cost of practice and insurance.

THE IDEAL RELATIONSHIP

The key word used in describing the relationship is *ideal*. On that note, the ideal roles of the 1) doctor, 2) patient, and 3) society, will be addressed in some detail, much of which is described in the *American College of Physicians Ethics Manual* and in the *Principles of Medical Ethics, The American Medical Association*. By revisiting the ideal roles of the participants in the relationship, many of the ethical issues requiring elimination can be addressed in order to establish a better quality of living en route to a more perfect semicircle of life modeled after the mathematical semicircle.

The doctor-patient relationship, in its ideal state, is one built on mutual understanding, moral and legal agreement, and absence of ethical issues. Therein lies the rub. In common practice, the relationship is a major area of potential conflict, resulting in a multitude of ethical issues in health care.

THE IDEAL PRIMARY ROLE OF THE PHYSICIAN

1) *Devotion* to the same ethical principles prescribed for everyone else in society (Chapter 8)

2) Meeting the required *standards* for all physicians within a community with regard to education, training, continuing medical

education, certification, licensure, hospital and/or medical school faculty appointments

3) *Competence*, under the responsibility of a departmental head in the institution where the physician is affiliated

4) In *compliance* with the rules and regulations of the medical staff and/or the institution, whether it be a hospital, a corporate entity, the military, or any other venue in which a physician may be employed part-time, full-time, temporarily, or permanently, and whether or not the physician is salaried or offering his professional services pro bono

5) Thoroughness in understanding the patient's complaints, in taking a history and performing a physical examination, in pursuing the problems, in evaluating the data and their interpretation

6) Meeting the scientific standards of the community in the selection of appropriate tests and procedures

7) Explaining the findings and making appropriate recommendations to the patient with clarity and tact

8) Obtaining informed consent

9) Avoiding discrimination, bias, paternalism and maternalism

10) Manifesting kindness, compassion, concern, responsibility, and hope

11) Understanding and respecting the patient's uniqueness and autonomy

12) Being respectful of the patient's rights to his cultural and religious beliefs

13) Keeping accurate medical records

14) Being available to the patient for medical service

15) Relieving pain and suffering

16) Treating and curing disease

17) Never harming the patient (raises the ethical issue of assisted suicide. See Chapter 25 for details)

18) Providing on-going care and guidance

19) Supporting the patient's best interest

20) Defending the patient against the adversarial role of an insurer

21) Participation in societal efforts to correct and improve a) health care for the poor, uninsured, and mentally ill, and b) unfair insurance practices

22) Help society achieve comprehensive, universal health care for everyone

FINANCIAL ARRANGEMENTS between physician and patient:

1) Fees should be clearly stated and known to the patient, preferably in advance of the medical services. Otherwise, issues arise unnecessarily.

2) Fees should reflect services accurately.

3) The physician should show concern regarding costs to the patient.

4) Compensation is an important aspect of medical service, but should not be the physician's primary consideration.

5) The physician has an ethical duty to be aware of the incentives of the system in which he/she practices and the possibility of obvious as well as subtle influences. This matter applies to compensation in fee-for-service as well as to capitation fees.

6) The doctor has an ethical duty to be aware of, and to avoid, personal conflicts of interest as they may relate to fees.

CONFIDENTIALITY

The rule regarding confidentiality is that all sessions between a patient and his physician are strictly confidential. The physician's required respect for the patient's *privacy* enables a patient to be candid. This matter can be appreciated, for example, in psychiatric illness, teenage pregnancy, etc. The issue, however, is not sacrosanct and can be *breached* legitimately

1) when a patient's health or life are at risk

2) when society can be benefited

3) when reporting is required by law, as with a) communi-

cable diseases including AIDS, tuberculosis, sexually transmitted diseases; b) gunshot wounds; c) suspected child abuse and abuse of the elderly.

INTIMACY

The greater the intimacy between the doctor and the patient, as with the doctor and his family or with his friends, the greater are the ethical issues for both doctor and patient. Primarily at risk are the doctor's *professionalism* and the patient's *independence*. The threat of mutual *respect* certainly becomes a factor in the relationship. Other issues include the risk of loss of *objectivity* and inability to avoid *bias*. Emotional reactivity may be unavoidable. Financial factors may certainly intervene.

ADVERTISING BY PHYSICIANS

The issue of advertising has declined from a totally *forbidden* circumstance in the past to its present *permissive* form that states simply, "It is unethical if the advertisement is false, deceptive, misleading, and unsubstantiated." Regrettably, societal customs now offer the medical profession approval of the use of the media for its advertising to the same extent as they do the business community. As a result, medical advertising is comparable in every way to industrial advertising. From the standpoint of its *dignity* and *professionalism*, it leaves much to be desired. Without going into great detail, it may take an ethicist to judge whether an advertisement is ethical or unethical, but any socially-minded person can tell good taste from bad taste.

Advertising brings medicine to a fork in the road. Is medicine losing its grip on its image as a noble profession in favor of its aim as a business? Are there merely a few rotten apples in the barrel? Medicine must decide whether it wishes to be a noble profession again or a new member of the business community. It cannot have it both ways without losing its identity.

THE PHYSICIAN AND CONFLICT OF INTEREST

Another activity which threatens the professional image of medicine is the unsavory engagements by physicians in any conflict of interest. It is clearly stated in the manual of The American College of Physicians that "the physician must avoid any personal commercial conflict of interest that might *compromise* his loyalty and treatment of the patient. *Collusion* with nursing homes, pharmacists or colleagues for personal financial gain is morally reprehensible." Furthermore, it states that "For a physician to own shares in a drug company or in a hospital in which he practices does not constitute unethical behavior of itself, but it does make him vulnerable to the accusation that his actions are influenced by such ownership. The safest course would be to avoid any such compromising situations."

Conflicts of interest are varied, and primarily must never be in violation of a patient's welfare and best interest. In the doctor-patient relationship, *trust* is fundamental, and any semblance of impropriety, such as involvement in a conflict of interest, would readily destroy the good name of the relationship as well as respect for the physician and the medical profession.

Examples of activity by physicians that may raise questions of conflict of interest include the following:

1) Financial interest in a facility, such as a medical laboratory to which the physician refers his patients for recommended studies (Ed: There may actually be no impropriety.)

2) Overutilzation of the fee-for-service arrangement in a private practice as well as underutilization of service in a managed care facility

3) Acceptance and use of gifts from a pharmaceutical company, and in return favoring the use of the company's products

4) Bias based upon personal interests in a consultation arrangement

5) Stock investments as an influential factor in the pre-scription of drugs

6) Ties with a drug company in a clinical research program for large fees particularly without a patient's informed consent and awareness of the physician's financial interest

7) Financial ties to a company with a product used in scientific research without revealing the researcher's connections prior to publication of the findings

In summary, concern for the patient's best interest must always take precedence over any personal financial consideration. In all instances that have the superficial appearance of a conflict of interest, there are valid exceptions that clearly show that the physician may be entirely justified in appearing to be primarily concerned in a conflict of interest. Each suspected circumstance must be evaluated individually without prejudgment.

The fundamental consideration in a questionable conflict of interest is whether or not the patients of the physician are benefitted, harmed, or are unaffected by the physician's extra-professional interests.

THE IMPAIRED PHYSICIAN
There is no circumstance more hazardous to a patient's well being or more disruptive of a doctor-patient relationship than is the occasional misfortune of the exposure of patients to an impaired physician. Several ethical principles are at issue, but the most important is that of *non-maleficence* or of first doing no harm (primum non nocere) to the patient.

FREQUENCY
The frequency with which impairment of the physician occurs is not really known and is hopefully rare, but most importantly must be quickly identified, and eliminated.

What constitutes impairment? First, and foremost, is the subtle, slowly evolving, progressive deficiency in the physician's ability to acquire new and maintain current scientific knowledge and skills. The difficulty is due predominantly to professional overwork, lack of time, and neglect by the physician to engage in his *continuing medical education (CME)* on a regular basis. A designated amount of CME is a requirement for renewal of his licensure and his hospital staff appointment, to say nothing of his primary obligation to the care and best interest of his patients. In this regard, it has been stated that a physician who has been out of medical school for ten years, has not kept up on his knowledge and skills in accordance with medical progress, but continues to practice what he learned ten years previously, will be entirely outdated because everything from ten years ago has been replaced, modified, or forgotten by the physician.

Unfortunately, patients assume that every physician is up to date in his current knowledge. They have no way of recognizing a physician's failing *cognitive skills*. The physician's peers, however, are likely to recognize such deficiency early-on, and are in a position of responsibility to seek corrective measures for the affected colleague before a calamitous event befalls a patient.

In the occasional instance wherein a physician's judgment and skill come into question, the physician himself is expected voluntarily to discontinue his service and obtain assistance or seek a solution. If the physician fails to do so, however, his colleagues, who are expected to step in as good *Samaritans*, often hesitate to become involved in a sensitive situation because of possible litigation.

The impaired physician must be identified, however, in the interest of the well-being of his patients and their protection from harm. There are legal mandates in various states pertaining to such matters as there are also regulations in all hospitals regarding the conduct and duties of all the members of its medical staff. The issue is an important one for the hospital's continued *accreditation*. State licensure generally has responsibility in such matters, although the removal of a physician's annual *relicensure* is not an easy matter to contest successfully.

In addition to loss of professional skills, a significant cause of physician impairment are the effects of *alcoholism*, or less often, illicit substance abuse. The disorder is usually due to the stressful burden upon the physician, resulting from the many hours he spends in the care of ill patients. The problem is rather overt and readily detectable, certainly sooner than is the more subtle impairment due to the diminution of skills. Here too, the dreaded issues are possible harm to a patient and the threat of the accusation of *negligence* and malpractice resulting in *litigation*—the most intimidating event in the life of a practicing physician.

Modern circumstances concerning impairment are such as to make the issue a small one that can be nipped in the bud before it materializes to a matter of concern to a patient.

Impairment may occasionally be due to a physician's *organic illness*, either temporary or permanent. Such impairments are generally readily identified and attended early, usually by the affected physician himself. Colleagues must always be alert to the need of providing aid to a fallen peer in the interest of patient protection.

In the rare matter of mental illness, everyone other than the physician is likely to become aware of the problem. Identifying and isolating the disorder can be extremely difficult, especially since the affected physician is totally unaware of his circumstances, as is usually the case. The matter must be attended promptly in the interest of patient care as well as the interest of the physician.

The reader knows that physicians at times normally engage a consultant when they have any concern regarding their patient's best care. The process has no bearing upon the subject of the impaired physician. By design, however a consultation would ensure the safest as well as the best patient care pending the removal and treatment of an impaired physician.

ROLE OF THE PATIENT IN THE DOCTOR- PATIENT RELATIONSHIP

How to be a successful patient in the patient's own best interest in his relationship with physicians is not taught in school, where the role of the ideal patient should be a part of social studies early in everyone's education. Simple matters of health are addressed, but many important details relating to a non-problematic doctor-patient relationship unfortunately are overlooked. This important matter is addressed in the forthcoming pages.

IDEAL ROLE OF THE PATIENT

1) The patient should learn to select a physician wisely and thoughtfully.

2) In establishing a relationship, the patient should be faithful to one physician and avoid hopping from one physician to another, especially among specialists without first consulting or at least notifying the primary physician, who should monitor the patient's overall care, including all of his medications.

3) The patient should have confidence in the physician's fulfillment of his professional role, to which, as a matter of fact, the patient has full rights.

4) The patient should be able to provide a detailed history of his illness accurately and with candor; he should avoid minimizing or exaggerating his complaints.

5) The patient should keep a diary pertaining to his health care, particularly regarding his medications. The diary will be invaluable to the physician.

6) The patient should be cooperative and compliant, and avoid resisting care.

7) The patient should be respectful, avoid undue criticizing and frivolous suing for damages due to imagined, non-existent, or dubious negligence and malpractice.

8) The patient should be realistic, reasonable, and rational.

9) The patient should know the extent of his insurance, including its precise coverage and its limitations.

10) The patient should be familiar with, respectful of, and cooperative with, the same ethical principles in health care, to which the physician and all other participants in health care may be bound.

11) The patient should understand the recommended treatment, benefits, risks, and alternatives before considering and authorizing informed consent.

12) Informed consent (see Chapter 11) must be given specifically for the physician's recommended treatment and procedures, disposal or use of tissues, organs, and removed body parts; for donation of organs for transplantation or research; for autopsy unless mandated by law, or opposed for religious reasons.

13) The patient should understand the fees in advance of the services and acknowledge the means of payment.

14) The patient should agree to fair compensation for services.

15) The patient should share with his physician and family the preparation of a Living Will, Advance Directive, Durable Power of Attorney, and the selection of a Surrogate or Proxy.

16) The patient should come to a decision during his mature years regarding his end-of-life care in terms of Sanctity of Life care and doing everything possible versus Quality of Life care and dying with dignity.

17) The patient should give serious thought to serving as an organ donor.

18) The patient should participate in society's primary role.

19) The patient, in understanding his rights, should assume appropriate responsibilities with each of those rights.

Following the patient's informed consent, the physician proceeds with the patient's approval of the physician's recommendations, which must be in compliance with state laws. Treatment without the patient's consent constitutes legal assault and *battery*. This is not inconsistent with the physician's application of the *doctrine of presumed consent*, as a result of which the physician may not seek formal informed consent. The doctrine generally applies to the physician's daily conduct of regular details, such as taking of blood, ordering a chest x-ray, performing an electrocardiogram, or any other routine procedure, which patients have learned to expect. Where indicated, the physician may make a presentation of recommendations to a member of the patient's family or the designated Surrogate, and must then be assured that consent is consistent with the patient's preferences and best interest.

JOINT RESPONSIBILITY

When informed consent is in order, a part of its preparation requires a *balance* between a) the physician's recommendations (representing his own autonomy, persuasion, and paternalism) and b) the patient's agreement (representing his own autonomy and self-determination). There may be an exchange of ideas, expressed and negotiated differences, and an actual sharing of power and influence.

The result will be a joint responsibility in the patient's best interest, leading to mutual agreement. Absence of mutual agreement leads to an imbalance between the physician's recommendations and the patient's agreement, a situation requiring resolution.

RESOLUTION OF DIFFERENCES IN THE PROCESS OF INFORMED CONSENT

Although the physician is obliged to assure *continuity* of care, he is not compelled to act in opposition to his own professional and ethical values. Hence, if he is unable to carry out his intent, the physician must choose among several *options*: 1) obtain a second opinion from an uninvolved, unbiased physician, 2) seek a court order in his favor, 3) appeal to his hospital's Ethics Committee, a group designated by institutional rules and regulations in compliance with the expectation of the Joint Commission on Accreditation of Health Care Organizations (JCAHCO) to prevent or settle ethical disputes and issues, or 4) withdraw from, and transfer the care of the patient to an appropriate physician, preferably selected by the patient. In any case, proper notification must be given to the patient, who should give his approval. The physician is ethically bound to the continued provision of care to the patient personally if no other doctor has been designated or is available, or if the care constitutes an emergency.

The patient, based upon his rights of autonomy and self-determination, is free to accept the physician's options, change physicians, or leave the hospital on a signed *discharged against advice*.

Under all circumstances, in exercising his rights, the patient must assume corresponding *responsibilities*.

IDEAL ROLE OF SOCIETY

Society plays a vital role in making a number of important contributions toward the improvement and success of every doctor-patient relationship:

1) By assuming the obligation of engaging in the on-going discussions pertaining to the critical need of health care reform

a) by working toward the provision of universal, comprehensive, cost effective, quality health care, especially for poor, uninsured, elderly, disabled and mentally ill patients

b) by helping to resolve the issue of burgeoning, misdirected health care costs

c) by helping to establish universal and comprehensive

health insurance at fair costs as a social necessity and not as a commercial enterprise

2) By demanding standardized qualifications of all health care providers

3) By scrutinizing and eliminating harmful practitioners in all categories of health care, who are untrained, incompetent, impaired, and generally substandard in the provision of care

4) By supporting scientifically valid medical research in its drive to advance good health for everyone and to eliminate disease in all

5) By making every effort to develop quality living so that everyone in society can live harmoniously among his neighbors

MEDICAL RISKS FOR THE PHYSICIAN AND
THE PATIENT
In the doctor-patient relationship, risks may occur both for the doctor and the patient.

RISK-TAKING BY THE PHYSICIAN
In undertaking the profession of medicine, the physician accepts the moral *commitment* to the treatment and care of all sick patients. Most doctors and nurses accept such responsibility and duty without qualification. Various risks may be required, however, by the physician in the care of a patient

1) who may be difficult to manage because he is non-compliant, uncooperative, demanding, hostile, litigious, or demented;

2) with a contagious disease, such as tuberculosis or AIDS.

As a matter of fact, it is unethical for a physician to refuse to care for an HIV-positive patient. (The risk of transmitting AIDS from the patient to the doctor is low-level). The physician, however, is not required legally to take risks in his decisions regarding his choice of patients. His freedom of choice is a matter of his *conscience*, upon which he may claim his right of refusal.

Failure by the physician to take risks suggests one or more of the following:

1) Lack of moral fiber and commitment
2) Bias
3) Fear of personal harm
4) Lack of concern that the doctor-patient relationship will be harmed

RISK-TAKING BY PATIENTS

The patient is not expected to accept risks when the physician is impaired as a result of 1) loss of his skills or 2) being the victim of alcoholism, substance abuse, mental illness, physical disease, or any other cause of impairment. A patient is likely to accept a risk inadvertently, but usually not knowingly. If he has in fact accepted a risk per chance, the patient should expect that the physician, on his own initiative, or with the help of colleagues, is removed from the responsibility of patient care, if the impairment warrants it. Furthermore, the patient has a right to expect that an impaired physician is prevented from continuing to serve as a risk as long as the physician is observed to be potentially hazardous to the health of the public.

A physician who is HIV-positive, for example, should of course seek expert guidance. His infection may actually pose a low-level of risk to patients, (just as an HIV-positive patient is probably at a low level of risk for the physician).

THE ROLE OF THE PHYSICIAN IN ABUSE OF THE ELDERLY

Abuse of the elderly is a form of *domestic violence*. It is usually overlooked in favor of child abuse, which is given considerably more attention and concern by society. There are three categories of elderly abuse, 1) physical, 2) psychological, 3) financial. They may be present singly or in combination.

Types of abuse are either *active*, in which the abuse is overt, or *passive*, in which the abuse is covert neglect, either intentional or unintentional. An example of the passive, unintentional type concerns the patient on drug treatment, perhaps for depression, who is subject to a high risk of falling and related injuries.

Intensity of abuse varies widely from mild and subtle to severe and violent.

Frequency of abuse is surprisingly high. In 1996, there was a reliable estimate of 820,000 cases in the United States reported by The National Council on Elderly Abuse. *Claims* of abuse are understandably very low, perhaps only ten percent being reported.

The incidence of elderly abuse is greatest among elderly who are *dependent*, as for example, confined to nursing homes.

Contributing factors to abuse include frailty of patients, complexity of medical problems, and side-effects from medications.

SIGNS 0F ABUSE (difficult to differentiate from self-imposed abuse or a developing psychiatric disorder):

1) Visible injuries (presumed to be accidental)
2) Malnutrition
3) Inappropriate clothing
4) Substandard care despite adequate resources
5) Poor personal hygiene
6) Withdrawal, depression, agitation, insomnia; evidence of harassment and intimidation
7) Lacking in knowledge of personal finances
8) Sudden transfer of assets, documents, wills
9) Prevented from seeing the doctor alone
10) Conflicting accounts between patient and abuser
11) Withholding or denying the patient his medication, food, assistance with hygiene, eye glasses, dentures, hearing aid, safety precautions, and access to medical care

12) Evidence of failure to allow the patient to make his own decisions, especially concerning financial matters

13) Denial of the patient's right to privacy, autonomy, and self-determination

14) Premature decision to place the patient in a nursing home

PREVENTION OF ABUSE

1) The patient should (be urged to) aim for and maintain independence in all physical, psychological, and financial categories.

2) Consider placing the patient in a close-knit, three-generation family and household, preferably by design, and not by necessity. This arrangement is regarded as the most desirable from the standpoint of a grandchild's maturity and development.

3) Need for general societal improvement in civility—respect for others, including the elderly.

4) The elderly must unite and organize toward a common goal of strength and influence.

TREATMENT OF ABUSE

1) The possibility of self-infliction and/or an evolving psychiatric disorder must be ruled out before charging anyone close by with abuse or blame.

2) The family should be assisted in exploring the aid of home health facilities, social service agencies, alternative living facilities, and geriatric centers that offer comprehensive care.

3) The patient should be provided with close contact, follow-up care, and continuing care by the physician.

4) The doctor-patient relationship must be preserved by respecting the patient's wishes and keeping the patient's trust.

5) If abuse continues, the circumstances may become reportable as neglect or abuse (a legal requirement of the physician in most states, as with child abuse statutes).

ETHICAL ISSUES

1) How to resolve the dilemma of whether or not to report abuse (often in the absence of verifiable proof)? Criteria for mandatory reporting must be clear. If not, the physician must use the patient's best interest as the standard.

2) How to balance the patient's best interest against respect for a competent patient's wishes?

3) How to resolve the conflict between the patient's right to confidentiality and the requirement of mandatory reporting laws?

4) Is reporting a violation of the patient's right to confidentiality?

5) How does reporting affect the fundamental principle of trust in the doctor-patient relationship?

6) Is the physician protected from liability and litigation? (Whether right or wrong, the physician is usually protected as long as the report is made in good faith.)

7) Is the protective agency (to whom the report of abuse is made) a)able to follow up properly? b) possibly worsen the situation? or c) guarantee its own confidentiality?

8) Is there justification for cynicism regarding the state's ability to handle reports of elderly abuse? (It is estimated that a state may spend ten times more in time and costs on the protective services for children than for the elderly, not withstanding the fact that there may be significantly more abuses among the elderly than among children.)

THE PHYSICIAN AS EMPLOYEE

As an employee, the most important ethical consideration relates to the matter of the physician's *independence*. As a solo practitioner, the physician enjoyed independence and could be totally concerned and occupied with the delivery of health care in a treasured doctor-patient relationship. Much of that has changed in recent years. More physicians have become full-time or part-time employees in many pursuits. As a result, numerous controversial issues have arisen that reveal ethical problems requiring resolution.

Ethical Issues

1) The employed physician is no longer a free agent, whether or not the physician is salaried for his service on a full-time or part-time basis, or even serves gratis.

2) The physician's care of patients is subordinated to the rules of practice determined by the employer or institution, among which are the military, industry, health maintenance organizations, academic facilities and hospitals.

3) Should a physician employed by a health maintenance organization, a hospital, or the military be:

    a) restricted to institutional policy and formulary?

    b) prevented from prescribing unauthorized drugs, tests or procedures?

4) The obligation of the physician is set forth in a job description, to which the physician may have reluctantly agreed to comply, and is beholden. Under such circumstances, there is no issue as long as the agreement contains no illegal, immoral or unprofessional expectations in violation of a physician's conscience and commitment to the ethical principles of beneficence and non-maleficence in accordance with his code of medical ethics.

5) Significant considerations include matters of trust, confidentiality, and the patient's rights.

6) The volume and/or quality of services may be reduced in the interest of cost containment while the corporation (employer) maintains prices to the purchaser to assure profitability.

7) Physicians may be subjected to limitations of access to technology, specialists, and new drugs.

8) Physicians may be in ethical conflict with institutional abuses of human rights;

    a) e.g., his expected role at executions in a prison, where it is unethical for the physician to administer lethal drugs, even in an emergency. It would be ethical only for the physician to certify death.

b) e.g., the physician is expected to determine fitness for military duty or an industrial job. Differences of opinion may easily arise and create conflict in favor of the employer.

9) As medical scientists employed full-time by a corporation, the physician

a) has a fiduciary duty to the employer,

b) must refrain from personal use of its confidential non-public research,

c) may not trade on the findings (in the stock market).

10) Academic medical scientists as temporary employees of a corporation (by virtue of receipt of grants) have the same restraints as in 8) above.

11) Physician-employees of medical journals are beholden in their duties to the journal (not to the funding source), and must refrain from using non-public information for personal gain (in violation of journal regulations). The primary responsibility of an employed physician is to his employer. There is no issue as long as the employer's rules and regulations do not conflict with the physician's professional, religious and moral standards in his relationship with patients and duties.

SECTION D:

SUBJECT II: DIET AND NUTRITION

We maintain with Plato, that reason has a natural and rightful authority over desire and affection; with Butler that there is a difference of kind in our principles of action; and with the general voice of mankind, that we must do what is right at whatever cost of pain and loss.

— William Whewell, 1794-1866

CHAPTER 13

THE IDEAL DIET:
VITAMINS AND MINERALS

Through the centuries, scholars, research workers, and martyrs of medical science have labored and died to overthrow superstition and to bring good health to all mankind.

— Anonymous

In the selection of seven major subjects in health care with ethical issues requiring resolution in order to achieve a high level of *quality living*, the author has selected the subject of diet and nutrition as *second* in importance to the doctor-patient relationship.

There is no modality in health care more valuable than one's diet and nutrition in the maintenance of health and in the growth, repair, and efficiency of body tissues throughout life. With the aid of proper nutrition, the body is able to be constantly vigilant in preserving its highest level of *immune* cell production and function in the body's perpetual battle against disease.

The primary aim of man is to reach his full and natural *life span*. In this regard, man is dependent upon his *diet* to assist him also in overcoming genetic and environmental adversities toward his goal of perfecting quality living in his *semicircle of life*.

Strangely, instead of accepting the best that science has to offer in its recommendation of an ideal diet, most Americans have departed into unscientific, bizarre, and harmful eating habits, while simultaneously seeking quick means of correcting the adverse effects of their misadventures. The ethical issues that have emerged are enormous and will be considered here.

THE AVERAGE AMERICAN DIET

1) *High in calories*: Many surveys are available which clearly demonstrate the excessive number of calories consumed in the average American diet, on the order of about three thousand calories per day. The result is storage of unused energy from the proteins, carbohydrates and fats, and a tendency to *overweight* and *obesity* (see Chapter 14).

2) *High in saturated fats and trans fatty acids*: The average diet is also excessively high in saturated fats and trans fatty acids (at least twice that of unsaturated fats). The common sources are mostly animal fats, eggs, milk, butter, cream, cheese, and mayonnaise, totaling a daily intake of more than 150 grams of fat, providing more than fifty percent of the caloric intake and more than 1000 mg. of cholesterol. The result is an increased tendency to *hyperlipidemia*: an *increase* in each of the lipid fractions, including total cholesterol, low-density lipoproteins (LDL-C), very low-density lipoproteins (VLDL-C), and triglycerides, and a *decrease* in the high density lipoproteins (HDL-C).

3) *High in sugars*: The average diet is too high in the intake of sugars, which tends to produce hyperglycemia.

4) *High in salt*: The average salt intake (sodium chloride) is high, exceeding ten grams of salt per day (the equivalent of four grams of sodium per day). Approximately twenty percent of our population is *sodium-sensitive*, and thereby tends to develop the essential type of *hypertension*.

5) *High in alcohol*: A high intake of alcohol, in addition to causing disease on the basis of its own toxicity (see Chapter 16) is a factor in the development of *hypertriglyceridemia*.

6) *A low intake of mono-unsaturated and poly-unsaturated fatty acids*: serves to support the adverse effect of a high intake of saturated and trans fats in their cause of *hyperlipoproteinemia*. All six of the above factors in the average American diet comprise *risk factors* for ischemic (coronary) heart disease, myocardial infarction, stroke, and other hazards, possibly even certain cancers.

7) *A low* intake of *complex carbohydrates*, found in fruits and vegetables, comprises less than the recommended fifty percent of the daily calories in the American diet.

8) A *low* intake of *fiber*, by at least fifty percent of the recommended 35 grams per day, found in fruits, vegetables, legumes, grains and bran of cereal grasses (wheat, oats, barley, corn, and rice).

Despite the above eight improprieties in the average American diet, there is evidently a surprising degree of *nutritional adequacy*. Malnutrition is uncommon as a result of a high American standard of living, education, the body's remarkable capacity for biosynthesis, and enrichment of many of the foods eaten with vitamins, minerals, and trace elements. *Malnutrition* does exist, however, among the poor, elderly, alcoholics, and in some patients with serious, debilitating illnesses.

ETHICAL ISSUES

The Food and Drug Administration (FDA) controls and regulates foods, drugs, and cosmetics, resulting in a minimum of problems. The FDA, however, does not control or regulate 1) nutrition, 2) weight, and 3) vitamins, minerals, and herbs (improperly designated by Congress as *"Food Supplements."*) The lack of regulation by the FDA in these categories creates a multitude of ethical issues, including mythical claims, exploitations and abuses extending to quackery and fraud.

The most egregious violations are perpetrated outside of scientific medicine, and have been referred to collectively as the "Great American Diet Hoax," which consists of:

1) Exploitation and swindling of the American public by a lucrative industry dominated by food-faddists, hucksters, and self-styled nutritionists

2) Preposterous claims and outrageous assertions of potentially hazardous benefits including the cure of cancers

3) The fastest growing snake-oil business in health care

4) Responsive public clamoring for weight reduction miracles

5) A national preoccupation with diets to provide for an ideal physical image, preservation of youth and for longevity

6) The public's fanaticism attracts a widespread promotion of bizarre departures from sound scientific dietary rules. Some even fail to mention the importance of monitoring by one's physician and following a regular exercise program. The promoters are often opportunistic, self-serving fringe practitioners including irresponsible physicians, and non-medical health food mongers. They make unsubstantiated claims (rarely based on study by application of the *scientific method*) of prevention and cure of a wide variety of diseases, and the promise of good health and long life. Their theories are often half-baked, and are given wide advertising among the media and the public because of their impressive charismatic style, and not because of data supported by the scientific community.

7) The claims are often imagined, exaggerated, irrational, and hazardous, based upon theories not taught in standard medical education.

8) Particularly and importantly noteworthy is the general absence of these promotions in valid scientific publications, with peer reviews and critiques, that would normally accompany reported studies in medical journals.

9) There is insufficient and lack of aggressive governmental enforcement actions against misrepresentation.

10) Greed (and/or self-aggrandizement) seems to be the dominant motive.

The author takes the position that all health care promotions should be looked upon with skepticism unless they have been the result of a controlled study with application of the scientific method and published in a respected scientific journal available for peer review and critique.

No attempt will be made to provide any details regarding any of the numerous diets alluded to in the above comments. Recommendations, however, can be made in the interest of quality living for the public to

1) learn to separate scientific fact from fiction,

2) distinguish between medically accepted, not accepted by organized medicine, and investigational,

3) distinguish between self-styled nutritionists and bonafide, qualified registered nutritionists including biomedical research scientists with no conflict of interest, valid and reliable nutritionists with academic stature as qualified medical specialists in metabolic and endocrine disorders. A college degree per se is not enough to qualify as an expert.

THE IDEAL DIET

The term "ideal"' is used in the diet because the components of the diet all represent the best that scientific medicine offers from the standpoint of nutritional value. Ideal caloric values and ideal weights are deliberately excluded because the subject of obesity, dieting, and weight control is addressed as a social factor in the behavioral class of the environment separately in chapter 6 and more thoroughly in Chapter 14.

The following material has been gathered from the standard, well known textbooks of medicine on the library shelves of medical schools, hospitals, and all physicians who care for patients. The author is not a nutritionist or a dietary expert and offers no personal opinions. The contents are the best that organized medicine

has to offer and currently expects all physicians to accept and follow, based upon established scientific evidence. The ideal diet has
been arrived at scientifically, based upon the intake of essential
dietary nutrients and calculated energy requirements.

BASIC DIETARY NUTRIENTS

The basic dietary nutrients may be 1) essential, i.e., cannot be
made by the body and must be taken in by diet, or 2) non-essential,
i.e., can be made by the body and need not be part of the diet.

ESSENTIAL DIETARY NUTRIENTS

These cannot be made by the body and include the following:

   a) Water: seventy percent of body weight

   b) Protein: ten amino acids

   c) Carbohydrates: sugars and starches

   d) Fatty acids: unsaturated: oleic, linolenic, linoleic, arachidonic

   e) Vitamins; thirteen complex organic compounds

   f) Minerals: fifteen inorganic

   g) Trace elements: approximately eighty inorganic

NON ESSENTIAL DIETARY NUTRIENTS

These can be made by the body. For example, seventy percent of
the blood cholesterol does not come from the diet, but is manufactured in the liver.

ENERGY REQUIREMENTS IN THE IDEAL DIET

The average calorie intake, based upon standard caloric expenditures, should be about 25-35 calories per kilogram of body weight
per day, depending upon sedentary existence or hard physical
work. For example, a 150-pound male (70 kg) white-collar worker
expends an average of 30 cal/kg body weight (30x70) or 2100
cal/day to maintain his 150 pounds of weight. The elderly require
fewer calories because of their lesser body mass and lesser activity.
Blue-collar workers of course require more.

COMMONLY CONFUSED TERMS IN DIET

Rice, wheat, oats, barley, and corn are *cereal grasses*. Within each grass is the *grain* or *seed* or *fruit*. The coat of the grain is *bran*. Removal of the coat or bran is called *hulled*. Peas, beans, and lentils are *leguminous* plants. Within each plant is a *legume* or *seed* or *fruit*. Grits are *grains*. *Hominy grits* are hulled corn. *Groats* are *hulled oats*.

METABOLISM OF THE ORGANIC NUTRIENTS: PROTEINS, CARBOHYDRATES, AND FATS

In digestion, *hydrolysis* (breakdown) of nutrients occurs, resulting in smaller particles by action of enzymes and bacteria mostly in the small intestine. Absorption and transport follow.

PROTEINS

Proteins are hydrolyzed by gastric hydrochloric acid and by enzymes including pancreatic trypsin, chymotrypsin, and peptidases. The end products are peptides and amino acids, which are essential for specific tissue formation, optimal growth, and nitrogen equilibrium. There are ten *essential amino acids*: leucine, isoleucine, lysine, methionine, phenyl alanine, threonine, tryptophan, valine, histidine, and tyrosine. Other amino acids include glutamine, cystine, asparagine, arginine, alanine, glycine, serine. cysteine, ornithine, and proline.

RECOMMENDATIONS for the intake of proteins are 1.0–1.5 gm/kg body weight/day, comprising *twenty percent* of the caloric intake. For example, in the 150 pound male on 2100 cal/day, twenty percent of 2100 cal = 420 calories, or 105 gm/day (1 gm protein provides 4 cal). The ten essential amino acids should be included.

SOURCES OF PROTEIN

Among the most frequently eaten are lean beef; fish; seafood; skinless chicken and turkey; legumes: peas, beans, lentils; nuts; non-fat cottage cheese, yogurt, and milk; egg white; soybean (tofu); chicken soup, bouillon. Shrimp and liver should be avoided because of their high cholesterol content (although the fat content is very low).

CARBOHYDRATES
Carbohydrates are mainly *starches* (polysaccharides) and *sugars*.

Hydrolysis of carbohydrates occurs by enzymatic actions of glycosidases: salivary amylase, pancreatic amylase, maltase, and lactase.

The end-products of metabolism in the intestine are monosaccharides, absorbed and transported by pancreatic hormones: a) *insulin* converts glucose to glycogen by glycogenesis, and b) *glucagon* converts glycogen to glucose by glycogenolysis. The aim in carbohydrate metabolism is a) *homeostasis*, maintaining a normal blood sugar despite eating or fasting, exercise or inactivity, and b) control and maintenance of body weight.

RECOMMENDATIONS
Carbohydrate intake should be restricted to *fifty percent* of the caloric intake. In the example of 2100 calories, that would equal 1050 calories or 260 gm/day (1 gm provides 4 cal).

SOURCES OF CARBOHYDRATES
1) All fruits, except avocado
2) All vegetables: steam, roast, avoid frying
3) Rice, cereals: except granola (high in coconut oil)
4) Desserts and snacks: angel food cake, air-popped popcorn, pretzels, gelatin
5) Pastas, bread, bagels. Avoid doughnuts, croissants, waffles
6) Beverages: all except chocolate and whole milk

SUGARS provide unneeded calories, but are useful in emergencies. They contribute to dental caries, and may improve mood via serotonin metabolism in the brain.

FATS

Fats are not more important than protein and carbohydrate in the diet, but are given considerably more attention in the text because of their controversial role in health care, their role as risk factors in the cardiovascular causes of death, and in the ethical issues they raise.

Fats are composed mainly of long chain triglycerides containing mostly saturated and unsaturated fatty acids and some cholesterol and glycerol esters. Fat metabolism may be either exogenous or endogenous.

EXOGENOUS FAT METABOLISM

1) Hydrolysis occurs by a) the enzymatic action of pancreatic lipase, which is activated by bile acids and b) intestinal lipase, nucleases, esterases, and phosphatases.

2) Release of secretin and cholecystokinin occur by action of hydrochloric acid. The flow of bile and pancreatic juice are stimulated

3) Emulsification of fat occurs with bile acids, which are synthesized from cholesterol made in the liver.

4) The end products of fat metabolism are fatty acids and monoglycerides.

5) Bile acids interact with the end-products plus cholesterol, fat soluble vitamins (D and K), and carotene. The products are *chylomicrons* (large lipoprotein particles).

ENDOGENOUS FAT METABOLISM

1) The end-products are esterified to produce tryglycerides, which are carried in the very low density lipoproteins (VLDL-C).

2) Intermediate density lipoproteins (IDL) form a cholesterol-rich, very low-density lipoprotein (VLDL-C) and also a low-density lipoprotein (LDL-C), which carries seventy-five percent of the esterified cholesterol. The high-density lipoprotein carries the

other twenty-five percent.

LIPIDS

Lipids are present in the blood plasma as a lipoprotein complex —a combination of lipids plus proteins. They consist of eight elements:

1) Cholesterol (C), 30 percent in free, insoluble, unesterified form, and 70 percent in soluble, esterified form in combination with fatty acids (25 percent with HDL-C and 75 percent with LDL-C and VDL-C) for transport and metabolism

2) Low Density Lipoproteins (LDL-C) originate as VLDL-C

3) Very low-density lipoproteins (VLDL-C)

4) Triglycerides are carried with VLDL-C

5) High Density Lipoproteins (HDL-C)

6) Phospholipids, especially lecithin, originate and are metabolized in the liver

7) Glycolipids in small amounts

8) Lipid soluble vitamins A, D, E, and K and steroid hormones

FAT AS A RISK FACTOR

Dietary Fat contains:

1) Fatty acids (FA), usually more than 100 gm/day, consisting of

a) saturated (long chain) FA's: myristic, palmitic, and stearic

b) unsaturated FA's: mono- and poly-: oleic, linoleic, linolenic, and arachidonic

c) partially saturated (trans) FA's (semi-soft vegetable oils)

2) Cholesterol (C): at least 1 gm/day

EXPERIMENTAL DATA:

There is a strong cause/effect relationship between 1) an increase in dietary *saturated* fat leading to an increase in serum lipids, especially LDL-C, and 2) the development of *atherosclerosis* of the coronary arteries, carotid arteries, and the aorta. It is of interest that the relationship varies greatly among different animal species. In man, an experimental decrease in dietary saturated fat causes *regression* of atherosclerosis in its early stage of formation. An increase in mono-unsaturated and in poly-unsaturated fatty acids is followed by a decrease in serum lipids, especially LDL-C and regression of early atherosclerosis.

CLINICAL DATA

In clinical (human) studies, an increase in calories and saturated fats produces hyperlipidemia (increased levels of LDL-C and cholesterol in the plasma), and an increase in the formation of atherosclerosis plus its complications: ischemic heart disease, myocardial infarction, and stroke. In primary familial hyperlipidemia, extensive atherosclerosis as well as its complications of ischemic heart disease, myocardial infarction and stroke occur early in life. The evidence that hyperlipoproteinemia is a major risk factor for atherosclerosis and its complications: ischemic heart disease, myocardial infarction and stroke is well established.

The clinical types of hyperlipoproteinemia are primary or secondary:

1) *Primary,* due to mutation of a single gene: apolipoprotein E2, 3, and 4; the last numbered, (E4), being the most atherogenic in the development of premature atherosclerosis.

2) *Secondary,* due to dietary fat excesses, diabetes mellitus, hypothyroidism, systemic lupus erythematosus, and cardiac transplantation.

CHOLESTEROL (TOTAL-C)

Cholesterol (total-C) is insoluble in free form, constituting 30 percent of the total-C. Seventy percent is in soluble form, three-fourths with LDL-C and one-fourth with HDL-C. The normal blood plasma level is 100-200 mg/dl, 70 percent of which is manufactured in the liver. The *exogenous source* of cholesterol is the diet and makes up thirty percent of the blood level. The foods highest in cholesterol include meats, egg yolk, butter, milk, cream, cheese, mayonnaise, liver and shrimp (low in fat). The maximum daily intake of 300 mg produces blood levels of 200 mg/dl in 50 percent of patients. Nuts are low in cholesterol but high in fat.

The *endogenous source* of cholesterol is the liver, where it is synthesized mainly, and provides 70 percent of the blood level. Cholesterol is vital in health, with intrinsic value (in normal amounts) for cell walls, nerve fibers, bile, and hormone formation.

TRIGLYCERIDES
The normal blood level of triglycerides is 40-200 mg/dl. It is a neutral fat carried in the plasma with VLDL-C.

The sources and causes of an elevation in the blood are dietary fat, alcohol consumption, and pancreatitis. An independent elevation in triglycerides per se may have little significance, although the relation of triglycerides to ischemic heart disease is highly suggestive. The mechanism would be its close relation to the digestion and metabolism of LDL-C, VLDL-C, and HDL-C.

TREATMENT OF HYPERTRIGLYCERIDEMIA
Consists of
1) the same diet as in the treatment of hyperlipidemia,
2) avoidance of alcohol intake,
3) use of drugs such as fibric acid derivatives, nicotinic acid, certain statins.

HIGH DENSITY LIPOPROTEINS (HDL-C)
The normal blood level of HDL-C is 35-60 mg/dl. It carries 25 percent of the esterified cholesterol. Its consideration as a good cholesterol is based upon the following:
1) It picks up cholesterol from body tissues and returns it to the liver for processing and excretion.

2) It is inversely related to premature atherosclerosis, especially of the coronary arteries. An increase in HDL-C tends to reduce ischemic heart disease whereas a reduction in HDL-C increases the risk of ischemic heart disease. Ergo, HDL-C is an anti-risk factor and is more significant than are the total C and LDL-C levels. HDL-C contains the sub-fractions apolipoprotein-A1 and apolipoprotein-A2, which appear to be better risk indicators than is HDL-C.

Certain factors unfortunately tend to lower the HDL-C level:
1) Male androgens
2) Menopause (reduced estrogens) in the female
3) Inactive life style
4) Smoking
5) Obesity
6) Low fat diet and certain cholesterol lowering drugs aimed at lowering the LDL-C and C levels

In order to raise the HDL-C level, correct all factors that lower the HDL-C level and to correct all risk factors concerning ischemic heart disease, hypertension and diabetes mellitus. Niacin, estrogens, alcohol in small amounts, and omega-3 fatty acids also tend to raise the level.

PROGNOSTIC CLUES REGARDING LIPOPROTEINS
1) The ratio of the total cholesterol to the HDL-C is normally 4.0 (eg: 200:50 respectively). The lower the number, the better is the outlook (lower cholesterol and/or higher HDL-C).

2) In post-menopausal women, the LDL-C level tends to be equal to or higher than in the male. Also, death due to ischemic heart disease has a higher incidence in the female than in the adult male.

3) In both sexes, after age 80, an increase in LDL-C poses little, if any, increase in risk of ischemic heart disease (as long as the patients have had no prior manifestations of ischemic heart disease).

4) The presence of the genetic protein, apolipoprotein E-4, portends an increased level of LDL-C.

INCREASE IN RISK FOR ISCHEMIC HEART DISEASE SUMMARY

Elements in the blood plasma predicting an increased risk for ischemic (coronary) heart disease are the following:

1) Increase in cholesterol (C)

2) Increase in triglycerides (TG) has little independent value per se; they carry VLDL-C

3) Increase in low-density lipoprotein cholesterol (LDL-C). This is known as *bad* cholesterol, and is a strong risk factor for ischemic heart disease. An increase in its sub-fraction, apolipoprotein-B (APO-B), is a better predictor of risk for ischemic heart disease than is an increase in LDL-C

4) Increase in very low-density lipoprotein cholesterol (VLDL-C)

5) Decrease in high-density lipoprotein cholesterol (HDL-C) is a better predictor of risk for ischemic heart disease than are increases in cholesterol or LDL-C levels; this is known as '*good*' cholesterol.

TREATMENT OF HYPERLIPIDEMIA

1) The primary type of hyperlipidemia must first be ruled out, and the causes of the secondary type then considered and treated accordingly: a) diabetes mellitus, b) hypothyroidism, c) nephrotic syndrome, d) obstructive liver disease, e) alcoholism, f) dietary indiscretion (the most common secondary cause).

2) Exercise regularly

3) Eliminate excess calories and maintain a standard weight

4) Saturated fats should be reduced to *ten percent* of the total caloric intake

5) Mono-unsaturated and poly-unsaturated fat intake should be increased to *twenty percent* of the total caloric intake.

6) Trans-fatty acid intake should be reduced to zero.

7) Approved common foods:

    a) Fish, seafood (except shrimp)

    b) Poultry: skinless white meat of chicken or turkey

    c) Dairy: egg white (occasional yolk), skim milk, non-fat cottage cheese or yogurt

    d) Grains and pasta: spaghetti, macaroni, rice, oat bran

    e) Soups: onion, chicken broth, beef bouillon, tomato, bean

    f) Breads and crackers: all except doughnut, croissant, waffle

    g) Cereals: all except granola

    h) Dressings: herbs, spices, vinegar

    i) Vegetables: all

    j) Fruits: all except avocado

    k) Nuts: walnut, almond, pecan

    l) Desserts and snacks: angel food cake, air popped popcorn, pretzels, gelatin

Fats and fatty acids should not exceed *30 percent* of the total calories. For example: 30 percent of 2100 calories = 630 calories = 70 gm fat/day (1 gm provides 9 calories).

HYDROGENATION

Hydrogenation (saturation) should be *reduced* in the intake of food. In the manufacturing process, hydrogen (in gas form) is added in order to convert oil from the liquid state to the soft or solid form in order to prevent *rancidity*.

A **SATURATED** fatty acid is solid at room temperature. It is fully hydrogenated, carrying all the hydrogen atoms it can hold. In the body, saturated fat is converted to cholesterol and LDL-C. The HDL-C is not reduced.

An **UNSATURATED** fatty acid is liquid at room temperature and may be a) a mono-unsaturated fatty acid with one pair of hydrogen atoms missing, or b) a poly-unsaturated fatty acid with two or more pairs of hydrogen atoms missing.

PARTIALLY SATURATED (TRANS) fatty acids are solid or soft at room temperature. They are partially hydrogenated. Their effect (like saturated fatty acids) is raising the LDL-C, and (unlike saturated fatty acids) lowering the HDL-C. The result is that they pose a greater risk for the development of ischemic heart disease, myocardial infarction, and stroke than do saturated fatty acids.

Trans fatty acids are found in solid or soft margarines, vegetable shortening, and in partially hydrogenated oils. Common sources include cookies, croissants, doughnuts, and french fries.

COMMON SATURATED FATTY ACIDS IN FOODS TO BE AVOIDED

(or at least reduced to ten or less percent of the total caloric intake daily):

Beef, pork, lamb, bacon, duck, lunchmeats, veal, sausage, poultry skin; eggs, butter, cream, whole milk, ice cream; cheeses; chocolate; mayonnaise; custard, cheesecake; cookies, potato chips, pies.

MONO-UNSATURATED FATTY ACIDS TO BE STRESSED IN THE DIET

Liquid vegetable oils: olive, canola (rapeseed), peanut, and liquid margarines.

POLY-UNSATURATED FATTY ACIDS TO BE STRESSED IN THE DIET

1) Poly-unsaturated omega-6 fatty acids contained in vegetable oils: soybean, corn, safflower, sesame, sunflower, linseed (flaxseed).

2) Poly unsaturated omega-3 fatty acids contained in

a) fish: salmon, tuna, mackerel,

b) nuts: walnut, almond, pecan,

c) legumes: peas, beans, lentils,

d) dark green, leafy vegetables contain the plant form of omega-3 fatty acids.

Mono-unsaturated and poly-unsaturated fatty acids should comprise at least *twenty percent of the thirty percent* of the daily calories in the diet recommended for intake of fats.

HINTS REGARDING DIETARY FAT

1) Avoid frying. Instead, bake, broil, steam, poach.

2) Beware of "no saturated fat." The product may still contain much cholesterol, e.g., shrimp, liver

3) Beware of "no cholesterol." The product may still be high in saturated fat, e.g., chocolate, although it does not raise the cholesterol level.

4) Read all labels carefully.

5) All fats contain saturated (S), mono-unsaturated (M), and poly-unsaturated (P) fatty acids, although one or another predominates. For example, olive oil contains 77 percent (M), 9 percent (P) and 14 percent (S). Canola oil contains 62 percent (M), 32 percent (P) and 6 percent (S). Chicken fat contains 31 percent (S), 22 percent (P) and 47 percent (M). Beef fat contains 52 percent (S), 44 percent (M) and 4 percent (P). Coconut oil contains 92 percent (S), 6 percent (M) and 2 percent (P). Palm oil contains 81 percent (S), 11 percent (M) and 2 percent (P). (Source: Composition of Food, U.S. Dept. of Agriculture.)

6) An ideal diet is well-balanced, nutritious and calorie controlled according to one's standard weight and medical status with approximately *20 percent protein, 50 percent carbohydrate* (mainly fruits and vegetables), and *30 percent fat* (predominantly *mono*-unsaturated and *poly*-unsaturated fatty acids). One's physician must approve and monitor the diet to the same extent as is required with medications. Registered dietitions are available to physicians and patients to fill prescriptions for diets, as are pharmacists for drug prescriptions.

THE ROLE OF FIBER IN THE IDEAL DIET

As noted at the onset of this chapter, fiber, an important

aspect of the ideal diet, is normally consumed in amounts about half as much as is recommended. Dietary fiber consists of cellulose, pectin, and lignin.

The *sources* of fiber are abundant and are found in the foods mostly recommended as part of the ideal diet: fruits, vegetables, grains and bran of cereal grasses (including wheat, oats, barley, corn and rice), legumes of peas, beans and lentils.

When present in an *insoluble* form, fiber has been considered as possibly having value in the prevention of colon cancer. This is an unanswered question. In the *soluble* form, fiber is valuable in suppressing an excess production of bile acids (lipids formed during the metabolic breakdown and reduction of cholesterol). Fiber also has considerable value in its addition of *bulk* to the stool and its aid to the process of evacuation. The recommended *dosage* of fiber is about 35 *grams per day*. As a supplement to fiber in its aid to bowel function, psyllium, one of the rare herbs used in traditional medicine, may be added to the diet. It is a mucilloid and is commercially available.

SALT IN THE IDEAL DIET

Salt, chemically *sodium chloride* (NaCl) is an essential component of the ideal diet and important in health (see Minerals later in this chapter). Salt circulates in the body in ionic form as Na+ and . Cl- (ions of sodium and chloride respectively). In routine studies of blood electrolytes, they are important components that are checked in cases of excess loss due to vomiting, diarrhea, excess sweating, during use of diuretic drugs, and in connection with head injuries (because of inappropriate secretion of antidiuretic hormone, responsible for a low sodium in the blood). *Thirst* is an easy and valuable clinical guide to the need of a deficient sodium ion in the blood. Ordinarily, it is not necessary to measure the blood level of sodium and chloride or to supplement the intake because it remains controlled by the normal homeostatic mechanism in man—a fundamental and remarkable process in our body chemistry. To be sure, if there is disease, especially cardiovascular or renal, or any other disorder in which electrolyte imbalance may be suspected, blood testing is easily performed.

As indicated at the start of this chapter, the ideal intake of salt is about *5 gm per day*, approximately half of the amount usually consumed in the average diet. Based on the atomic weight of the sodium ion (23) compared with that of sodium chloride (58), 5 gm of salt has about 2 gm or *2000 mg of sodium*, the average daily requirement in the ideal diet. The source of salt is abundant in most foods in a normal diet. An excess intake, as is common, is not particularly harmful in the absence of heart or kidney disease. A common manifestation of an excess intake is ankle *edema* (usually caused more commonly by other less serious conditions). Edema is due to the presence of water, the carrier of the sodium ions.

A great concern about salt is in its relation to high blood pressure. It is not normally the cause of *hypertension,* although in about twenty percent of the population who are *sodium-sensitive,* salt may be an important factor in the cause. In such cases, salt restriction and a specifically controlled intake are an important part of the therapy. Hence, the normal intake of 2000 mg of sodium per day may need to be reduced to 1600 mg or to 1200 mg or even less if heart function is sufficiently impaired. For most people, a diet low in salt intake is troublesome in its lack of taste. Common spices can make up for the deficiency, and *salt substitutes*, especially spices, are available as safe and satisfactory seasoning agents. Their feature is that they are devoid of sodium.

Hint: for those who require a restricted amount of salt daily, the sodium content of canned foods should be scrutinized carefully for their high sodium content. As a rule, fresh fruits and vegetables have considerably less sodium than equivalent amounts in most canned foods.

WATER IN THE IDEAL DIET

Water comprises *70 percent* of man's body weight, and is vital to health. Its chief function is as a *solvent* for the transport and circulation of blood and its contents, and it has many other important roles in the body's physiology and chemistry. It serves also to carry wastes from the body by way of the kidneys and bowel. It is also essential in respiration and body temperature control.

The *intake* of water is usually in compliance with need and is guided by the perception of *thirst* as well as by habit, for example, with meals for a desirable total of *eight glasses of fluids per day.* Excessive *loss* of water during illness, especially associated with fever, sweating, vomiting, and diarrhea, demands special consideration because of the attendant loss of electrolytes with water, which may require replenishment at times by parenteral means in place of the oral route.

An interesting point about water intake and excretion is its loss via diuretic drugs and certain diets for weight reduction. Some crash programs in dieting take advantage of *diuresis* in claiming benefits in weight reduction. Of course, when the water is restored, as is inevitable, the weight will also be restored. The reference to one's *medical status* is enormously important in the role of water in the construction of a dietary program. The ideal diet and its components are for a healthy person without any medical disorder. Everyone should check with his physician, who would modify the recommended breakdown of the constituents including water in the ideal diet in accordance with the patient's medical problems, drug treatment, and physical activities.

TEA IN THE IDEAL DIET

After water, tea is the most consumed beverage world-wide. As far as the body is concerned, it can be a suitable replacement for water. It comes most frequently as black, green, or oolong. Herbal tea is not tea. Like coffee, tea has *caffeine*, but generally about 50 percent less. Hence, like coffee, it serves as a central nervous system stimulant. Tea also contains *phytochemicals*, theaflavins, thearubigins, and antioxidants in very small amounts. Antioxidants, also present in vitamins C and E and in beta-carotene (precursor of vitamin A), are considered theoretically to act in combination with oxygen-free radicals released during metabolism, thereby hypothetically reducing the oxidation of LDL-C, and finally reducing the tendency to atherosclerosis.

Tea has still other features including *anti-clotting* effects (favorable or unfavorable, depending on circumstances), a high *fluoride* content beneficial to teeth, and *oxalates*, which may cause kidney stones, a complication that can be offset by adding milk to the diet. The calcium in milk can bind the oxalates and prevent stone formation.

COFFEE IN THE IDEAL DIET
Coffee is a popular beverage world-wide, more so than tea in the United States. The *caffeine* in coffee, twice as much as in tea, accounts for its primary role as a *stimulant* of the central nervous system. For many, the day's activities cannot start or be maintained without a cup or two of coffee. The flavoring of coffee is due to its content of volatile oils and tars, which can be eliminated by the process of filtering. There are no harmful effects that can be attributed to moderate amounts of coffee, the intake of which should be a matter of discussion with one's physician.

ALCOHOL AND THE IDEAL DIET
The *hazards* of alcohol (see Chapter 16) as a cause of disease and destroyer of many lives may be offset slightly by the *benefits* of a controlled intake of small amounts, which have a favorable effect on reducing LDL-C and even increasing HDL-C levels in the blood and thereby hopefully reducing the risk of ischemic heart disease. The effect of alcohol in increasing the levels of *triglycerides* is certainly not desirable and, as pointed out previously, may not be too important as an isolated circumstance per se.

Studies have shown that the daily intake of 2 ounces of whiskey, or 6 ounces of wine (especially red), or 12 ounces of beer, may be beneficial in reducing undesirable elevations of lipids in the blood. To many, the problem with alcohol consumption is the frustration of reducing a joyful intake of an alcoholic beverage to a relatively minute medicinal dosage for an uncertain benefit.

A major question that has never been answered satisfactorily concerns the control most people have over their daily intake compared with the few who develop *alcoholism*.

Ethical Issue: An important ethical question relates to the dearth of livers available as organs for transplantation and where patients with self-abused alcohol related end-stage liver disease should be placed on the waiting list as recipients of a donated liver (see chapter 21).

PHYTOCHEMICALS IN THE IDEAL DIET

More than one hundred organic compounds known as *phytochemicals* are present in some of the most favored foods in an ideal diet including fruits, vegetables, cereal grasses (rice, oats, wheat, barley, corn), and leguminous plants (peas, beans, and lentils). The phytochemicals are considered to have beneficial properties in their contribution to the prevention of ischemic heart disease and possibly of certain cancers.

Included among the phytochemicals are *indoles*, isothiocyanates, saponins, phytosterols, phytoestrogens, polyphenols, capaicin, allyl sulfides, carotenoids, and phenolic acids.

ORGANIC FOODS AND THE IDEAL DIET

A great deal of publicity has been given to so called organic foods. The claim is that the *organic* growth of food with *manure* instead of *pesticides* and chemical fertilizers is safer for the workers, the consumers, and the environment, as well as being more nutritious and tastier for the consumer.

Skeptical farming experts allege that the claims of the organic food enthusiasts are mythical or half-truths designed to sell farming products at premium prices, and are primarily entrepreneurial. The basis for the opposing opinion is that there are reported flaws in the concept:

a) The nutrient value and flavor of a food are in the plant genes, not in the manner of growth.

b) The amount of pesticide residue is generally insignificant and easily washed.

c) The manure itself that is used to supplant the pesticide may be unsafe.

The status of organic food is an ethical issue for the consumer to reflect upon, fortunately with the rights of autonomy and self-determination.

IRRADIATION OF FOOD

As with organic food, an ethical issue exists concerning the public's reluctance to accept the concept of irradiation of food as an improvement in the quality of the food to be eaten.

It should be realized that over six million cases of food poisoning caused by infection with salmonella, campylobacter, and E. coli and about 10,000 deaths occur annually. These are astounding figures that have led to drastic considerations in the prevention of infection by the food industry's recent introduction of exposing food to irradiation with an ionizing source of *gamma rays*.

In *support* of this process is that a) the irradiated food has no radioactive properties and is not harmed or altered in any manner, and b) the procedure is endorsed by the U.S. Department of Agriculture, The Food and Drug Administration, and The American Medical Association.

In *opposition* to the process is widespread skepticism and fear on the part of the general public. Their concern should be allayed by the recollection that there was public opposition in the past to the pasteurization of milk, to fluoridation of water, and to microwaving of food. To these innovations there is no longer any opposition. The processes are all safe, as is the irradiation of food for its *antibacterial* benefits.

MONOSODIUM GLUTAMATE (MSG) AND THE IDEAL DIET

Monosodium glutamate is the salt of glutamic acid, one of the important amino acids present naturally in human cells as well as in many foods: chicken, milk, tomatoes, peas, hydrolyzed vegetable protein (soy, wheat, corn).

It is *not an allergen* as is commonly suspected. Instead, a small percentage of the population is *sensitive* to MSG and reacts to it by developing facial pressure, burning, nausea, weakness, headache, and drowsiness. The condition is known as an *MSG Symptom Complex* The reaction is temporary and there is no published record of serious harm.

DRUG SUPPLEMENTS TO THE IDEAL DIET

In addition to the maintenance of proper nutrition and an ideal weight, an aim of an ideal diet is to correct *abnormal lipid levels* in the blood. A number of drugs are available as supplements to the ideal diet if abnormal blood lipids fail to return to normal levels and the person concerned is at risk for ischemic heart disease, myocardial infarction, or stroke.

The reader is reminded that as far as fat is concerned, the aim in the ideal diet as emphasized earlier in this chapter is to establish normal serum lipid levels:

a) Cholesterol under 200 mg/dl

b) LDL-C level under 130 mg/dl

c) HDL-C level over 35 mg/dl

d) Tryglyceride level under 200 mg/dl

WHEN SHOULD DRUGS BE USED?

The addition of drugs should be considered for use if the lipid levels fail to attain a normal range after six months of strict adherence to the diet. Drugs are necessary in about twenty-five percent of people who, despite following an ideal diet, continue to have lipid levels considered to be in a hazardous range. There are a number of effective drugs for use in lowering abnormally high lipid levels in addition to (not instead of) an ideal diet:

1) Bile acid-binding resins (also known as *sequestrants).* Their benefit is in lowering the total cholesterol and the LDL-C. Two examples are cholestyramine (Questran) and colestipol (Colestid). The dosage is 8-10 gm / day before meals. There may be mild gastrointestinal side effects.

2) Fibric acids reduce the levels of tryglycerides and VLDL-C. Two examples are gemfibrozil (Lopid) and clofibrate (Atromid-S).

3) 3-hydroxy-3-methylglutaryl Co-enzyme-A reductase, in a normal early step in the brosynthesis of cholesterol, catalyzes the conversion of HMG-Co A to mevalonate. The reaction is inhibited by HMG-Co Enzyme-A reductase inhibitors known as *statins.* They lower the cholesterol and LDL-C levels.

An example of one of the early-marketed statins is lovastatin (Mevacor) in a dosage of 20-40 mg, taken in the evening (when cholesterol is made by the liver). An adverse effect is mild liver dysfunction. Other statins include simvastatin (Zocor), fluvostatin (Lescol), pravastatin (Pravacol), atorvastatin (Lipitor). Still others have continued to appear on the market. In large amounts, some may be carcinogenic experimentally, but in recommended doses they are relatively safe and highly effective.

4) Nicotinic acid (Niacin, Vitamin B3) is effective in lowering total cholesterol, LDL-C, and tryglycerides. It may raise HDL-C. The dosage is 1 gm three times daily. Side effects include flushing, pruritus, gastrointestinal distress, mild liver toxicity, and hyperglycemia.

5) Estrogens in the post-menopausal state inhibit endothelial

hyperplasia, retard osteoporosis, and are effective in lowering LDL-C and raising HDL-C blood levels. Their increased risk of cancer of the uterus, and questionably of the breast, are unsettled effects.

6)Plant sterols, including sitosterol, stigmasterol, and campasterol inhibit cholesterol absorption. They are marked by an unsavory taste.

7) Probucol (Lorelco) lowers cholesterol, LDL-C, and HDL-C. The dose is 500 mg twice daily. They may induce cardiac arrhythmias.

8) Omega-3 fatty acids (fish oil), derived from salmon, tuna and mackerel, in a dosage of 1 gm three times daily, lowers lipid levels, cholesterol, triglycerides, LDL-C, VLDL-C, and may increase HDL-C levels. The drug may also inhibit platelet aggregation effecting an increase in fibrinolytic activity and decrease in blood viscosity. The mechanism of action is attributed to eicosapentaenoic acid and to docosahexaenoic acid (long-chain polyunsaturated fatty acids).

The reader is referred to Chapter 14 for a discussion of dieting and drugs in relation to obesity and weight control.

VITAMINS, MINERALS, AND TRACE ELEMENTS
Basis for Current Status
The basis for the current usage of vitamins (V), minerals (M), and trace elements (T) is the revolutionary Congressional Dietary Supplement Health and Educational Act of 1994, in which, sad to say, V, M. and T, along with herbal drugs, totaling over a thousand preparations, were declared to be "dietary supplements," not drugs. The unfortunate result of such legislation is that The Food and Drug Administration has been removed as the regulator and premarket tester for such vital issues as safety and efficacy, as is the FDA's responsibility with all drugs and foods.

The industry responsible for the manufacture of vitamins,

minerals and herbs may make claims without FDA approval and they may cite favorable physiologic effects of their products. (They may not, however, claim that their product cures a specific disease.) The law is bad enough in its application to vitamins, which are, after all important in health, although they do have side effects, but the law is really an inexcusable reason to remove herbs from their true identity as drugs and mislabel them as food supplements.

Furthermore, the Act permits the industry to market vitamins, minerals, and herbs with suggested dosages without *standardization* (as required with drugs) and without evidence that would be required by the FDA for proof of safety and efficacy if they were labeled as drugs. The Act also fails to provide guidance for assurance of reliability. The Act, in the judgement of many reliable drug watchers, was not made in the best interest of the health of people or in their quality of living, but rather in support of the pharmaceutical and especially of the herbal industries. In partial correction of their grave error, Congress established an office of dietary supplements at the National Institutes of Health in 1995 with an annual budget to enable standards to be set for the recommended daily allowance (RDA) of vitamins and minerals, based on age, weight, and sex. Their responsibility does not include the herbal market. (See Chapter 17 for a detailed discussion of herbs.)

IDENTITY of Vitamins (V), Minerals (M), and Trace Elements (T):

1) There are thirteen commonly known vitamins: A (retinol), Beta-carotene (precursor of vitamin A), C (ascorbic acid), D, E (tocopherol), K, B1 (thiamine), B2 (riboflavin), Niacin, Pantothenic acid, B6 (pyridoxine), B12 (cyanocobalamin), Folic Acid, and Biotin.

2) There are fifteen commonly known minerals: sodium chloride (Na, Cl), iron, calcium, phosphorus, potassium, magnesium, manganese, iodine, zinc, copper, selenium, cobalt, chromium, molybdenum.

3) Trace elements total about eighty. They are essentially catalytic. Examples are fluorine, lithium, nickel, germanium.

MINIMUM DAILY REQUIREMENTS

The minimum daily requirements (MDR) for V, M, and T are minute, easily met, and widely *available* in a balanced diet.

A dietary intake of food with less than the MDR can lead to a deficiency resulting in illness. Such diseases are rare in the United States, although they may occur in disorders associated with wasting, starvation, malnutrition, food faddism, anorectic states, chronic alcoholism, and to some extent in association with the needs of pregnancy.

VITAMINS AND MINERALS AS FOOD SUPPLEMENTS

Vitamins and minerals, as designated food supplements, are not foods and are certainly superfluous as supplements in an ideal diet because of their abundance, especially in fruits and vegetables.

Indeed, as unnecessary supplements, they are not entirely harmless. For example, Vitamins A and D, iron, and calcium may interfere with the absorption of zinc, a mineral needed in immune function, protein synthesis, and wound healing.

Some *advertising* is subject to ethical questioning. For example, the over-the-counter sale of vitamins with a *stress formula* suggests (falsely) that the preparation cures physical and emotional stress. (Ed: The FDA would surely oppose such mislabeling if it had the authority.)

VITAMIN PROFILES

The profiles of the vitamins are as follows:

A (Retinol): US Recommended Daily Allowance, (RDA) 5,000 IU; uses: for vision, skin, bones, red blood cells, and immune system; found in dairy products, liver, fish oil; deficiency causes night blindness, dry skin, infection.

Beta-carotine: RDA up to *5 mg*; precursor of Vitamin A; found in carrots, sweet potato, spinach, squash, kale, cantaloupe, and in green leafy vegetables; deficiency, same as Vitamin A.

C (Ascorbic Acid): RDA *60 mg*; serves in collagen, bones, teeth, healing, iron absorption, as antioxidant; found in citrus fruit, melon, tomato, cabbage, potato, broccoli; deficiency causes bleeding of gums and impaired healing.

D: RDA *400 I.U.*; functions in calcium and phosphorus metabolism, and bone growth; found in dairy products, herring, salmon; deficiency causes retarded bone growth.

E (Tocopherol): RDA *30 I.U.*; functions in blood cells and tissues, and as antioxidant; found in green leafy vegetables, wheat germ, nuts, cereal grains; deficiency questionably causes muscle and CNS disorder.

K: RDA *20-80 mg*; functions in blood clotting; found in green leafy vegetables, liver; deficiency causes abnormal blood clotting.

B1 (Thiamine): RDA *1-2 mg*; functions in carbohydrate metabolism, in brain and in muscle; found in whole grain, meats, peas, beans; deficiency causes disorder of CNS, muscle and heart.

B2 (Riboflavin): RDA *1.5-2.0 mg*; functions in carbohydrate, protein and fat metabolism, in tissues, red blood cells, and skin; found in dairy products, fish, poultry, green vegetables; deficiency causes dry skin, inflammation of mouth.

Niacin (Nicotinic acid): RDA *20 mg*; functions in skin, CNS, gastro-intestinal tract, and in metabolism of carbohydrate, protein and fat; found in fish, meat, liver, peas and beans; deficiency causes skin and mental disorders.

Pantothenic Acid: RDA *10 mg*; functions in carbohydrate, protein and fat metabolism and in hormone production; found in peas, beans, whole grains; deficiency is rare and causes weakness.

B6 (Pyridoxine): RDA *2 mg*; functions in protein metabolism; found in chicken, fish, whole grains, peas and beans, bananas; deficiency causes inflammation in mouth and skin; anemia.

B12 (Cyanocobalamin): RDA *6 ug*; functions in making red blood cells; found in dairy products, meats, liver; deficiency causes CNS disorders, anemia.

Folic Acid: RDA *400 ug*; functions in DNA, RNA, red blood cells, CNS, protein metabolism; found in green leafy vegetables, peas and beans, liver, and citrus fruit; deficiency causes CNS disorders, diarrhea, anemia, heart disease, stroke; a decreased intake may increase the risk of a neural tube defect in the fetus during pregnancy; in the elderly, an increase in the blood level of *homocysteine*, a component of folate metabolism, results in an increased risk of coronary heart disease.

BIOTIN: RDA *30 mg*; functions in carbohydrate, protein, and fat metabolism; found in green leafy vegetables, liver; deficiency causes dry skin, hair loss.

One of the most popular dietary pastimes is to take one *multivitamin daily*. Conventional wisdom dictates to "join the crowd, it wouldn't hurt." The reader should bear in mind that all vitamins in excess dosage have a toxicity potential, and that megadosage *supplements*, a recommendation of some alternative medical practices, are certainly unnecessary, definitely unproved, and dangerously unsafe.

A FEW HAZARDS OF VITAMIN OVERDOSAGE

Vitamin A: toxic to brain, liver, bone, muscle, skin.

Niacin: flushing, headache, nausea, diarrhea, gastrointestional bleeding, liver toxicity, cardiac arrhythmias.

Pyridoxine: severe nerve damage.

Folic Acid: may mask signs of B12 deficiency, reduce benefit of methotrexate in cancer chemotherapy, interfere with anticonvulsant treatment.

Vitamin C: diarrhea, hyperoxaluria, decreased immunity, reduce beneficial effects of chemotherapy in breast cancer.

Vitamin D: risk of kidney stones, kidney damage, mental retardation in children, arteriosclerosis in elderly.

Vitamin E: headache, dizziness, blurred vision, fatigue, nausea, gastrointestinal disorder, muscle weakness.

ANTIOXIDANTS

Beta-Carotene (precursor of Vitamin A), *Vitamin C*, and *Vitamin E* are considered as antioxidants, based upon the physiological *hypothesis* that the body utilizes oxygen in the production of energy, and in turn releases *oxygen-free radicals* (molecules with unpaired electrons) that serve as oxidants. Most are *neutralized*, but an excess of oxidants may accumulate and cause damage to cell membranes and DNA. A further consideration of the hypothesis is that low-density lipoprotein cholesterol (LDL-C), which is deposited on arterial walls, becomes oxidized, and attracts monocytes, which engulf the oxidized LDL-C. An atherosclerotic *plaque* is then formed on the arterial wall. The oxidized LDL-C is more atherogenic than native LDL-C, resulting in an increased amount of thrombus and clotting (somewhat analogous to the oxidation of iron and the formation of rust).

According to the theory, the antioxidants intervene in the above process by detoxifying the free radicals, leading to a reduction in the oxidation of LDL-C, thereby reducing any increased tendency to atherosclerosis.

An added theoretical consideration is that an excess accumulation of oxidants may be a factor in the cause of cancer. By detoxifying the free radicals with antioxidants, cancer may be prevented. The same concept has been applied to cataract of the lens of the eye and to macular degeneration of the eye (cause unknown in both conditions).

In summary, antioxidants may defend against oxidative stresses by scavenging free radicals and interrupting the chain reactions induced by the free radicals.

SUPPORTIVE VIEWS

There are data in support of the antioxidant theory:

1) In several studies, patients with an increase in their intake and increase in their blood levels of antioxidants have been shown to have decreased rates of coronary heart disease, cancer, cataract, and macular degeneration.

2) A study of a poorly nourished population in China showed a decreased risk of cancer with Vitamin E and beta-carotene. (They also received the mineral, selenium.)

3) Chocolate, high in polyphenol oxidants may reduce the risk of developing heart disease, although its saturated fat content may be an opposing factor.

OPPOSING VIEWS

On the other hand, some studies show opposing views to the evidence for support:

1) Tocopherol (Vitamin E) and beta-carotene, in a cancer prevention study, showed no benefit regarding risk of cardiovascular disease or cancer. As a matter of fact, there was a 50 percent increase in cerebrovascular hemorrhage and a decrease of 34 percent in the incidence of cancer of the prostate.

2) In a cancer prevention study with beta-carotene and retinol, antioxidants may have been harmful to smokers.

3) In the health study conducted by Harvard's Department of

Public Health on 22,000 physicians, published in 1996, there was no effect of beta-carotene in the risk of cardiovascular disease or cancer after twelve years. There was a possible benefit in the risk of prostate cancer among those tested with reduced blood levels of beta-carotene. (The author is pleased to have been a part of this study.)

CURRENT ASSESMENT

The current assessment of data regarding the antioxidant theory is that it is not clear that antioxidants alone are the protectors of disease. Studies to date are inconclusive. Further studies are indicated, and are in progress.

MINERALS

The fifteen minerals of importance to body health are as vital as the vitamins, but for some reason are not as well known or emphasized as much.

The best known, however, are the *sodium* and *chloride* ions. They are very prominent in the daily lives of people because of the general awareness of the importance of *salt*, especially in hypertension and in heart failure. (See salt in Ideal Diet). Similarly, *potassium* is well known to most people because of its tendency to loss by urination along with sodium in the use of diuretics in hypertension. *Calcium* and *phosphorus* are of concern to people with knowledge about bone growth in children and with bone injuries in accidents, particularly among post-menopausal women and the elderly because of osteoporosis.

IRON deficiency results in anemia, and may occur in children, in pregnancy, and in blood loss especially due to heavy menses.

Little attention is paid to the remaining minerals. Some people are aware, however, that many reliable multivitamin preparations have varying amounts of minerals incorporated in the preparations designed for daily use. One should be cautious about their uses.

Their needs are easily met in the ideal diet. Supplementary intake is generally unnecessary, except as indicated previously.

NaCl (SALT): The recommended daily allowance *(RDA)* is about *5.0 gm* (one level teaspoonful), or *2000 mg* sodium per day.

POTASSIUM, RDA *4000 mg*, is essential for growth, muscle contraction, alkalinity and healthy skin. It functions in the transmittal of oxygen to the brain. Food sources include green leafy vegetables, oranges, whole grains, potatoes, bananas, nuts, meats.

CALCIUM, RDA *1000 mg*, essential for teeth and bones and function of muscle, CNS, and blood. Food sources include milk, dairy products, green leafy vegetables, peas, and beans.

IRON, RDA *18 mg*, is essential for blood and muscle function. It is found in beef, poultry, eggs, fish, green leafy vegetables, liver, beans, enriched-flour breads and pastas, and fortified breakfast cereals.

IODINE, RDA *150 mcg*, functions in thyroid and in metabolism; found in iodized salt, seafood.

COPPER, RDA *2 mg*, for utilization of iron and development of bones, nerves, and connective tissue; found in whole grain cereals, green leafy vegetables, seafood, eggs, peas, and beans.

MAGNESIUM, RDA *400 mg*, essential for muscles and nerves, and for teeth and bones; found in leafy green vegetables, apple, corn, almonds, soybean.

MANGANESE, RDA *2 mg*, activates enzymes, important in reproductive function; found in leafy green vegetables, whole-grain cereals, egg, nuts, beans.

SELENIUM, RDA *0.2 mg*, helps in regulation of metabolic processes; found in cereal bran, broccoli, onion, tomatoes, tuna.

ZINC, RDA *15 mg*, essential for growth, and reproductive function; found in nuts, liver, eggs, milk, whole-grain cereals, shellfish.

CHROMIUM: Widespread in foods as well as in water.

One readily notes that the foods containing minerals are the *same* as those containing the vitamins, and constitute many of the recommended foods in the ideal diet.

HAZARDS OF MINERAL OVERDOSAGE

As with vitamins, more is not better, and there are definite hazards in ingesting an overdosage of minerals:

Sodium Chloride: edema, hypertension, congestive heart failure.

Potassium: muscle weakness, cardiac arrhythmias.

Calcium: reduced absorption of iron and zinc; mental impairment; renal dysfunction.

Zinc: nausea, vomiting, diarrhea, fever, impairment of immune response; reduced level of protective HDL-C (good cholesterol).

Copper: Dysproteinemia; hepato-lenticular degeneration (Wilson's disease); malabsorption.

Iodine: thyroid dysfunction.

Magnesium: diarrhea.

Manganese: Parkinsonism and other CNS disorders.

Cobalt: nausea, vomiting, diarrhea, hearing loss, thyroid dysfunction.

Iron: siderosis, damage to the liver and other organs; hemochromatosis: a common genetic disorder with overload of the liver (occurs in less than one in every thousand births). One should be cautions not to take a vitamin preparation containing iron unless one has need of iron as determined by a blood hemoglobin level

less than *14 gm/dl,* or a blood *ferritin* of less than 30 percent saturation. In suspected blood loss usually by way of the gastro-intestinal tract, a simple diagnostic test is a stool occult blood determination. The role of a guiding physician is essential.

Another commonly advertised mineral that presents an ethical
issue is the promotion of *chromium* picolinate with great claims of
its merit as a dietary supplement (within the law because Congress
decided that it should not be a drug under FDA control). It is falsely claimed to promote weight loss, reverse diabetes, reduce cholesterol, and build muscles. With such claims, it is no wonder that
it has an enthusiastic following. Scientific studies, however,
demonstrated that the claims are all unsubstantiated. As a matter
of fact, hamsters showed damage to their chromosomes and possible cause of cancer. The responsible agent was considered to be the
picolinate, not the chromium.

HAZARDS OF TRACE ELEMENT OVERDOSAGE
As the name implies, some eighty *trace* elements are found in
traces among the ideal foods we eat normally. It may also be noted
that the food sources are the same as those containing the vitamins
and minerals.

Specific mention is made of *nickel,* which plays a role in the
development of lung cancer, and of *fluorine,* which contributes to
neurologic disease, although it is beneficial in dental disease.

Particular attention is given here to *germanium,* which is found
in common herbs, such as sea algae, ginseng, and garlic. In the
1920's it was tested as a remedy in anemias and infections, and
was found ineffective therapeutically, but toxic to the kidneys.
Special attention is called to its current poularity among some
herbalists, who promote germanium as a *miracle* drug for the prevention and cure of cancer, AIDS, allergies, arthritis, osteoporosis,
heart disease, fatigue, and sex dysfunction, at a cost up to twenty

dollars per day. A requirement for its efficacy is that the patient must be relaxed and have faith in the remedy. The assessment of germanium by scientific medicine is that its supplementation is useless and potentially harmful. If the reader learns of any benefits, he will understand that the virtues are based upon an anecdotal reference, and not a scientific study.

Selenium has received some attention based upon suggestive and inconclusive evidence that it may reduce the risk of certain cancers, e.g., prostate, colon, and lung. Only 55 micro-grams (a microgram is one-millionth of a gram) are needed daily and are easily met by eating grains, seafood, meats, and poultry. An excess intake in supplement form may cause nausea, vomiting, hair loss, and dental loss.

EXPLOITATION OF FOOD SUPPLEMENTS
The exploitation of the food supplements: vitamins, mineral, trace elements, and herbs, is the most lucrative and ubiquitous *snake-oil* mongering business in the United States. In 1996, the mega-vitamin (and mineral) and herb mania reached a $6.5 billion expenditure by 100 million Americans in over-the-counter purchases. Surely in part at least, it is due to the Congressional creation in 1994 of The Dietary Supplement Health and Education Act and its weakening of the strong and valuable arm of The Food and Drug Administration in drug control.

What makes the entire issue even sadder is the failure for concern by anyone other than organized medicine over 1) the hazards of vitamin and mineral overdosage and 2) the absence of scientifically studied benefits, safety factors, and hazards of overdosage in connection with the herbal market (see Chapter 17).

COMMON MYTHS regarding Vitamins (V), Minerals (M), and trace elements (T) are the result of widespread exploitation and false claims by certain promoters of food supplements. They claim (without scientific evidence of safety, efficacy, and essentiality to health) that the intake of *megadoses* of V, M. and T may be used for multiple beneficial purposes, especially in the prevention of cancer and heart disease, enhancement of immunity, improvement of energy, bone strength, sexual power, and longevity. Surprisingly, the claims fail to include the logical circumstance of treating a specific vitamin deficiency (perhaps neglected because of the rarity of a deficiency).

FINAL WORDS of wisdom regarding vitamins, minerals, and trace elements:

1) They are not substitutes for, or essential supplements of, a balanced nutritious diet of 20 percent proteins (chicken, fish, cheese, beans), 50 percent complex carbohydrates (five servings per day of fruits and vegetables), and 30 percent fats (predominantly mono-and poly-unsaturated oils, and a minimum of saturated fats and trans fatty acids),

2) The minimum daily requirements (MDR) are minute and easily met with the ideal (scientific) diet.

3) A supplement of one-a-day multivitamin-mineral preparation with 25-100 percent of the MDR is generally more than adequate, adds little to the benefits, and wouldn't hurt.

4) An excess intake of V, M. and T is superfluous, ineffective, mostly excreted, and may be harmful.

5) Many V, M, and T preparations on the market are unapproved by the FDA, and lack the basic standards for dosage accuracy, efficacy, and safety (as required of all drugs by the FDA).

6) Everyone should be cautious of any unproved claims of benefits made by health care providers other than properly qualified professionals in organized medicine and allied professions.

CHAPTER 14

WEIGHT CONTROL: ROLE OF EXERCISE

Out of water and earth and air and fire mingled together arose the forms and colors of all mortal things.

— Empedocles, 5th Century BC

INTRODUCTION

In considering the *ideal* diet in Chapter 13, there was reference to the *average* caloric requirement of 25 to 35 calories per kilogram of body weight per day for people engaged in activities ranging roughly from a white collar job to a blue collar job.

It was also stated that the average American diet exceeds in calories the number needed to maintain the average person's weight, the result being that unused energy is *stored* in the body. The tendency is for the individual to become *overweight* or even *obese*.

In this chapter, the subject of overweight, obesity, dieting, and weight control will be elaborated as *adjunctive* to diet and nutrition, which is second to the doctor-patient relationship as a major subject in health care with many ethical issues relating to quality living. The elimination of the ethical components of the problem would go a long way toward the goal of quality living for everyone in pursuit of a perfect semicircle of life.

WEIGHT CONTROL

Weight control, primarily by dieting and exercise, is an outstanding concern of all people, whether one is 1) under one's standard weight, 2) at one's standard weight, or 3) above one's standard weight. It is a major factor in the minds of everyone in consideration of good health.

Since *two* out of every three Americans consider themselves above their standard weight (and certainly above their desired weight), the weight problem is a serious behavioral and societal issue, as well as an important medical disorder. In the minds of most people, the pursuit of weight reduction and weight control is regarded more as a social problem than a medical one. The issue is even more one of physical appearance than a health hazard.

OBESITY AS A HEALTH RISK

Does an increase in one's weight above normal pose a health risk? There should be some comfort in appreciating that *overweight*, or *up to twenty percent* above one's standard weight, is not really a significant risk factor (especially if only up to ten percent). More than twenty percent above one's standard weight, however, constitutes *obesity*, and is definitely a risk factor for ischemic (coronary) heart disease and in the aggravation of potential hypertension and diabetes.

STATISTICS

Obesity is second to smoking as the leading cause of preventable death (over 300,000 per year).

The *average* weight of adults also known as "the girth of a nation":

1) In the United States is fifteen pounds greater than in Europe,

2) In Europe is five pounds greater than in South America,

3) In South America is five pounds greater than in Africa

4) In Africa is ten pounds greater than in Asia

5) In the United States is thirty-five pounds greater than in Asia

The *average* adult population in the United States (according to actuarial tables) is:

1) Five percent underweight
2) Thirty percent within the range of standard weight
3) Twenty-five percent overweight
4) Forty percent obese

In summary, one-third of the adult population in the United States is at or below the standard weight, and *two-thirds* is above the standard weight. Four out of ten people are at risk for complications of their obesity, a percentage greater than in any other continent on earth.

IDEAL WEIGHT

What is ideal weight? It is actually a narrow range in weight based upon age, sex, height, and body build, and found in *actuarial tables*. A contributing factor, and perhaps a more realistic one, is an opinion of what each person sincerely believes he should weigh. A reliable scientific formula, however, is the *body mass index (BMI)*, an equation in which the actual body weight (in kilograms) divided by the square of the height (in meters) is equal to *21-24* in a person of normal or standard weight. In an overweight person, defined as twenty percent or less above the standard weight, the BMI is *25-28*. In an obese person, defined as more than twenty percent above the standard weight, the BMI is greater than *28*. The correlations decline in persons older than 75 years.

PATHOPHYSIOLOGIC EFFECTS OF OBESITY

1) Tends to a sedentary life style, leading to a vicious cycle of increase in weight and inactivity.

2) Tends to an increase in body fat and a body mass index greater than 28.

3) Tends to increase in blood pressure and heart rate.

4) Tends to increase in insulin resistance.

5) Tends to increase in blood sugar.

6) Tends to decrease in insulin sensitivity and in glucose tolerance.

7) Tends to increase in lipid levels: cholesterol, LDL-C and triglycerides.

8) Tends to decrease in HDL-C.

CLINICAL EFFECTS OF OBESITY

1) In overweight (less than twenty percent above standard weight), the ill effects may be none or few.

2) In obesity (greater than twenty percent above standard weight), the effects may be significantly increased in morbidity and mortality, especially in young people, thereby becoming a major risk factor in aggravating potential or existing:

a) diabetes mellitus via hyperglycemia and increase in insulin resistance,

b) ischemic heart disease via hyperlipidemia: increase in production of lipoproteins rich in LDL-C, VLDL-C, triglycerides, and increased synthesis of cholesterol and its resulting hypercholesterolemia,

c) hypertension and stroke,

d) gall bladder disease,

e) degenerative joint disease,

f) osteoporosis,

g) sleep apnea,

h) bias factor: presumed repulsive physical appearance.

The impact is greater in young patients than in elderly adults.

ETIOLOGY OF OBESITY

The causes of obesity are not really known. This may at first be surprising. There are a number of complex interactions among environmental, behavioral, cultural psychological, and genetic components that have been given consideration as *contributing factors* as follows:

1) *An extravagant life style* with peer pressure is quite apparent.

2) *A low normal metabolism* is a reasonable consideration, but is not consistent with studies.

3) An obvious consideration is that the *caloric intake exceeds caloric expenditure*, accompanied by excess eating, a sedentary life style, and minimal exercise.

4) There is an increase in incidence on a *familial* basis. It is really not certain that the same environment is the prevailing factor, although the same heredity may be the actual circumstance.

5) *Genetic* factors have supporting studies. For example, an *Ob gene* has been identified. It is an adipocyte—specific gene that encodes *leptin* (a protein that regulates body weight). Experimentally, mutations in the Ob gene in mice have been noted to result in a reduction in circulating leptin and a corresponding decrease in the control of satiety. Obesity is the result. The bone volume of the mice is increased as a result of increased production of osteoblasts (overweight people have a reduced likelihood of osteoporosis).

Furthermore, in mice, the administration of recombinant leptin results in an increase in the control of satiety by a reduction in appetite. The result is weight loss. Genetic factors have supporting evidence clinically. The serum leptin concentration correlates with the percentage of body fat by showing an increased level in obese patients, suggesting insensitivity to endogenous leptin production.

A setpoint theory as a contributing factor is of interest. It is based on the theory that hunger stimulates a set point or adipostat in a *feeding center* in the hypothalamus of the brain, and eating is stimulated. An increase in plasma glucose, gastric distension, and beta-adrenergic stimuli ensue, activate the satiety center in the hypothalamus, and eating is inhibited.

Experimental destruction of the feeding center in mice results in a reduction in feeding, and wasting. Experimental destruction of the satiety center results in an increase in feeding, and obesity. To translate this to a clinical hypothesis, obesity would occur if abnormalities were present in the normal hypothalamic control of hunger and eating in the *feeding* and *satiety centers*.

THERAPY OF OBESITY

The cost of health care in the overall treatment of obesity is astronomical. The national expenditure for treatment of the disorder is estimated as $40 billion per year. The therapy of obesity is as complex as is the etiology of obesity. Despite all of the variabilities, its essential component is the *diet*. Dieting has been referred to facetiously as "the rhythm method of girth control.", and as "the great American weighting game." The popular approach by most Americans to the treatment of obesity is to engage in one or more of the following:

1) Compulsive obsession with avoiding weight gain and becoming obese

2) Pursuit of thinness as a primary driving force

3) Constant preoccupation with food and restriction of calories

4) Suffering of guilt over eating rich desserts

5) Drinking artificially sweetened beverages and using sugar substitutes

6) Searching endlessly for a magic pill that would melt off fat, despite years of failure by the drug industry to produce such a miracle without harmful effects

7) Infatuation with an endless procession of bizarre (often irrational) diets with promises of rapid weight loss. Most are a) not generally published in any leading scientific journal, and b) not based on application of the scientific method with controlled studies and an opportunity for peer review and critique. Instead they claim benefits that are entirely anecdotal, testimonial and privately observed.

8) Compulsive considerations of enrolling in ritualized exercise programs and commercial weight–loss clubs featuring physical activities

9) Indulging in periodic binge eating out of frustration, as a reward, or as punishment

10) Attending expensive fat farms and spas where fellow sufferers gather periodically for temporary benefits, socialization, and commiseration

11) Failure to distinguish between relatively harmless effects of overweight and more harmful effects of obesity

12) Regarding every additional pound of weight as a bane

13) Willingness to resort to a variety of surgical procedures in desperation or as a last resort

14) Unfortunate tendency to forego strict dieting and exercise programs on a long-term, life-long basis in favor of short-term crash programs, however ill-advised, and new drugs, not a single one of which has ever withstood the test of time for safety and efficacy

PREVENTION OF OBESITY

Despite the mounting evidence that obesity is a serious risk factor in the cause of coronary heart disease and other disorders, there remains a surprisingly low level of attention to the prevention of obesity.

More than the health factor, there is too often a prevailing psychological factor of embarrassment over one's so called "repulsive" physical appearance as obesity advances in an individual. It is difficult to comprehend the enormity of the bias by a society that is itself generally inclined to be overweight. The bias factor, more than the health factor, then becomes the driving force in the pursuit of treatment for obesity by many, when in fact, much could have been accomplished in prevention. (The reader is reminded that obesity is proffered as an example in the behavioral or societal class of environmental disorders in Chapter 5.)

The collective wisdom of scientific medicine is in agreement that any prophylactic concern about obesity should begin *early* in life, the earlier the better. Everyone should:

1) Aim for maintenance of an ideal or standard body weight by the use of the scientifically recommended dietary measures of organized medicine and a mandatory exercise program on a regular basis under the care of one's family physician with the aid of expert dietetic consultation.

2) Be alert to an unexplained tendency to an increase in weight, blood pressure, blood sugar, and blood lipids.

3) Heed the published experimental findings in rats, in which a standard, maintained weight is achieved by a calorie-controlled diet based on adequate nutrition with proteins, carbohydrates, and fats, and containing the necessary vitamins and minerals. In controlled studies, the properly treated rats had a life span greater than the rats permitted to eat freely without control of diet. In addition, remarkable changes were noted in the controlled group in learning ability, blood glucose control, female reproductive capacity, muscle mass, and immunity. Most surprisingly, there was a delayed onset of late-life diseases including cancer, diabetes, hypertension, cataracts, and kidney failure in the weight-controlled group.

One would hope that these experimental studies in rats can have at least a semblance of meaning for man. If not, however, they at least suggest that the maintenance of a *standard weight* is the aim of everyone in order to have a meaningful quality of living and approach to the perfect semicircle of life.

FINAL THOUGHTS ABOUT DIETING

1) For most people, there is inability to maintain one's selected ideal diet permanently. The more stringent and limited is the diet, the shorter in duration is the adherence to it. After five years of dieting, the failure rate has been reported as 60-90 percent, greater in females than in males. Why not be encouraged by the success rate of 10-40 percent after five years of dieting?

2) Be wary of the numerous and endless array of self-styled experts with their unique concepts of diet and their incredible influence upon vulnerable and gullible sufferers of obesity. (Why are there so many available? If only one were sound and successful, would there be any need for all the others?) Perhaps each may be effective for a brief period in a minority of cases.

EXERCISE

In comparison with diet and drugs, exercise has a remarkably low ranking in the order of interests for the obese patient, despite its importance. As a matter of fact, it took until 1992 for the American Heart Association to grade a physically inactive life-style as a major *risk factor* for coronary heart disease and stroke on a level with such risk factors as smoking, hypertension, and diabetes.

Exercise does not come second to dieting in importance in weight control, but should be practiced side by side with calorie control. According to R.N. Butler, "If exercise could be packed into a pill, it would be the single most widely prescribed and beneficial medicine in the world."

The problem is not that everyone fails to appreciate the enormous value of exercise in the promotion of good health, but rather to many it does not represent a priority as high as the diet or anorexiant drugs, mainly because of the required effort and commitment.

In order to engage in exercise, one must call upon one's sources of energy:

    1) With low intensity exercise, (a good starting point for newcomers to exercise): fat storage is in interstitial spaces

    2) With high intensity exercise: glycogen (carbohydrate) storage is within muscles and the liver

EFFECTS OF A SEDENTARY EXISTENCE
(THE COUCH POTATO)

It is estimated that more than *sixty percent* of adults live an inactive, sedentary existence, which is statistically correlated with the following:

1) An increase in the rate of sudden death

2) Osteoporosis and osteomalacia

3) Obesity

4) Muscle wasting

5) Doubling of the risk of heart disease and stroke

6) A reduced mental performance

7) Emotional instability (greater moodiness)

HEMODYNAMIC STAGES IN EXERCISE

1) The cycle may be started with the pumping action of the exercising heart, which continues to pump throughout the cycle.

2) Increase in heart rate and blood pressure (see stage 16)

3) Increase in cardiac contractions and stroke volume

4) Increase in cardiac output

5) Increase in blood supply and oxygen to exercising muscles (heart does more volume work and less rate work)

6) Arteriolar dilatation in exercising muscles

7) Extraction of oxygen in the exercising muscles resulting in increase in oxygen utilization by muscles

8) Venous engorgement in muscles (followed by venoconstriction)

9) Increase in venous return to right side of heart

10) Blood from right side of heart via pulmonary artery is pumped to lungs

11) Increase in respiratory rate and hyperventilation

12) Oxygen is extracted from lungs by pulmonary veins and returned to left side of heart

13) Increase in left ventricular filling occurs

14) Increase in activity of sympathetic nerves to heart

15) Increase in concentration of circulating catecholamines

16) Increase in heart rate (see stage 2)

17) Cycle goes round and round

The beauty of the complex hemodynamic changes in exercising is that the one exercising need have no concern with the autonomic process, and need only be concerned with the risks of exercise: shortness of breath, chest pain, and injuries.

EXERCISE TIPS

1) Any movement is better than none

2) Avoid elevators: use stairs, especially in going up

3) Park your car in order to walk

4) Take exercise breaks from desk or sofa; stretch and walk around

5) Take a stroll instead of a snack

6) Stand or walk around when using the telephone

7) Walk your pet at an increased pace

8) Drink water throughout the day. The perception of thirst decreases with age

9) Get up to get your own drink

10) Advance to an increased level of activity: do housework, mow the lawn, swim, walk two miles

11) Get more exercise than just running to the doctor

12) How fast should you walk? "Walk as though you have someplace to go." (President Truman) Brisk walking is the best exercise for the elderly.

CLINICAL BENEFITS OF EXERCISE

In order that exercise be beneficial, it must be:

1) Appropriate, neither too short nor too long; neither too low nor too high in intensity (strenuous overactivity may cause complications)

2) Safe, with no physical barriers

3) Convenient, accessible; otherwise, it is postponed or deferred

4) Regular, at definite times every day or on alternate days; a matter of habit

5) Methodical, systematic, routinized

6) Pleasant and enjoyable

7) Indicative of achievement and serve as further encouragement

8) Indicative of psychological benefit: improvement in mood, emotional stability, and possibly in mental performance

Possible mechanisms for improvement of mental performance by physical exercise:

1) Flow of oxygen-rich blood to the brain is enhanced

2) Ability of gray matter in brain to use oxygen is boosted

3) Production and function of neurotransmitters such as serotonin, to transmit brain signals are enhanced

4) Nerves and response—conveying nerve endings are better maintained

PHYSICAL AIDS TO EXERCISE

A number of external physical supports are available as aids to exercise:

1) Three-pronged walking stick

2) One or two canes

3) Walker

4) Joint braces

5) Ankle-foot orthotics

6) Massage

7) Physical therapy

DRUG TREATMENT OF OBESITY

There are few diseases that have as poor a track record

regarding efficacy and safety of their drug therapy as does obesity. The reference relates not only to cure of the disease, but also to improvement and prevention. The aim of all drugs for obesity is evidently to control the appetite, even though that would seem to be the least rational approach to the problem. Accordingly, the drugs are designated as appetite suppressants, anorexigenics, anorectics, and anorexiants.

In the past, as a matter of desperation, some well-known drugs were used even though they were irrational and dangerous for obesity. Among these were diuretics, laxatives, thyroid, digitalis, and amphetamines.

Despite the bad track record, new drugs continue to be marketed because the drug industry understands only too well the patient's mentality and hope for a magic pill. The best advice (besides avoiding them) is for all new anorexiants to be FDA approved and to be taken only for a temporary period at best, and never, never be used as a permanent appetite suppressant. Drugs must never be used instead of a well-chosen, permanent diet and exercise program under a physician's guidance. In other words, they must never be more than a crutch for a brief period, as a starter for encouragement and surely not as a substitute for an established way of eating and exercising. An organized group in strong opposition to obesity drugs includes members of The National Association to Advance Fat Acceptance. The title of the organization is self-explanatory.

Still another matter to emphasize in the need for caution is that there is very little, if any, information regarding the long-term effects (possible delayed toxicity) of any drug used for a protracted period.

That brings us to two of the recently marketed drugs, fenfluramine (Pondimin) and phentermine (Fastin). Fenfluramine is a sympathomimetic amine, which has a significant effect upon the central nervous system in increasing the activity of the satiety center and decreasing the activity of the feeding center, decreasing the uptake of *serotonin*, and increasing glucose utilization. Phentermine is also a sympathomimetic amine and resembles fenfluramine. Although both drugs have FDA approval with a warning for use only over a brief period, the combination of the two, called *Fen-Phen*, was not approved, but was used extensively with great success in suppressing the appetite. The side effects, however, were very slow and subtle in their development of toxicity, and produced *devastating* results: damage to heart valves and pulmonary hypertension in about thirty percent of the people who used the combination. (The author is reminded of a drug used many years ago that 'melted away the fat', but caused blindness many months after onset of use.)

In case the reader is still interested in learning about anorectics, another drug, dexfenfluramine (Redux), chemically related to fenfluramine, was available, based upon experimental evidence in rats, in whom it produced damage to brain cells. The drug was recalled after alarming reports of damage to heart valves appeared (as with Fen-Phen). The estimated loss in sales and in lawsuits will be in the hundreds of millions of dollars, to say nothing of the loss of lives.

The drug, Orlistat, prevents the absorption by the intestine of about one-third of the fat consumed. (Ed: How about eating one-third less fat?)

Beta-3 adrenergic agonists function by speeding up the expenditure of body energy (reminiscent of the action of addictive amphetamines). A drug is available to promote the enhancement of CCK-A, a hormone in the gut, the function of which is to inform the brain when the patient is satiated.

Mazindol (Mazanol, Sanorex) is similar to amphetamines. It

inhibits the uptake of norepinephrine. Side effects include increase in blood pressure, tachycardia, dry mouth, constipation, headache, insomnia, nervousness, and blurred vision.

Sibutramine (Meridia) inhibits the uptake of serotonin and norepinephrine. It produces a feeling of fullness and appetite suppression. Side effects are varied and include elevation of blood pressure.

Appetite suppressants containing phenylpropanolamine have been linked to hemorrhagic stroke.

An interesting preparation, which functions as a fat substitute, is Olestra, which is incorporated into food snacks such as corn chips, potato chips and crackers. The drug is synthesized from sugar and fatty acids, and has the physical properties resembling mineral oil. It has no caloric value. Upon ingestion, it passes through the body without being digested or absorbed. It is able to withstand high cooking temperatures like frying. Olestra has qualified FDA approval. The disturbing news about the agent is that it can deplete the body of fat—soluble vitamins such as A,D,E, and K as well as carotenoids. It can also cause changes in liver cells and be a risk for hepatitis and possibly cancer. Diarrhea and abdominal cramping may occur. (Ed: Are food snacks really necessary at such cost?)

The *problems* with the pursuit of an anorexiant are obvious by now. They include:

1) The reliance is primarily on the simplicity of a pill and secondarily on the more important and more demanding *life-long* commitment to a diet and exercise program.

2) The natural history of obesity is measured in years, whereas the proper concept of drug usage is best measured in weeks.

3) Anorexiants, like drugs in general, have a tolerance factor, so that the rate of weight loss declines with continued usage of the

drug, which then would necessarily require an increase in dosage—a hazardous decision.

4) An over-all assessment of anorexiants is that their effect is temporary, disappointing, and risky. At best, they should be used, as warned by the FDA, for short periods.

5) If the patient is not satisfied with the fundamental treatment of obesity with diet and exercise, and drugs fail him, the three radical choices he has, all for desperate consideration are,

a) starvation (as in anorexia nervosa) for limited periods and intermittent application. Its production of keto-acidosis, a potentially serious metabolic disorder, may also be attained with certain popular diets that are very low in carbohydrate and excessively high in protein and fat.

b) purging and catharsis (compare binge eating and bulimia)

c) surgery by liposuction (a plastic surgical procedure designed more to improve physical appearance than to reduce weight), gastroplasty (shortening the stomach), intestinal by-pass (preventing absorption of digested food by sending it to the colon for excretion), and/or ablation of the lateral hypothalamus of the brain (no effort will be made to explain this operation).

GENERAL PRINCIPLES IN THE SUCCESSFUL TREATMENT OF OBESITY:

1) The approach must be multi-faceted.

2) Motivation, motivation, motivation.

3) A well-balanced, nutritious diet with a fixed calorie intake commensurate with an energy expenditure based on maintenance of a standard weight.

4) Back-to-school education in nutrition based on multiple sessions with a registered dietitian under the supervision of the family physician.

5) Behavior modification requiring private and group counseling with psychologic help.

6) Physical activity program properly monitored and part of a permanent regimen of exercise, exercise, and exercise

7) Life-long guidance and medical care by a family physician, internist or board-certified specialist in metabolic diseases. Obesity is a chronic disease and must be followed carefully like hypertension or diabetes in a life-long commitment.

Remember, the subject is obesity and not overweight, which some people are more successful in correcting by themselves than is obesity.

Finally, the great American diet hoaxes must be distinguished from reliable scientific data in order to achieve and maintain an ideal weight and permanent good health, i.e., in the search for a more complete quality living by aiming toward the goal of the perfect semicircle of life.

SECTION D

SUBJECT III: MEDICATION

Man does not need a machine to manufacture happiness, or an oracle to tell him where to find it; it is a byproduct of life needing only to be separated from a dross of want and pain.

— Homer W. Smith, 1952

INTRODUCTION

The third subject among the seven major medical subjects in health care with many ethical issues that relate to quality living concerns the medications we take 1) by a physician's prescription and 2) by self-treatment with over-the-counter drugs and herbs.

The medications or drugs we take actually comprise the largest category of therapeutic measures available to us, upon which we depend for the benefit of our illnesses. It also has a proportionately large number of ethical issues which require resolution as we proceed en route to our highest level of quality living in our hypothetical goal of a perfect medical semicircle of life.

No one can dispute the fact that never before today in our long history of health care has the use of medication drugs for the treatment of our illnesses been as successful in their benefits over a wide range of diseases. They are of particular value in the treatment of our most serious medical disorders: coronary artery disease, acute myocardial infarction, stroke, cancer, leukemia, diabetes, infections, psychiatric illnesses, muscle and joint conditions, et al. The pharmaceutical industry should be commended for its cooperation and response in addressing the needs presented to it by the medical profession pertaining to the problems most essential to health care, that could be benefited by medication.

In appreciation, the industry is the benefactor of the constant support of its endeavors by a cooperative federal government with favorable patent laws, a Food and Drug Administration that guards against drug toxicity and protects the safety and efficacy of drugs, a medical profession eagerly awaiting its products with a ready prescription pad, and enthusiastic public ready to take a pill for every ailment, and an elderly population with multiple disorders, each of which receives a carefully designed medicament.

Not under consideration in the text, even though they have a destructive role in health care, are abused illicit drugs including cocaine, heroin, lysergic acid diethylamide (LSD), and phencyclidine (PCP), et al. Their sale and usage are matters of criminality and illegality, not of ethical concern.

CHAPTER 15

PRESCRIPTION DRUGS

The desire to take medicine is perhaps the greatest feature which distinguishes man from animals.

— Sir William Osler, 1904

STATISTICS

A review of the extent to which drugs are used in health care reveals astonishing information. Prescription drugs alone represent an $80 billion industry. Approximately 2.5 billion prescriptions for drugs are written annually. The average cost of a prescription for every patient is approximately $40. The average cost of a prescription for a *new* drug exceeds $70.

Most patients over sixty-five years of age fill an average of *more than one* prescription per month. This is a higher number than is taken in any comparable age group under sixty-five years of age.

When the enormous drug market of self-treatment with over-the-counter drugs and herbs is added to the costs of our medications, the numbers become astronomical, and so do the ethical considerations they raise, especially among the non-prescription drug users.

DEFINITION OF A DRUG

It is important that we define a drug so that everyone understands fully what he is ingesting, injecting, inhaling or applying to his body for the benefit of his ill health. The *standard* definition of a drug is any chemical compound or biological substance administered to or taken by a human being or animal 1) as an aid in diagnosis, prevention, control, or improvement of any pathological condition, or 2) for the relief of pain or suffering.

The author is quick to point out to the reader that there are numerous drugs that actually cure disease and relieve pain and suffering. They should not be overlooked or reduced in prominence by the myriad of drugs that are less beneficial, of little benefit, or of no benefit. Never mind the harm that many may cause. Our concern in the text is less with the quality of the drugs we take than with the ethical issues they raise in affecting our quality of living. The reader is also urged to note that the definition of a drug truly applies also to the congressional designation of vitamins, minerals, trace elements, and herbs as food supplements. (The issue of having removed herbs from the category of drugs where they truly belong and designating them as *food supplements,* will be addressed in Chapter 17 when self-treatment is discussed.)

**ROLE OF THE FOOD AND DRUG
    ADMINISTRATION (FDA)**

Following a calamitous event in health care in which death was caused by poisoning resulting from an elixir of sulfanilamide, Congress was prompted in 1938 to pass *The Food, Drug, and Cosmetic Act.*

It took another calamitous event—that of congenital birth defects among children of pregnant women who took thalidomide (in Europe, not in the United States, thanks to the FDA)—to prompt Congress again to take action and pass the *Kefauver-Harris Amendments* in *1962,* further strengthening the role of the FDA.

The primary role of the FDA is to assure the *safety* and *efficacy* of every new drug before marketing by a manufacturer. (Please note how this mandate fails to apply to food supplements, even though they fit the definition of a drug.)

FDA REQUIREMENTS

The FDA has a clear set of requirements to be met prior to approval and the release of drugs to the public:

1) Proprietary and generic names

2) Description

3) Clinical pharmacology

4) Indications and usage

5) Contraindications

6) Warnings

7) Precautions

8) Adverse reactions

9) Overdosage

10) Dosage and administration

11) Manufacturer's name and address, batch and lot number of drug, date of expiration of drug

12) An *insert* with the above data must be included with every package. The same data is duplicated in *The Physician's Desk Reference (PDR)*, published annually by Medical Economics. Editions prepared specially for *consumers* are available for purchase by everyone interested in checking on available prescription drugs.

THE PLACEBO: ITS USE AS A DRUG IN THE PAST

(See Chapter 23 regarding the *current* use of the placebo in medical research.) The placebo (Latin, 'I please', English, 'placate') is an inert, *inactive* substance, not a drug, used as a therapeutic agent in the *past* to please or gratify a patient. It was offered in a prescription as treatment for anxiety, emotional stress, and other *non-organic* or psychosomatic disorders, but never for any organic disease. The physician may have revealed the diagnosis, but never the identity of the treatment. Hence, informed consent was deliberately withheld. Obviously, if a patient were told whether or not he is receiving a placebo, the point of the treatment would be lost. To be sure, failure to inform the patient actually constituted deception (in a bland manner with beneficial intent).

The *bases* upon which benefits were anticipated by the physician in prescribing a placebo were many and varied:

a) Expectation of the patient's improvement via his confidence and trust in the immediate environmental symbols of healing including the physician's office, diplomas, the doctor, nurse, white coat, stethoscope, physical examination itself, and *ambience* of the hospital.

b) Patient's passion for medications despite costs: drugs in general, antibiotics, analgesics, vitamins, sedatives, stimulants, and herbs despite 1) their unproved efficacy or safety and 2) the physician's lack of their endorsement.

c) The power of suggestion: "This will help your cough."

d) Encouraging and optimistic reassurances by the doctor: "You will be all right."

e) Doctor with favorable traits: compassion, interest, concern

f) Patient's own optimistic expectations regarding good health: "Everyday in every way, I'm getting better and better."

g) "Cost is no object," even if startlingly high.

EXAMPLES OF THE POWER OF THE PLACEBO

Two shameful and unethical examples illustrating the benefits and power of a placebo without obtaining informed consent are the following research studies:

1) Use of a placebo as the drug being tested and a known antidepressant used as the control in a double blind study. The placebo produced greater improvement of depression than the control (antidepressant)!

2) Expectation of beneficial treatment of angina pectoris by splitting of the chest and ligating the internal mammary artery.

In the controls, the chest was incised and no ligation of the internal mammary artery was performed. Surprise! The controls, with no ligation, showed greater benefit than did the procedure with the ligation.

In both experiments, results were subjective and judged on the basis of *symptoms*, not on objective findings. This may explain the unexpected results, but does not excuse the *immorality* of the procedures. The current requirement of informed consent would preclude such studies.

CURRENT USE OF THE PLACEBO

(*See* Chapter 23 for more detail regarding the current use of the placebo in contrast with its therapeutic use in the past.) Two *criteria* are basic:

1) The placebo is used exclusively as a control in scientific studies to determine the efficacy and safety of a medicinal substance to be tested.

2) Explanation is given to the patient regarding the planned procedure in a research project leading to *informed consent*—a mandatory requirement in compliance with modern principles which include respect for a patient's rights of autonomy and self-determination.

ETHICAL ISSUES

1) Should the placebo be used again as in the past without informed consent as therapy in appropriate situations for non-organic disorders? This decision has not been totally abandoned because of its occasional benefits.

2) How often are prescriptions really serving as placebos unintentionally when they are written a) as shot-gun treatments for lack of diagnosis or in frustration for lack of adequate treatment and a desire to do something that might by chance be beneficial? or b) for want of doing something that may be expected by the patient?

3) Since disclosure of the intended use of a placebo would wreck the point of the treatment, would not the failure of disclosure be a form of deception on the part of the physician? Might the physician be excused on the basis of his therapeutic privilege in the best interest of the patient?

DRUGS AND THE ELDERLY PATIENT

Patients over 65 years of age comprise 34 million people (13 percent of the population) and they take 30 percent of prescription medicaments. They also buy 70 percent of the over-the-counter drugs, as compared with 30 percent purchased by the remainder of the population. They are not as inclined, however, to delve into the herbal market as do younger patients.

PHARMACOKINETICS

Older patients differ significantly from younger patients in the pharmacokinetics of drug action by manifesting a) impaired absorption, distribution, and metabolism; b) impaired excretion (biliary and renal), as a result of which older patients tend to show an increase in vulnerability to morbidity and mortality; and c) impaired protein-binding action at the target receptors, causing a reduction of efficiency of drugs.

OTHER DRUG PROBLEMS AMONG THE ELDERLY:

The elderly also tend to have multiple chronic illnesses often requiring multiple drugs prescribed by multiple physicians in various specialties. Too often, unfortunately, these patients may lack a highly recommended relationship with a single physician (a family doctor or a general internist), who would serve as a monitor and overseer (often called a gatekeeper in a managed care facilities) of all medications as well as the patients' medical conditions. To complicate the situation and further impair the quality of care, the patient may be adding his own medications purchased over-the-counter or in health stores. In addition, chronic disorders often require drugs for long-term use, and the likelihood of drug interactions may become a factor in an increased incidence of adverse drug reactions (ADR's).

A still further complication in the older patient's drug therapy program is the frequent tendency to skip doses because of a) cost as well as b) forgetfulness.

THE PHARMACEUTICAL INDUSTRY AND NEW DRUGS MANUFACTURING ISSUES

The pharmaceutical industry has the fortunate role of manufacturing products designed to improve health and save lives, never mind that the industry is in a highly competitive business primarily profit-driven like all commercial enterprises. As a result, there is constant, endless manufacturing of *new* drugs, many of which are often similar chemically and in action to the products manufactured and already marketed by competitors. The chemical changes are often minor but never identical because of patent rights that protect against duplication. New drugs are given new proprietary names and presented to the public with claims of advantages, often marginal at best, over marketed drugs they really mimic. As a result, the drug market is flooded, thereby creating a glut and a state of confusion, especially for the physician, who is generally obliged to acquaint himself with relatively few of the similar drugs for limited use among his patients. He could not possibly become an expert in all marketed drugs, and he need not be one. In specialty practices, the physicians necessarily are familiar with a wider understanding of drugs used in their limited areas of expertise.

ADVERTISING of new drugs by manufacturers is extensive in journals and in the media. There is also constant lobbying among medical, dental, pharmaceutical, and nursing personnel in offices and hospitals with *samples* accompanied by blurbs.

The advertising, as expected, results in great use of the products and profit for the industry. The enormous cost of the advertising and promotion ($8 billion per year) is added to the cost of research and development of new drugs ($24 billion per year), The total cost is then transferred to the pricing of the drug to the patient (after the industry takes its profit). That is of course the American business way. Should drugs intended for the health of all people, including the poor and the elderly, be treated like automobiles or any other commercial product not intended primarily for health care?

As an advertising ploy, the pharmaceutical industry mimics other (non-medical) industries in using attractive models and celebrities, including athletes, to endorse their products. The consumer is expected to believe that if the model takes the drug and if it is good enough for a celebrity, it should be good enough for the consumer. The consumer is then expected to pressure his physician for a prescription. Whether or not this activity is a matter of good taste, it is still an ethical question.

THE SCIENTIFIC METHOD

A saving feature in the control of the commercialization of drugs are the rigid research requirements of the FDA prior to marketing of a drug by industry with the aim of assuring the *safety* and *efficacy* of all drugs. The key to the requirements for industry, which are the same as for academic institutions, is the *mandatory* application of the *scientific method*. Its requirements are as follows:

1) A plausible proposal

2) Approval by The Institutional Review Board where the research scientist plans to perform the study

3) A sufficient number of subjects

4) Random selection of subjects

5) Controls with or without placebo

6) Double-blind technique

7) Statistical analysis

8) Clinical trials

9) Approval by the FDA

10) Valid publication, peer review, critique, replication, and modification; a continuing, on-going process

It is important here to note that the scientific method in the study of drugs does not exist in connection with the marketing and the advertising of herbs and other food supplements, which do not come under FDA control.

DIRECT-TO-CONSUMER ADVERTISING
BY THE PHARMACEUTICAL INDUSTRY

A new device in the marketing of new pharmaceutic products is the practice of direct-to-consumer (DTC) advertising of prescription drugs via the media and the Internet. According to the drug industry, a number of factors favor the practice:

1) Industry has the right and responsibility to inform the public of new products requiring a prescription and physician supervision.

2) The process has educational merit in that it meets the growing demand by patients for medical information.

3) Patients are given an increase in responsibility, which they seek, for their own health.

4) The doctor-patient relationship is improved by the increase in communication.

5) Patient compliance with drug regimens is improved.

6) Public health is enhanced.

The medical establishment is strongly *opposed* to the DTC practice by the industry because of a number of factors:

1) The drug industry's favoring of the practice (see above) is entirely a figment of the industry's imagination.

2) The bottom-line of the DTC practice is not for better health, but for profit.

3) The merit of the promotional material far outweighs the merit of the educational material, which is often negligible.

4) The information in the DTC ads compared with that of similar

drugs available in scientific journals is often of suspect quality, misleading (by subtle distortion), of minimal benefit, low in accuracy of predicting efficacy, lacking in warnings and precautions, and low in evidence to justify the claims.

5) The industry's aim to create consumer demand tends to *undermine* the physician's role as the system's safety net in preventing the use of an improper drug for the patient. The patient's demand for the drug is likely to result in a prescription that may not really be the physician's choice.

6) There is a tendency for the DTC ads to diminish the primary role of the physician in selecting and monitoring the drugs best suited to the patient's specific needs.

7) There is dubious public health value in the DTC ad.

8) The patients, according to the physician, should place their trust and responsibility entirely in the hands of their physician for their care; and certainly not badger him for drugs with which they are impressed by advertisements that often are not in the patient's best interest.

The DTC advertising process may be legal, but is it ethical?

There is insufficient public awareness that a number of members of the pharmaceutical industry provide free medications to the Pharmaceutical Research and Manufactures of America. Physicians can prescribe drugs gratis for needy patients by consulting the available Directory of the Prescription Drug Patient Assistance Program. The pharmaceutical industry must be commended for such altruistic conduct.

Throughout the text, the author has found numerous opportunities to lament over the unfortunate positions of the poor in relation to their diminished capacity to obtain drugs needed for their survival as well as their health care. A striking example is the case of a transplantation of a kidney to an impoverished recipient who could not afford the price of the anti-rejection drugs essential for the preservation of the donated kidney. The patient lost the kidney and her life.

It is common knowledge that among patients on Medicaid, doses of drugs are skipped frequently as a money-saving necessity. Other examples abound.

FDA REQUIREMENTS IN CLINICAL TRIALS

Another dubiously ethical practice is the enrollment by the pharmaceutical industry of community-based physicians as research investigators, a highly euphemistic term for physicians who utilize their patients in clinical trials required by the industry to obtain final FDA approval of their drugs.

FACTORS FAVORING the process, as claimed by the industry (and obviously supported by participating physicians):

1) Doctors are involved in cutting-edge research vital to a doctor's growth as part of his continuing medical education.

2) Patients have ready access to potentially life-saving measures.

FACTORS OPPOSING the process:

1) Is not the quality of the clinical research diminished by a) the straying of the physicians far from their field of expertise, b) poorly executed studies, and c) providing poorly collected data?

2) Are doctors really enhancing patient care?

3) Is patient safety in jeopardy?

4) Is the requirement of informed consent fully met?

5) Are all the patients aware that they are "guinea-pigs" in a trial, or do some believe that they are merely getting a free sample for treatment of some complaint?

6) Does the physician have sufficient time needed to execute his research role, or does an office assistant fill out a company form by consulting the patient for required information?

7) Doctors generally receive lucrative stipends for their assis-

tance to the industry. Does this attraction outweigh the physician's research role?

8) Do lucrative stipends create conflicts of interest?

9) Is the clinical judgment of the physician clouded by his enticement of influencing patients to enroll in the research studies?

10) Are physicians furthering science or are they participating in a commercial venture similar to the sale of products out of office?

11) Do (and should) doctors make financial disclosure to the patients they enroll in the studies?

12) Should not doctors share their stipends with the patients participating in the studies?

13) Where applicable in hospital-based studies, are The Institutional Review Boards able to track the number of patients from each physician participating in the study?

14) Except for requesting the data, the FDA has no control over the procedure other than to be informed when any investigator receives more than $25,000 (reputedly a common occurrence).

15) Should the physician serving as a research investigator with us of his private patients in a private arrangement with a pharmaceutical company be expected to submit his study to his hospital's Institutional Review Board for approval as would be expected if the study were hospital-based.

All ethical doubts could, and should, be eliminated if the industry were challenged to restore quality in their clinical research with an ethical and practical scenario involving the industry, the physicians and their patients.

A final point in the industry's role in the manufacture of new drugs is to remind them that the world awaits an expansion of genetic engineering by the pharmaceutical industry in the manufacture of new drugs similar to the established production of human insulin, wherein the DNA of a non-disease-producing strain of E. coli bacteria is genetically altered by adding a human gene.

ROLE OF THE PHYSICIAN REGARDING NEW DRUGS

In the physician's constant survey of new drugs:

1) Should he not be conservative, cautious, prudent, and follow the dictum to "be not the first by whom the new is tried, nor yet the last to cast the old aside?"

2) Should he not have rational and guarded skepticism regarding pharmaceutical claims?

3) Should he not be guided by scientific literature in lieu of company samples?

4) Should he not be expected to know the pharmacokinetics of the drugs to be prescribed, especially as they relate to the patient for whom the drug is intended?

5) Should he not be expected to know the patient's total medical picture before writing a prescription?

6) Should he not be obedient to FDA approval and guidelines (recorded in the drug inserts)?

7) Should he be expected to consider the cost and the possible use of available generic drugs?

8) Should he be expected to know the possible synergistic actions and adverse interactions of drugs prescribed in combinations? (Ed: Little is known about the interactions among three or more drugs taken simultaneously.) The result may be an increase in efficacy, decrease in efficacy, or increase in toxicity.

9) Should he not respect and be alert to side effects including allergies and adverse reactions?

10) Should he not follow the rule of matching the 'size' of the drug with the 'size' of the illness. (Ed: "More is not necessarily better.")

11) Should he not be expected to keep accurate records regarding the patient's drugs? (Ed: The record may be available to the patient upon written request.)

12) Should he not be able to predict potential adverse drug reactions (other than allergic reactions) by way of knowing the drug's pharmacology: absorption, distribution, metabolism (liver), and excretion (urine, bile)?

13) Should he not be aware that the pharmacological mechanism that is responsible for the drug's efficacy may be the same as many of its toxic effects?

14) Should he be expected to keep in mind that, in the diagnosis of a patient's illness, adverse drug reactions should be included in every differential diagnosis he offers in considering the etiology of the patient's complaints?

ROLE OF THE PATIENT REGARDING NEW DRUGS

The patient has specific guidelines to be followed regarding new drugs:

1) He must understand that prescriptions are required for drugs a) that are considered unsafe without a physician's supervision, b) that are administered by parenteral route, and c) that have a high abuse potential.

2) All drugs taken by a patient should be monitored by or at least known to one primary physician.

3) The patient should be knowledgeable regarding the drugs he is currently taking: their indications, time of administration (with reference to meals or fasting, day or night, frequency, etc.), mode of action, and side effects.

4) The pharmacist can be helpful as a valuable consultant.

5) Drug inserts and the consumer copy of The Physician's Desk Reference are available to the patient for reference.

6) Patients should not be bashful to shop around a) for comparative costs of expensive new drugs and b) for possible use of generic drugs, (which are best known to pharmacists). The patient should receive the physician's approval.

7) Patients should be respectful of all drugs.

8) Patients must realize that drugs should be taken seriously and as a matter of necessity. Drugs should not be taken casually or frivolously. Every patient should know with certainty what he is putting into his body for his health.

9) The prolonged or indefinite use of any drug should be avoid-

ed. The physician prescribing the drug should be consulted periodically regarding its continuation or replacement.

10) A prescribed regimen should be adhered to strictly. The added use of over-the-counter drugs and self-treatment with herbs should be avoided.

11) The patient should be alert to new and unexpected symptoms. They may represent a) possible toxicity or an allergic reaction to a new drug, or b) symptoms of some ailment.

12) A diary should be kept carefully and accurately of all drugs used (for the benefit of the patient and available to the physician).

13) Multiple drugs prescribed by multiple physicians for multiple problems should be avoided unless the patient's primary physician is monitoring and has knowledge of the entire regimen.

14) The patient has rights regarding access to the physician's record or the hospital's record of the patient. (The legal limit for record keeping by the physician or the hospital is seven years.)

ADVERSE DRUG REACTIONS (ADR)
(Formerly called Adverse Drug Events)

"There are some remedies worse than the disease."
— Publius Syrus, 1st Century B.C.

It bears reemphasis that many drugs are lifesaving, *curative* of disease, and of great benefit in the relief of *pain and suffering*. There are no panaceas, however, and there is no drug that is entirely beneficial without any side effect or potential for harm. Every drug is in reality like a double-edged sword with expected benefits on one side and unexpected or undesirable effects (toxic or allergic) on the other side. There are no exceptions (not even if a placebo is used therapeutically as a drug).

In the entire drug market, *prescription* drugs offer the largest area of health care benefits, but may also be *sixth* among the causes, or contributing causes, of death (approximately 100,000 per year). The following are the more common causes: 1) cardio-vascular disease, 2) cancer, 3) stroke, 4) pulmonary disease, and 5) accidents. Pneumonia is seventh and diabetes is eighth.

The severity of reaction may range from a) mild to b) intense, disabling, and fatal. In the pregnant patient, congenital anomalies may occur.

TYPES OF DRUG REACTIONS

There are two types of adverse drug reaction: Type A: toxic, and Type B: allergic.

Type A ADR (Toxic):

1) Predictable

2) Common

3) An extension of the drug's known properties; hence, can be expected

4) Dependent upon dosage and/or route of administration

5) May be aggravated by drug-drug interactions and by drug-food interactions

6) Rarely life threatening

7) Occasionally disabling

8) Disappear with decline in plasma concentration

9) Avoidable

10) Usually listed in the product's labeling

Type B ADR (Allergic)

1) Unpredictable

2) Uncommon

3) Usually not an extension of the drug's known pharmaco-logic activity

4) Independent of dosage or route of administration

5) Dependent upon patient's sensitivity

6) Rarely avoidable

7) Includes the following reactions: idiosyncratic or allergic, anaphylactic, carcinogenic, teratogenic

8) Organs usually affected are the liver, skin and blood, less often the kidney and central nervous system

9) May be life-threatening in liver, skin, and bone marrow toxicity

TIME OF REACTION

1) Anaphylactic (type B): immediately

2) All others (types A or B): minimum of five days to a maximum of twelve weeks. Rarely is there a prolonged delay. An unfortunate exception is the prolonged use of *fen-phen*, a combination of fenfluramine (Pondimin) and phentermine (Fastin), used as an appetite suppressant in obesity. Although the drugs were approved individually by the FDA, a caution was issued that their usage was only approved on a short-term basis. The delayed toxic effects were serious: pulmonary hypertension and multivalvular heart disease.

INCIDENCE OF ADR'S

An unfortunate circumstance is the apparently low incidence of adverse drug reactions (less apparent than real). The reasons are as follows:

1) Frequent failure of recognizing ADR's, which may be obscured, hidden or masked by the underlying medical condition.

2) Misdiagnosis: renal failure may be present and not recognized as due to an ADR

3) Frequent neglect of consideration of ADR in a differential diagnosis

4) The acknowledgement of an adverse drug reaction is an admission of a possible error in treatment.

5) Failure of reporting as required (an illegal act) may raise the possibility of negligence and malpractice.

REPORTING OF ADR'S

1) Reporting is a requirement based upon the FDA's responsibility of ensuring safety of all manufactured drugs.

2) Drug manufacturers are responsible for notifying the FDA of all known ADR's.

3) Hospitals, medical staffs, and private physicians are responsible for a) reporting serious ADR's to the FDA and b) maintaining an ADR surveillance system.

4) The Joint Commission for the Accreditation of Health Care Organizations (JCAHCO) establishes standards for the monitoring of ADR's by hospitals, nursing homes, and all organizations seeking its accreditation (without which the health care facility would not be eligible for reimbursement by Medicare, Medicaid, or other federal funds).

DRUG-DRUG INTERACTIONS (INCOMPATIBLES)

Drug-drug interactions between *two* drugs are common, and mostly well-known. Examples include fenfluramine and phentermine, Viagra and nitrates, Mevacor and Lopid, aspirin and Coumadin, Seldane and antibiotics, insulin and Inderal, Tagamet and Dilantin, codeine and alcohol, Gingko and Warfarin, Ginseng and digoxin, Echinacea and cyclosporine, Ginseng and Phenelzine, St. John's Wort and Prozac.

Drug-drug interactions among *three* or more drugs, however, are much less well known, if at all, but often may be surmised. Although most interactions are not harmful, some may neutralize each other's actions, others may reduce the action of each of the drugs, and still others may compound the effects of the drugs.

RECOMMENDATIONS by experts in pharmacy have been offered to offset the unwelcome effects of interactions:

1) The actions and side-effects of every drug prescribed should be known to the physician and to the patient.

2) The patient must be alert to new symptoms and the consid-

eration that a drug may be the cause.

3) New combinations of drugs must be checked with the physician and the pharmacist.

4) Multiple combinations should be avoided. Drugs should be taken separately, as far apart from each other as possible. This matter should be discussed with the physician prescribing or monitoring the drugs.

5) All available information provided by the manufacturer in the inserts and in the PDR should be checked and heeded.

DRUG ERRORS

The commission of errors in the use of drugs conjures up the frightening thought of mistakes causing terrible results in the care of innocent people.

The *frequency* of any errors at all is rare in the physician's office practice and in the issuing of prescriptions. There are built-in *controls*, especially by alert registered pharmacists, who double check all drug requests from offices as well as in hospitals, nursing homes, and hospices. The registered nurse, a responsible professional, is often involved between the drug order and its delivery, and serves as still another overseeing mechanism and safeguard.

Reliable studies indicate that drug errors in hospitals occur at the average rate of three per ten thousand drug orders. The rare error is most often of little or no significance as far as patient effect is concerned. Data from nursing homes suggest a slightly higher rate of errors than in hospitals.

Reports of drug errors increase in numbers when patients control their own selection of drugs as with the 1) unsupervised consumption of over-the-counter drugs and vitamins, 2) care-free use of herbs, 3) wreckless compliance in taking prescribed drugs (skipping doses, missing times of administration), and in taking multiple prescribed drugs from multiple sources in the absence of a monitoring primary care physician.

TYPES OF DRUG ERRORS

1) *Dosage*: if the prescribed dosage is reduced, the effect of the drug will be diminished and possibly eliminated. If the dosage is increased, the danger of toxicity is present (noted by Paracelsus, 16th Century).

2) *Improper Selection*: The risk of selecting the wrong drug is obvious. In practice, this error is not infrequently the case with the wrong selection of an appropriately needed antibiotic. There is too often a dependence on chance as in spinning the wheel in gambling.

3) *Allergy*: Unfortunately, this complication cannot be predicted and its frequency is not well known. A thorough history can be helpful.

4) *Drug Interactions* are most common in the use of multiple drugs, which are best taken at reasonable intervals (unless approved by the physician for combined intake).

5) *Inaccurate Diagnosis*: This is not excusable, and occurs most often in self-treatment with over-the-counter drugs and herbs.

REASONS FOR ERRORS

Errors in hospitals, although rare, are most often attributed to illegible writing of orders, misunderstood ordering by telephone, and by poorly communicated verbal orders. The more severe an illness, the more likely there may be haste, increase in numbers of drugs, and complexity of medications.

EFFECT OF ERRORS

If the error is a small one, as is usually the case, and if there is no apparent effect upon the care of the patient, the error need not be disclosed (according to The Physician's Code of Ethics). On the other hand, if the error influences the care of the patient, the code of ethics mandates that the error be *disclosed* honestly.

PHYSICIAN'S REACTION TO AN ERROR

The physician's primary concern is first and foremost doing no harm in the care and well-being of the patient. An error rarely poses a problem. Occasionally, however, the physician may be plagued by the dreaded claim of *negligence*, the most unwelcome experience for any physician. Accusations of malpractice are most often initiated by angry and upset family members of a patient they believe was mistreated. If sufficiently vindictive and litigious, they may initiate a lawsuit with the aid of a willing and cooperative lawyer. In most instances, such suits are determined to be *frivolous*, and the physician is exonerated. The rare serious error gets magnified attention.

PREVENTION OF DRUG ERRORS

A number of valuable suggestions have been collected and are offered as means to prevent drug errors:

1) Improvement of monitoring

2) Adherence to the use of the Standard Hospital Formulary

3) Orders should be written in undisputed clarity and accuracy.

4) Telephone and verbal orders should be clear, used at a minimum, and only when urgently needed.

5) Installation of computerized physician order entry systems to check drug spelling, dosage and interactions

6) The registered nurse and the pharmacist can be relied upon as checking factors in the prevention of drug errors.

7) Improvement in patient education beginning early in life, especially regarding the hazards of self-medication with over-the-counter drugs and scientifically unproven herbs and other food supplements

8) Avoidance of combining similar-sounding drug names by writing both generic and brand names

9) Adherence to required reporting of errors (and adverse drug reactions) to USP's medication errors reporting program and to FDA's medication errors committee

It has been stated wisely that the best doctor is the one who a) commits the fewest errors, and b) provides patients with the best drugs in correct dosage for treatment of an accurate diagnosis.

OFF-LABEL DRUGS
DEFINITION

A number of drugs have been approved by the FDA and in use for *Purpose-A* and found by chance to be useful, but unapproved, for *Purpose-B*. Such drugs are known as *off-label* drugs.

Our Congress has allowed the pharmaceutical industry to promote *off-label* drugs in order to make the distribution of the drugs easier and faster (an action of dubious wisdom). Availability of the unapproved off-label drugs, because of their lack of scientific evaluation for Purpose-B has resulted in an increase in the number of prescriptions of drugs with unproved value and the threat of mistreatment and negligent practice. Thus, the minimum *standard* for safety and efficacy of drugs is lowered, as is everyone's well being as well as quality of living.

Such was the case when approved fenfluramine was combined with approved phentermine in order to improve the control of weight in obesity. Instead, the unapproved combination known as *fen-phen* caused serious disease of the heart (see delayed action of drugs). The allowance of off-label drugs is a serious ethical issue, and certainly not in the best interest of good health care.

Another troublesome example of the hazards of off-label drugs needs to be related here. The pituitary growth hormone is approved by the FDA for use in treating a proved deficiency of the hormone. Its approval for AIDS-related wasting has opened a door to questionable ethical practice. It is unapproved by the FDA for claims made by self-appointed specialists in anti-aging medicine for body-building, increase in energy and mental acuity, and as preservers of youth.

Organized medicine considers the use of the hormone for such unproved claims as exploitative and unscrupulous promotion. Although its usage is not illegal, since it is an approved drug, it is surely controversial, questionably ethical and possibly dangerous as an off-label drug.

Other similar examples of the dubiously ethical use of well established hormones and steroids as youth elixirs are available, hazardous, and regrettably used, despite their risks, by fringe practitioners whose motive is not in the best interest of patient care according to standard medical practice.

COMPLEX PROCESS OF NAMING DRUGS

Every drug is given *three* names: brand name, chemical name, and generic name.

BRAND NAME

1) The brand name or proprietary name is owned by the manufacturer with exclusive rights to the product for a seventeen year life period of the patent, after which the drug can be duplicated and the generic name can be used as, for example, with the availability of aspirin.

2) The name must be approved by the FDA.

CHEMICAL NAME

The chemical name is the molecular structure used by the research scientists. It is available in standard manuals, as in The Physician's Desk Reference.

GENERIC NAME

The choosing of the generic name is usually initiated by the manufacturer, who does not own the name. Since 1961, the name has been given and approved by the *U.S. Adopted Name Council* (consisting of The American Medical Association, The United

States Pharmacopoeia, The American Pharmaceutical Association, The Food and Drug Administration, and by The World Health Organization), leading to an assigned non-proprietary name.

The criteria used in naming a drug require that the name:

1) be appropriate for the drug's specific usefulness,

2) be short, easy to pronounce,

3) be euphonic and not sound like any other generic or brand names,

4) not be confusing or misleading, and

5) be used (by law) in advertisements, labels, and brochures.

GENERIC DRUGS

Generic drugs become available when patents on brand-named drugs expire. They are presumed to be (and should be) *bio-equivalent* to the proprietary drug, with the advantage of having a *lower cost*. They require FDA approval.

Who should suggest or initiate the usage of a generic drug? The pharmacist is better informed about its availability, but the physician decides whether or not he wishes to prescribe it. The patient should have a voice in the final approval.

PROBLEMS WITH GENERIC DRUGS

1) Duplication can be a complex process.

2) A limited percentage of proprietary drugs have available generic forms.

3) Physicians at times prefer that the patient take the drug with a proprietary name as a matter of judgment because the reliability of the generic product cannot be ascertained. (The name of the manufacturer may not be available.)

4) Instances are reported of corporate efforts to block the manufacture of generic drugs, claiming that the studies are flawed.

5) There are no authentic reports of any *lack* of equivalence between brand name drugs and FDA approved generic drugs.

DRUG SAMPLES

The promulgation of drug samples by the pharmaceutical industry is a significant and universal *promotion* technique as part of their advertising campaign. It is primarily performed by office sales-representatives called detail men and women and by mail at a cost to the industry of $10 billion per year. The issuance of samples is supplemented by extensive advertisements in publications (medical and non-medical) and in the media as well as in the Internet.

ETHICAL ISSUES:

1) The intention of the sample is to serve as a *starter dose* with a maximum supply for a few days, then requiring a prescription to complete the therapy. It is also accompanied by literature for educational information about the product. Most physicians take advantage of the process because of its convenience for treatment of self, office staff, and family, as well as for patients, who tend to look upon the samples as cost-saving, despite the fact that the overall cost of promoting the drug will ultimately be channeled to the patient when paying for the filled prescription. The issuing of free samples may serve as an easy path to gifts and gratuities with no defined limits, except for the conscience of the physicians. The question has been raised whether or not the process may be akin to the ethical issue of political lobbying for influence peddling.

2) A common practice by the pharmaceutical industry is to persuade (often readily willing) physicians with *rewards* to provide their patients with free drug samples as part of a drug company's clinical investigation prior to FDA approval. From the patient's standpoint, he is receiving a free sample. He may or may not realize that he is an experimental subject in a clinical study requiring informed consent. The physician assumes the dubious role of research investigator.

3) Although drugs represent the largest area of therapy in health care, perhaps deservedly so, should the costs reflect their high therapeutic status above the total cost of every other area of therapy including surgery, physicians' office care, and hospitalization? Should

the cost of drugs be a major factor in the overall cost of health care to the tune of $1 trillion per year? Should the most important therapeutic modality be unavailable to millions of people because they cannot afford them? Should insurance coverage of drugs be unavailable to almost everyone, especially since drugs are everyone's most needed therapeutic concern? The lack of coverage for drugs adds enormously to everyone's cost of health care, and is a great burden for many. Granted that the industry endures great costs in their research and development program (commendable indeed, but thanks to the FDA for its rigid requirements regarding drug efficacy and safety), should the cost to the patient be reflected in the excessive marketing and advertising? For example, is there need for television advertising of drugs directly from industry to consumer without the essential component of the physician's primary input? Should the cost reflect the amount of profit the industry is enjoying to the extent of one of the most lucrative of all industries? Should not the health care of everyone be a consideration in the amount of profit in the industry?

4) Granting the need for a seventeen year patent on every new drug for the protection of the manufacturer, should pharmaceutical drug companies closely simulate (without actually duplicating) every successful drug marketed by competitors, thereby creating a glut of drugs that pretend to have advantages over each other, often marginally?

5) Should not Congress recognize the herbs (which the members of Congress themselves determined to be food supplements) are really drugs with toxicity potential and dubious benefits, and should therefore be under the total control of the FDA as are all other drugs?

FINAL THOUGHT

After all is said and done, drugs remain at a peak in popularity despite their outrageously high costs, toxicity, glut, limited usefulness, abuse by enormous usage of unmonitored over-the-counter drugs and herbs of unproven value.

CHAPTER 16

SELECTIVE DRUG ISSUES

A cheerful heart is good medicine, but a downcast spirit dries the bones.

— Proverbs 17:22

A number of commonly used drugs, some good (beneficial), some bad (harmful), need discussion because they present ethical issues that cry out for resolution legally, medically, and socially in order to upgrade our quality living.

Many such drugs are available for consideration but several are outstanding examples that illustrate the issues involved, and are presented here.

MORPHINE

Morphine is the *gold standard* for relief of *acute pain* states, but controversial in the treatment of chronic pain. It is a *Schedule II* substance with a high *abuse* potential and severe psychic or physical *dependence* liability.

The recent trend has been to give the patient the sufficient dosage needed for *relief* of his pain in a) terminal illness despite the threat of death, and in b) chronic pain states despite the threat of addiction. On a medical basis, both trends are reasonable, but on an ethical basis, both trends are controversial in consideration of the *double effect* rule wherein the aim is to produce a good and desirable effect, i.e., the relief of pain. The bad and undesirable effect, possible addiction or even death, is unintended, but is approved by the patient. It would be unethical, in fact illegal, if the bad effect were caused intentionally, and the good effect incidentally. Another example of the double effect is the administration of chemotherapy to a pregnant woman with cancer, and incidentally causing the death of the fetus (bad effect). The patient has improvement of the cancer (good effect). The double effect rule remains an ethical issue in the application of the first example pertaining to morphine, depending upon state laws, which vary.

An attempt has been made in our Congress (which sometimes seems to want to practice medicine without a license) to pass a bill known as The Lethal Drug Abuse Prevention Act, that would impair good medical practice and tie the hands of good and compassionate physicians who would be restricted from relieving pain in the management of terminal illness. The bill has been opposed by a number of health care organizations despite the threat by Congress to revive the bill.

The physician's reliable judgment in the relief of chronic pain with morphine is greatly limited legally. This problem needs resolution in the best interest of patient care.

MIFEPRISTONE (RU-486)

Mifepristone, or RU-486 is also known as the early *abortion* pill. It is an abortifacient developed by Roussel-Uclaf Laboratories in France in 1981 and marketed in 1985. Despite its 1) remarkable history of highly successful results in several thousand cases throughout the world in trials conducted in many centers, 2) testing by The

World Health Organization world-wide and found to be safe and effective, 3) highly successful use throughout Europe, China and India in recent years and 4) approval by a number of American medical organizations, entry of the drug into the United States was opposed in 1989 by The Food and Drug Administration with an *important alert*, implying euphemistically that there is no evidence of any medical problems with the drug, but that opposition is based presumably upon great political pressure. In addition, there has been violent public reaction by pro-life opponents despite its favor by pro-choice supporters. As a result of intimidation and threats of boycott, licensing of the drug has been turned down by all phar-maceutical manufacturers.

The drug acts by preventing an embryo from developing as a result of its pharmacological opposition to the action of *progesterone*, a hormone needed for development of the embryo.

The current status of the drug world-wide is that it is as safe as and cheaper to use than the acknowledged safety of a surgical abortion. The procedure requires the oral administration of 600 mg. of the drug, followed 48 hours later by a vaginal supposito-ry of misoprostol, a prostaglandin that causes uterine contrac-tions, resulting in a miscarriage. Misoprostol is an approved drug but is an off-label drug (unapproved) as an abortifacient. Results with RU486 are best if the drug is taken within the first 55 days of post-coital amenorrhea.

Proponents of the use of RU-486 regard it as the moral right of women to own the drug and to use it privately as a matter of their conscience on the basis of their right of self-determination.

The Clinton administration reversed the previous opposition to women's abortion rights that occurred during the Reagan and Bush administrations, and supported the marketing of the drug.

It then became legally available in 1997, but was still not marketed by any drug company. Right or wrong, the years of unavailability of RU-486 has been an unfortunate obstacle in quality living for thousands of women who have sought its use unsuccessfully, not for medical reasons, but for political reasons. In 2000, the FDA finally approved the drug without restrictions, but its ready availability has remained an issue. (The reader is referred to Chapter 20 for an informative discussion of reproduction.)

MARIJUANA

There is an enormous amount of writing in support of the legalization of marijuana, based entirely on claims of its health benefits. There is an equivalent amount written in opposition to its value in health care. The impact of the dispute upon quality living deserves some thoughtful considerations.

Marijuana is an *herb* from the hemp plant, Cannabis sativa, and is also known as pot, joint and weed. It is an *illegal* Schedule I substance (addictive and without medical value). It contains more than sixty *cannabinoids*, the most active of which is delta-9-tetrahydrocannabinol (THC). Dronabinol is chemically synthesized THC. Like morphine, it is a Schedule II substance and legal. Unfortunately, the synthesized form is less effective clinically than is the herb.

The uses of THC are regarded as the same as smoking marijuana. Its dosage is 2.5 mg per day. The problems with THC, however, include erratic bioavailability, slow onset of action, and it has side effects, such as orthostatic hypotension, tachycardia, and conjunctivitis. It is also costly.

LEGALIZATION OF MARIJUANA

The legalization of marijuana has a number of **supportive claims**:

1) Smoking marijuana offers relief of a variety of symptoms in many patients with advanced stages of illness:

a) it increases appetite and forestalls wasting in AIDS,

b) it eases nausea and vomiting in patients on cancer chemotherapy,

c) it counters muscle spasms in patients with epilepsy and multiple sclerosis,

d) it helps control the dangers of increased intraocular pressure in glaucoma.

2) It often provides better results than do many prescription drugs and their side effects.

3) There are no recorded deaths from overdosage.

4) Its use is approved in several states, where doctors are free (legally) to recommend it by prescription.

5) A large segment of the population favors its availability by prescription for medicinal use only. In so recommending it, marijuana would be transferred from Schedule I (addictive, with no medical use, e.g., heroin) to Schedule II (addictive, with medical use, e.g., morphine).

6) It is easily home grown inexpensively.

The views in **opposition** to the legalization of marijuana, thereby making the subject an ethical issue, are many:

1) As an appetite stimulant in AIDS, anabolic steroids are more effective.

2) For nausea and vomiting in cancer chemotherapy, Zofran intravenously is at least as effective.

3) For the pressure of glaucoma, Xalatan is as good and does not lower the blood pressure like marijuana does.

4) For the pains and muscle spasms of neurologic disorders, many drugs are available and effective.

5) There is no scientific evidence of the medical usefulness of marijuana.

6) Its requirement as a cigarette for smoking contributes to its harm to the lungs by its higher concentration of tars, carbon monoxide, and carcinogens than are present in cigarettes with nicotine.

7) Its use would lead to the further liberalization of the drug laws (slippery slope effect).

8) Marijuana has other side effects, such as hormonal and reproductive damage, injury to the immune system, reduction of blood flow to the optic nerve and reduction of vision, impaired cognition and judgment, and possible leukemia in newborn infants of pregnant drug users.

9) Rejection as a medicinal by The American Medical Association on the basis that the benefits do not warrant the risks.

The pros and cons regarding the medicinal use of marijuana remain at a stand-off, and present an issue which continues to be a thorn in the advancement of the quality of living for all. Resolution of the issue does not seem imminent, despite recent decisions by the U.S. Supreme Court.

NICOTINE

The smoking of tobacco has been regarded for many centuries world-wide as one of the highest forms of quality living by way of happiness. Not only has it been socially acceptable among men and among women, but it also became a social achievement in the coming of age among boys and girls.

Only in the past fifty years has it been appreciated that cigarette smoking had serious side effects for most smokers. It actually took the past twenty-five years to really understand that nicotine is powerfully addictive, carcinogenic, and detrimental to the health of most smokers. In one of the most serious displays of immorality, many leaders in the tobacco industry fought bitterly to deny it caused addiction despite overwhelming scientifically supportive evidence of its toxic effects. It is astounding that everyone is aware that nicotine is the most poisonous substance that enters our bodies, yet an enormous number of people continue to smoke cigarettes (50 million in the United States). It is also astounding that the tobacco industry continues to promote and market one of the greatest poisons to health, surely one of the most important obstacles in our effort to approach quality living in the perfect semicircle of life.

Everyone should be reminded and impressed with the fact that cigarette smoke contains more than 15 *carcinogens*, most notably *nicotine*, an *addictive*, toxic, carcinogenic alkaloid. Another astounding fact is that the addiction and relapse rate (in quitters of smoking) is the same as with heroin and morphine.

Specifically, nicotine is the principal cause of *preventable* disease and of premature death. It is also a *risk* factor for ischemic heart disease, acute myocardial infarction, and stroke (via its role in causing disorder of lipid metabolism). Nicotine is the cause of lung cancer in over twenty percent of smokers. It is the causative factor in ninety percent of lung cancers (in ten percent, pollutants, especially radon, are the cause). Another astounding fact is that lung cancer causes the greatest number of deaths from any cancer (at least 150,000 per year). The figure represents twenty-five percent of all cancer deaths—500,000 per year, two-thirds in males, one-third in females. Lung cancer is the *leading cause of death* due to cancer in the male; prostate cancer is second, and colon cancer is third. In the female, cancer of the lung is the second cause of death due to cancer; breast cancer is first, and colon cancer third.

The distressing continuation of cigarette smoking accounts for 175,000 new cases of lung cancer annually in the United States.

And that's not all. Nicotine is the most important factor in causing chronic obstructive pulmonary disease (COPD), a terribly debilitating disorder, chronic and life-terminating after prolonged suffering.

Nicotine is a commonly known contributor to the frequency

and chronicity of bronchitis and sinusitis, pneumonia, and pulmonary complications after general surgery.

Nicotine is definitely linked to cancer of the mouth, larynx, pharynx, and bladder.

In 1995, an attempt by the Clinton administration to give the FDA jurisdiction over tobacco as a drug delivery device failed in a U.S. Supreme Court decision in support of the opposition by the tobacco industry.

PASSIVE SMOKING, the smoke inhaled by non-smokers subjected to the smoke exhaled by smokers, causes over 300,000 respiratory infections per year.

How does one know about the effects of smoking on non-smokers and the cause of 5000 deaths per year as a result of *passive* smoking? An examination of the urine of non-smokers at any time will reveal varying amounts of *metabolites,* or breakdown end-products of nicotine—the same findings as in smokers. The final astounding figure is that cigarette smoking and its poisonous nicotine accounts for $80 billion in the annual cost of health care.

ETHICAL ISSUES

The subject of nicotine cannot be allowed to pass unless some attention is given to the ethical issues that emerge:

1) Is it not unethical (perhaps even illegal, or even criminal) for some leaders in the tobacco industry to deny the addictive and carcinogenic power of nicotine despite overwhelming scientific evidence (shown to be present in the files of the industry according to some attorneys-general in their lawsuits)?

2) Did not some tobacco company executives perjure themselves in swearing before Congress that, in their opinion, nicotine is not addictive?

3) Are cigarette manufacturers less criminal than if they were manufacturing and selling heroin?

4) Do smokers have the right to spread the toxic fumes of cigarette smoking in public places and cause passive lung disease and deaths among non-smokers?

ALCOHOL

As with cigarette smoking, alcohol has been an important social enhancer almost since the origin of man. The difference, however, is that the evils of cigarette smoking have not been appreciated until recently, whereas drunkenness, as a temporary disability and alcoholism as a chronic disability, have always been known.

The long-term effects of alcohol in relatively few consumers is a serious burden upon society especially now that those with alcohol-related end-stage liver disease may be anxious to be candidates for organ replacement (see Chapter 21).

ALCOHOL IN SMALL AMOUNTS:

Another difference between cigarette smoking and alcohol is that small amounts of alcohol may actually be *beneficial* by increasing HDL-C (good cholesterol) levels, thereby reducing the risk of ischemic heart disease, myocardial infarction, and stroke. Small or mild amounts of alcohol are estimated on the order of two ounces of hard liquor or six ounces of wine (preferably red) or 12 ounces of beer per day.

The mechanism of the effects are based primarily on, fibrinolytic and anti-thrombic actions of alcohol:

1) Increase in the ratio of prostacyclin to thromboxane

2) Increase in tissue-type plasminogen activator

3) Reduction in platelet aggregation leading to a reduction in clot formation (The theoretical possibility of increasing the risk of a hemorrhagic stroke is a conflicting effect.)

SOCIO-PATHOLOGY OF ALCOHOL

The socio-pathologic factors pertaining to alcohol ingestion, especially more than the small beneficial amounts, are well known and worthy of emphasis:

1) Highway accidents (50 percent of the deaths are due to drunk driving).

2) Domestic violence.

3) Abusive behavior (approximately 10 million people are affected on any given day in highway accidents and/or domestic violence)

CHRONIC INTAKE OF ALCOHOL

The chronic intake of high doses of alcohol has adverse effects upon multiple systems. The points at which the effects are irreversible are regrettably not known:

1) Cardiovascular System

    a) Increase in heart rate

    b) Increase in systolic blood pressure

    c) Increase in cardiac output

    d) Increase in cardiac arrhythmias, especially atrial fibrillation

    e) Cardiomyopathy

    f) Cutaneous vasodilatation (accounts for feeling of warmth in cold weather)

    g) Increase in hyperlipidemia: high triglycerides and lowered HDL-C levels

    h) Increase in risk factor for ischemic heart disease and stroke

    i) Increase in risk of death due to cardiovascular disease

2) Gastro-intestinal Tract

    a) Increase in gastrin and in hydrochloric acid, resulting in acute gastritis, nausea, vomiting, hematemesis (Mallory-Weiss syndrome)

    b) Esophageal varices and hemorrhages

  c) Poor healing of an ulcer

3) Liver and Biliary Tract

  a) Impaired lipid metabolism: hypertriglyceridemia

  b) Impaired carbohydrate metabolism leading to hypoglycemia or hyperglycemia

  c) Lactic acidosis

  d) Hyperuricemia

  e) Hepatitis, cirrhosis, cancer

  f) Hepatic coma

4) Central Nervous System

  a) Depressant effect by inhibiting sub-cortical structures;
never a stimulant

  b) Decreased mental function and judgment

  c) Decreased motor function

  d) Abstinence or withdrawal syndrome: delirium tremens,
tremors, hallucinosis, seizures

5) Respiratory Tract

  a) Increased risk of pneumonia

6) Hematopoietic system

  a) mild macrocytosis

  b) mild to severe anemia

  c) mild bone-marrow effect: leucopenia, thrombocytopenia.

7) Electrolytes and kidney

  a) Increased urinary excretion of phosphorus, magnesium, and ammonia

  b) diuresis

  c) metabolic acidosis

CHAPTER 17

SELF-TREATMENT WITH OVER-THE-COUNTER (OTC) DRUGS, UNAPPROVED ANTICANCER DRUGS, HERBS AND OTHER SO-CALLED FOOD SUPPLEMENTS

Truth often suffers more by the heat of its defenders, than from the arguments of its opposers.

— William Penn, 1644-1718

The track record regarding prescription drugs is well documented and easy to follow. Self-treatment, however, is difficult to assess because it includes the engagement of patients in the *over-the-counter* market of drugs, the extensive and rather mysterious market of *unapproved anti-cancer drugs*, and the *herbal* market.

All together, the extent to which people undertake to treat their illnesses on their own volition is judged to be considerably greater than the number of drugs people take by prescription given them by their physicians. The ethical issues emerging from such ventures are many, some of which will be explored in this chapter.

The *bases* for the availability of medications without a physician's prescription include the following:

1) Granting patients the *right* of self-treatment without medical supervision, based on the ethical principle of autonomy

2) Giving patients the *responsibility* for accuracy of self-treatment, based upon presumed correctness of self-diagnosis

INTENT

The original intent in making OTC drugs available was for 1) minor, self-limiting symptoms and for 2) *temporary short-term* usage. These two criteria have been ignored and abused. The number of OTC drug sales is estimated at *ten times* the number sold by prescription. Their most common use for the most frequent complaints are the following:

1) Respiratory: common cold, cough

2) Gastrointestinal: heartburn, diarrhea, constipation

3) Musculo-skeletal: aches, pains, muscle and joint stiffness (generally called arthritis)

4) Neuropsychiatric: headache, insomnia, anxiety

5) Food supplements, including vitamins and minerals, herbs including so-called "natural" products available for whatever ails one, and fountain of youth elixirs. It is never, or hardly ever, recommended by those who promulgate food supplements that everyone should first check with his physician for approval before taking any medication on one's own volition.

POPULARITY

Reasons for the popularity of OTC drugs:

1) Excessive advertising by the industry

2) Easy access

3) Convenience of self-treatment

4) Relatively low cost

5) Relative safety (a debatable factor)

6) Beneficial in temporary relief of most symptoms treated

7) Favored by many insurance coverages in eliminating costly medical care

8) Has FDA approval (often conditional)

9) Many are traditional drugs previously available only by prescription, and have suffered an expiration of their seventeen year patent period.

10) Generally not seen as serious or dangerous drugs (although many have potent ingredients and serious side effects)

PERILS OF SELF-TREATMENT

Some perils of self-treatment with OTC drugs are the following:

1) Weakening of the safety factor inherent in frequency of misdiagnosis and misuse

2) Toxicity is not sufficiently well emphasized, but is a real issue

3) Benefits are often exaggerated

4) Overdosage is common because of its easy accessibility and low cost

5) Delay in proper treatment may invite early complications of existing illness which the OTC drug is presumed to treat

6) Tendency to ignore warning labels (in small print) and expiration dates

7) Drug-drug interactions, especially among elderly on multiple medications. For example, the common use of non-steroidal anti-inflammatory drugs for pain taken together with an alcoholic beverage (a common practice) risks gastrointestinal bleeding.

RECOMMENDATIONS

Suggestions by opponents of the use of OTC drugs in their concern regarding the *hazards* of pill popping of OTC and non-prescription medications including food supplements, are as follows:

1) Best taken on professional advice, at least with the knowledge of one's physician

2) Read inserts carefully and heed label warnings

3) Use only temporarily and consult physician early regarding their use. Never engage in self-treatment over a prolonged period

4) Keep detailed records of drug usage (for self and for physician)

5) Keep physician informed, especially if taking prescribed medications at the same time

6) Depend on drugs tested by the scientific method to be more certain of safety and efficacy

UNAPPROVED ANTICANCER DRUGS

Oh, what a tangled web we weave, when first we practice to deceive.

— Sir Walter Scott, 1771-1832

BACKGROUND

A very sad commentary on the cancer scene is the long list of unapproved drug treatments promoted by unscrupulous, exploitative quacks and frauds upon vulnerable and desperately ill victims of cancer who are searching in vain for some hopeful aid. It is reported that $4 billion is spent in this tragic, futile sea of iniquity. The number of unapproved, valueless, and potentially harmful anticancer therapies are far too many to describe, suffice it to say that a) other than currently approved drugs and therapeutic modalities, and b) exclusive of scientific, experimental drugs under investigation, not a single unapproved drug has been found throughout the years that has cured or even improved cancer. All are condemned by organized, scientific medicine, practicing oncologists, the American Cancer Society, and every knowledgeable, well-meaning supporter of the best interest of patients with cancer.

DIFFERENCES FROM APPROVED DRUGS

The following are clues to the identity of unapproved anticancer drugs:

1) The ingredients are secret and are never identified by the hawkers.

2) Drugs and accompanying therapies are vaguely, certainly never specifically, defined.

3) The developers of unproven treatments refuse to allow their products to be studied or even made available.

4) Unproven treatments remain unproven permanently.

CLAIMS

The claims made by practitioners of unapproved drugs and treatments of cancer are many and should be identified:

1) A favorite claim is that the product maximizes the function of the immune system. (Ed: With no scientific evidence.)

2) The product minimizes the adverse effects of cancer chemotherapy. (Ed: Not a shred of proof.)

3) Improves the quality of life (Ed: Precisely what they fail to do!)

4) Alleviates helplessness and hopelessness (Ed: If only it were true!)

5) Claims of benefits are glowing (Ed: All are supported by anecdotal and testimonial references, never by proper study.)

6) Claims never mention side effects, toxicity or any failure of treatment (Ed: Except when it is convenient to blame the patient for the failure.)

7) Claims sound too good to be true (notwithstanding the fact that the treatment is for a serious disorder)

8) Promises are made with money-back guarantees

9) The promoter displays suspicious credentials (Ed: Be on guard!)

10) The practitioner and promoter of the product also sells the preparation.

11) Eye-catching promotional terms are used: natural, revitalizes, purifies, balances, rejuvenates, stimulates

12) The therapies are often touted as cures for other medical disorders in addition to cancer, e.g., AIDS.

13) Publications are reprinted over and over without editing or revisions—even with the same typing errors.

14) The concept of detoxification is a favorite offering. The body, particularly the colon, collects deadly toxins. (Ed: A long discarded theory in medicine.) It is the basis for the irrational prescribing of frequent cleansing coffee enemas. (Ed: The approach to this therapy may be extreme, e.g., colonic machines are used to pump as much as 20-40 gallons of water. The dangers include electrolyte imbalance, infection, perforation of the bowel, obstipation.)

15) The concept of hyperoxygenation is another favorite, based upon the belief that the body needs more oxygen to survive, hence, their recommendation of drinking and bathing in hydrogen peroxide. (Ed: A totally false premise.)

16) The ingredients of their product, when occasionally known, often do not correspond to the promotional claims.

17) Claims that therapy does not work unless a) the patient has the right mental attitude, or b) the therapy is strictly adhered to.

MOTIVE

The only motive is greed. Deceit is difficult to prove, and its punishment is relatively small.

PROTECTION AGAINST FRAUD IN UNAPPROVED CANCER DRUG THERAPY

The protection of the public against fraudulent measures in cancer therapy is limited and includes the following:

1) A few states have laws barring the use of any unproven treatment of cancer. (Ed: All states should develop such laws.)

2) The American Cancer Society and certain other respectable and responsible organizations, oncologists, and research scientists maintain a close vigilance over research, development, and promotion of cancer treatments. (Ed: Attention should be given their findings.)

3) One must distinguish among cancer treatments between 1) unapproved, 2) approved, and 3) under investigation and not yet approved.

HERBAL THERAPY
INTRODUCTION

The author gave serious thought to the location of the subject of herbs in this text. Despite its legal and popular use as a *food supplement* (vide infra), *herbs* are discussed here under the heading of *self-treatment* with medications because the purpose of an herb is precisely the definition given to a drug. It is presumed and expected to act like a drug and *perform* like a drug. Since an herb looks like, smells like, tastes like and quacks like a drug, then it must be a drug. Drugs are not food supplements and, despite what our Congress has claimed, neither are herbs. They are drugs except for those among them available as spices for food flavoring.

HERBS AS FOOD-FLAVORING SPICES

We are all well aware of the wonderful value of many non-medicinal herbs that are used for food *flavoring*, e.g., rosemary, tarragon, basil, parsley, dill, thyme, pepper, et al. These do not pose any ethical issues.

HERBS AS DRUGS:

There are numerous ethical problems in the use of herbs as therapeutic agents in health care, despite their long popularity.

MYTHICAL CLAIMS BY HERBALISTS

1) Since they have been used for centuries in folk medicine, they must be valuable. (Ed: A previously noted fallacy derived from the historical principle of *empiricism*, which incidentally became the basis for the concept of quackery.)

2) Herbs are not drugs, but are food supplements as declared

by our Congress. (Ed: Disputed by organized medicine.)

3) They perform and contribute to thousands of improvements in health. (Ed: All anecdotal, none tested scientifically, or proved.)

4) Herbs are natural, not artificial like all drugs; hence they are beneficial and safe without side effects. (Ed: An untrue, illogical concept.)

5) There is an herb for every disease. (Ed: This may eventually prove to be true if and when all herbs are subjected to research based upon application of the scientific method.)

6) Combinations of herbs (shot-gun therapy) improve the chances for cure. (Ed: Lack of concern for overdosage, interactions, or specificity of treatment make this a dangerous recommendation.)

MAJOR ETHICAL ISSUES WITH HERBAL MEDICINE

1) In 1994, herbs (along with vitamins and minerals) were grouped and classified by Congress as *dietary supplements* in their Dietary Supplement Health and Education Act. In removing herbs from the category of drugs (where they really belong according to the definition of a drug), they were removed from the strict FDA requirements of all drugs, including testing, the approval mechanism, and overall regulation. As a result, important concerns about herbs were eliminated, including the establishment of objective criteria regarding safety, efficacy, potency, and standardization of dosage. Purveyors of herbs do not have to perform and report reliable and essential studies derived from the application of the scientific method, as is required of all drugs manufactured by the pharmaceutical industry; nor are they required to report side effects.

2) Parts of the plant used (root, stem, leaf, or flower) vary widely in potency from inert to toxic.

3) The contents contain a) metallic elements, such as iron and copper, b) the active pharmacologic components, if any, and c)

impurities and contaminants including animal parts and drop-
pings.

4) Batches of the same herbs vary in potency or in lack thereof.

5) In recent years they have been increasing in popularity in
the United States and are used and touted especially by herbalists and some practitioners of alternative medicine for a wide
variety of medical illnesses.

6) They are a growing segment of the health food industry.
Their annual sales exceed $2 billion per year. Their popularity is
even greater in Europe, where several hundred varieties are in
common use.

7) Benefits of herbs remain anecdotal and testimonial, and are
never based upon scientific study.

8) Side effects are ignored.

9) Most do not perform as advertised.

10) The active chemical components responsible for the
claimed pharmaceutical and/or clinical effect, including alkaloids
or glycosides, are known to be present in varying amounts in
many herbs.

11) No attempt has been made to identify the active chemical
component, if present, in many herbs in use today. The reward of
such effort would be:

a) ability to isolate the purified chemical compound, b) to prepare it synthetically, as is done with all drugs, c) the exact dosage
could be standardized, d) the exact potency desired to provide the
level of efficacy and control of safety could be achieved, and e) toxicity could be determined.

12) Packaging and labeling are poorly regulated, rarely carry
guidelines for proper usage, and lack warnings regarding toxicity
(compared with tight and explicit FDA controls over standard
drugs).

13) Medically untrained and medically unqualified sales staffs at
health food stores and at nutrition centers have been reported to offer
advice on the use of numerous herbal products available for every

conceivable health disorder about which they lack necessary knowledge and qualification (compared with the required education, training and licensing of registered pharmacists). Are they practicing medicine without a license?

14) Herbalists prescribe herbal remedies in the absence of an established diagnosis made by a responsible licensed physician.

15) Herbal medicine is actually in competition with scientific medicine, and should be held equally accountable, or else outlawed.

TOXICITY OF HERBS

In view of the general absence of public awareness or the promoter's admission of toxicity caused by herbs, the findings in a few available *reports* are worth citing:

1) Hepatotoxicity due to Yerba tea, germander, mistletoe, skull cap, comfrey, margosa oil, thornapple, chaparral tea, sassafras

2) Reduction in blood platelets and resultant bleeding due to milk thistle

3) Serious anaphylactic reactions caused by royal jelly

4) Inhibition of iron absorption caused by St. John's Wort

5) Respiratory and cardiac abnormalities caused by jin bu huan

6) Cardiac damage due to adonis vernalis

7) Nephrotoxicity due to aristolochia fangchi

8) Epilepsy-like seizures and renal failure due to yohimbe

9) Cardiovascular disease and deaths due to ephedra

10) Respiratory paralysis and death due to lobelia

11) Cancer caused by aristolochia fangchi, a Chinese herb, available in the United States, barred in many countries; the carcinogenic effect is due to content of aristolochic acid, mainly involving the urinary tract

Congress to date has shown little evidence of interest in protecting the public from the hazards of herbs. Will it take a catastrophic event for legislative action as occurred in the establishment of The

Food and Drug Administration in 1938?

BACKGROUND IN THE USE OF HERBS AS DRUGS:

Herbs have been used as therapeutic agents for the treatment of illness in *folk medicine* and especially in Chinese medicine for many centuries. It is therefore assumed without scientific evidence that they must be effective. (This is a clearly illogical concept.) To some extent, however, that concept may have validity. It is a popular empirical fallacy that long experience is proof of value. For the most part, the common use of herbs today, despite their long usage, is scientifically unproved, particularly in *efficacy and safety*. Their presumed value would be better served if they were scientifically tested in the same manner that the FDA requires by application of the scientific method in standard drug research by the pharmaceutical industry.

Historically, in our own American use of herbs in medicine prior to 1940, about fifty percent of the drugs we used in treatment were herbs derived directly from plants. The best-known example is digitalis, the leaf of the foxglove plant. Since 1940, however, new plants are no longer used in therapy in scientific medicine. Instead, about thirty five percent of drugs used are *synthesized* from plants and sixty five percent are chemically *manufactured*. A good examples is digitoxin, a glycoside, which is synthesized from digitalis, and is an important drug in the treatment of heart disease as a cardiotonic and diuretic agent.

A few examples of pharmaceutically active components of herbs that have been isolated, purified, synthesized, standardized for dosage, safety and efficacy by scientific testing, and approval for medicinal use are the following:

1) *Morphine*, an alkaloid of opium from the poppy plant; a potent analgesic. Others in the same group include codeine, which is also antitussive, and papaverine, a smooth muscle relaxant.

2) *Penicillin*, from the mold of penicillium; used as an antibiotic (the first one).

3) *Digitalis*, from the leaf of digitalis purpurea. Others in the group include digitoxin, a glycoside from D. purpurea, and digoxin from D. lanata.

4) *Dicumarol*, from spoiled sweet clover; used as an oral anticoagulant.

5) *Quinine*, an alkaloid from the bark of the cinchona tree, used in malaria. Others in the group include quinidine, an isomer of quinine, used in the treatment of certain cardiac arrhythmias.

6) *Colchicine*, an alkaloid from the seed of meadow saffron (colchicum autumnale), used in gout.

7) *Ergotamine*, alkaloid from ergot (claviceps purpurea), a parasitic fungus on rye, used as an oxytocic, and in migraine.

8) *Atropine*, from the solanacea plant, deadly nightshade (atropa belladonna); others in the group: belladonna, ('fair lady'), same as atropine; hyoscyamine, from henbane (hyoscyamus linne); scopolamine, from thornapple (datura metel); used as a smooth muscle relaxant and antispasmodic, in anesthesia, as a mydriatic, and as a central nervous system depressant.

9) *Aspidium*, from the male fern, used as an anti-helminthic.

10) *Ephedrine*, alkaloid from ephedra equisetina, also known as ma huang; used as a central nervous system stimulant, and as a broncho-dilator in asthma.

11) *Physostigmine*, alkaloid from calabar bean (physostigma venenosum); used in myasthenia gravis, and as a mydriatic.

12) *Pilocarpine*, alkaloid from leaf of pilocarpus microphyllus; used as a parasympathetic nerve stimulant, as a cholinergic, and as a miotic.

13) *Ipecac*, from the root of ipecacuanha; used as an emetic.

14) *Taxol*, from the bark of the yew tree; used in the treatment of ovarian cancer.

15) *Curare*, from the bark of strychnos toxifera; used as an arrow poison and in anesthesia in order to paralyze nerve endings.

16) *Cascara sagrada*; from the bark of rhamnus purshiana, used as a cathartic.

17) *Castor Oil*, from the castor bean (ricinus communis); used as a cathartic.

18) *Chaulmoogra Oil*, from the taraktogenos kurzii tree; used in leprosy.

19) *Vincristine*, alkaloid from periwinkle (vinca rosea); used in cancer chemotherapy, in acute leukemia.

20) Caffeine, in coffee and tea, used as a central nervous system stimulant.

21) Nicotine, alkaloid of the tobacco plant (nicotiana tabacum), used for centuries as one of our greatest joys and addictive poisons.

The author selected only a few of the many drugs that have been *synthesized* from plants and are valuable in the treatment of a broad variety of medical conditions. The lesson is apparent. Herbs have the *potential* of serving as the base for many needed medical disorders. To date, approximately one third of our drugs are synthesized from plants. The other two thirds are manufactured chemically. The author has no doubt that somewhere in the rain forests surrounding the Amazon River of South America, an herb exists, not yet discovered, that will cure cancer, and become our most valuable drug. The point is again made that all herbs currently used in the treatment of medical disorders should be subjected to study by application of the *scientific method* so that the active chemical component, if present, can be isolated, purified, synthesized and standardized. To be sure, many will be determined to have pharmacologic activity with beneficial as well as undesirable or even harmful effects. Many will be found to be inert, and can be discarded from use in health care.

CONVENTIONAL WISDOM REGARDING HERBS

1) Most are *old*, having been a part of folk medicine for centuries. Many have been highly recommended without interruption and

without revision or replacement, presuming that they have efficacy, no side effects, and in no need of improvement.

Drugs, on the other hand, the most dependable source of therapy in scientific medicine, are constantly being replaced or modified because of scientifically documented evidence of improvement in efficacy and safety or because of toxicity. Hence, most are *new*.

2) The lack of isolation, purification, and identity of the active chemical components of herbs (as is done with all drugs) prevents necessary standardization for dosage, efficacy, and safety.

3) As is the case with common drug practice of taking two or more drugs, the use of herbs taken along with drugs may pose incompatibilities. Everyone indulging in the use of herbs should so inform his physician, who will be well aware of drug-drug interactions.

4) Herbs should be reestablished by Congress as *drugs*, their true status, in order that the FDA can regulate their standards as with all drugs, primarily for efficacy and safety.

5) The sale of herbs should be under the jurisdiction of registered pharmacists with the required knowledge and qualifications in pharmacology in order to be available for professional advice.

6) Terms such as natural should be abolished because of their misleading intent as safe and unproved claim of benefit.

7) The application of the scientific method in the study of all herbs presumed to have medicinal value would be a boon to the herbal industry and would certainly enhance everyone's quality of living. On the basis of established successes cited early in this chapter, many could be shown to have potential value.

8) In deference to the herbal industry, an office has been established by Congress at our National Institutes of Health and named National Center for Complementary and Alternative Medicine with an annual budget. A number of prestigious academic institutions have been designated as affiliated centers for research in herbal medicine as a part of alternative medicine. Only

good can come from this experiment, which is long overdue. Their findings are eagerly awaited.

9) Should any preparation be taken as a drug or even as a food supplement which is not recommended by or known to one's physician? If any agent intended to improve one's health a) lacks scientific proof based upon controlled studies, b) has never been documented in an established scientific journal, and c) has no FDA approval, should it be taken without a physician's advice?

10) Congress should be urged to reexamine its decision to regard herbs as food supplements and redefine them as drugs, thereby placing them under complete control of the FDA, as with all drugs in use. This action would best serve the health interests of all people in the United States.

AROMATHERAPY

A variant and lesser known form of herbal medicine is Aromatherapy. It is based on the use of *aromatic oils* for the prevention and cure of many illnesses. The oils contain *resins* derived from roots, barks, leaves, and flowers of plants and trees, diluted in vegetable oils, which are *inhaled or rubbed* into the skin—not *digested*. The selected oil (rosemary, camphor, thyme, lavendar, eucalyptus, or rose) is chosen by a strange decision made from the patient's lock of hair or sample of handwriting. There is no valid evidence to support the claim of benefit, which is regarded by pharmacologists as a placebo effect.

SECTION D

SUBJECT IV:

ADVANCES IN BIOTECHNOLOGY

The existence and validity of human rights are not written in the stars. The ideals concerning the conduct of men toward each other and the desirable structure of the community have been conceived and taught by enlightened individuals in the course of history.

— Albert Einstein, 1879-1955

The fourth subject selected among seven important areas of health care encompasses biotechnological advances in the diagnosis and treatment of disease (Chapters 18-22). Like the other six subjects, it too is sated with many unresolved ethical issues reflecting adversely upon an incomplete quality of living.

CHAPTER 18

DIAGNOSTIC TESTS AND THERAPEUTIC PROCEDURES

If all printers were determined not to print anything until they were sure it would offend no one, there would be very little printed.

— Benjamin Franklin, 1706–1790

INTRODUCTION

The well-established history of predictably favorable public reaction to biotechnologic advances such as diagnostic imaging (magnetic resonance imaging, computed tomography, positron emission tomography), ultrasonography, and therapeutic innovations such as non-invasive surgery and organ transplantation in the sole interest of benefitting health and prolonging life, is expected. It is strangely ironic and perplexing. On the one hand, the populace eagerly awaits pharmacologic, radiologic, laboratory, and surgical advances in their best interest. On the other hand, however, there is certain to be a vociferous outcry from skeptical and cynical doubters, always ready with dissension and naysaying. The bases for opposition are predominantly legal, religious and moral. They are well intentioned and not without merit. The resultant issues then demand resolution by adjudication, arbitration, negotiation and by whatever means necessary for eventual universal societal acceptance, particularly when the new means of diagnosis or treatment of disease may be remarkable.

In general, the more revolutionary and advanced the concept of the innovation, the more audibly and visibly reactive is the antagonism and the longer is the process of settlement, which sometimes may be never. On this pessimistic note, ethical issues can be expected to flourish indefinitely.

The focus of this chapter is not on the actual biotechnologic advances, which have been and continue to be enormous, but rather on the ethical issues arising from their conflicting receptivity. Their lack of resolution impacts heavily on their adverse effect upon 1) the goal of quality living and 2) achieving a perfect semicircle of life.

The basic reasons for the plethora of ethical issues that arise with biotechnological innovations in diagnostic and therapeutic medicine can be categorized as disputes over, disagreements with, and violations of, the modern ethical principles of non-maleficence, beneficence and respect for rights—principles that serve as a bench-mark for the prime considerations of efficacy (high benefit) and safety (low risk) in the evaluation of every new modality in health care.

HISTORICAL BACKGROUND

The progress of medicine has been driving steadily from conversion of an art form to a full science. In the mid-twentieth century, a giant step in its climb was the introduction and full application of the *scientific method*. It was first applied in the evaluation of drugs (Chapter 15) and in the assessment of diagnostic tests and therapeutic procedures (current chapter).

Correlatively, a major turning point in the rapidity of the advances in medical science was the creation of the *Food and Drug Administration* in 1936 and its mandated role in the *regulation* and approval of manufactured health products. Prior to then, strange, unscientific, uncontrolled practices were in vogue, some for many centuries, rooted in folk medicine. They were never tested, questioned, improved, modified or discarded until the criteria of the scientific method were applied.

Modern scientific medicine is anxious to close its chapter on embarrassing therapeutic measures employed as major forms of unscientific treatment before the mid-twentieth century. Some reference is made herewith to a few of them to illustrate the significance of the advances made since their usage: 1) *leeching* (the use of leeches as a form of blood-letting), 2) *cupping* (for its rubefacient action), 3) *purging* and *puking* (ridding the body of imagined ptomaines, a term still heard today in connection with bacterial putrefaction), and 4) *bloodletting* (ridding the body of *toxins*, also presumed to be present without a demonstrated basis).

In the eighteen century, bloodletting was among the important and most popular forms of therapy. It may actually have hastened the death of George Washington when it was used by his eminent physician, Dr. Benjamin Rush, who, in his large practice, may have shed more blood in therapy than did any general at war. Of course, bloodletting was practiced by all physicians.

The concept of ridding the body of toxins by way of bloodletting, purging, and puking has been abandoned as lacking in scientific fact (besides contributing to the hazards of the treatment). The concept, however, may still apply to some extent, for example, in modern renal dialysis, a life-saving measure in the correction of failure of the kidneys to remove metabolic wastes from the blood as in the normal renal creation of urine. The toxins, really metabolic end-products, are well known, and need to be eliminated in order for the patient to survive while waiting for a kidney transplantation.

Many other non-scientific, unproved modalities were practiced and are now long discarded. A large number are still in use today in folk medicine and in alternative medicine, well illustrated in the popularity of herbs. An example of the discarded toxin theory is in current practice in alternative medicine in the form of cleansing enemas with large volumes of water and with coffee—not only without basis, but hazardous.

The basis for discarding or not accepting any therapy or procedure in modern scientific medicine is primarily that it lacks established, reproducible proof of efficacy and safety. Before such a 'holier than thou' attitude is assumed, one should look seriously at the various bizarre modalities in use today in the treatment of arthritis, for example, outside of organized medicine.

Before we leave the historical background, we must narrate the practice of *four radical* procedures still in vogue in the late 1930's and early 1940's. The excuse for their use was that they were desperate measures for incurable diseases, even though there was little if any evidence of benefit and much risk. (Little benefit and much risk are unacceptable criteria for any approved modality today.) Currently, patients' rights based upon informed consent would preclude their consideration without research evidence of a high benefit to a low risk ratio.

The four radical therapies were 1) fever therapy for syphilis of the central nervous system, 2) insulin shock therapy for some forms of insanity, 3) electroshock therapy for manic depressive psychosis, and 4) pre-frontal lobotomy for schizophrenia. (It is evident that modern antibiotic and psychotropic drugs with their own benefit versus risk issues were not yet available.)

1) Prior to the discovery of penicillin, in the late 1930's, *fever therapy* produced by the introduction of malarial parasites into the patient's blood stream was a common practice for syphilis of the central nervous system. The aim was to induce about ten vigorous rigors of malaria. There was little if any evidence of significant

benefit, certainly not a curative one. The risk of great harm was real (but so of course was syphilis of the brain).

2) During the same era, *insulin shock therapy* was a highly recommended treatment for certain mental disorders including chronic schizophrenia (for want of anything better to do). The aim was to induce about two hours of hypoglycemic coma with insulin intravenously per session. Here too there was little evidence of benefit and real evidence of risk of harm.

3) *Electro-shock therapy* for manic-depression psychosis (now more commonly known as bipolar disorder) was an accepted form of therapy. The aim was to induce convulsions (probably to shake things up in the brain). The experience was frightening to patients (in whom fractures of the vertebrae occurred) as well as to observers. Electro-convulsive therapy is still in common use in severe depression, although the relapse rate is high.

4) *Pre-frontal lobotomy* for advanced schizophrenia was developed by a Portuguese surgeon named Moniz in 1935, who received the Nobel Prize in Medicine in 1949. There was at least an experimental basis for the concept. Removal of the frontal lobe of the brain in chimpanzees had a calming effect on the apes. The procedure sounds as frightening as it really was. It was actually performed by driving an icepick or a sewing needle under the supra-orbital ridge of the skull (just above the eye-ball) into the patient's frontal lobes and macerating the brain tissue (not an exaggerated term). The procedure might possibly have been continued despite its terrifying consequences, if it were not made obsolete by the introduction of a series of new psychotropic drugs.

After the 1950's, explosive and dramatic progress in drug therapy (Chapter 15) and patient's rights (chapter 11) were advanced and the ineffective, unscientific, hazardous, aforementioned procedures used in medicine as the best in modern treatment were forsaken, forever, to be sure. (One wonders whether sophisticated drugs and procedures used today will appear as primitive 50 years hence.)

HOME TESTING DEVICES

Our first consideration in the application of modern diagnostic tests and procedures is the evaluation of home testing devices, selected because of their ethical implications. The basis for their availability and popularity is the emergence of the principles of the patient's *rights* and the patient's *autonomy* or freedom of action, provided, of course, that the patient understands the requirement of *responsibility* to go with his rights.

In response to the right of self-treatment and the right of self-diagnosis, a number of tests for home use have been introduced in recent years and are now available without restriction for the diagnosis of a variety of medical disorders. They have been referred to by the crass term of 'do-it-yourself kits', but are known officially as *home testing devices.*

Their aim is rational, enabling anyone, who now has rights, to indulge in self-diagnosis. They are of course easily available and convenient. Ideally, they can serve as monitoring devices for a patient to follow the course of a disease diagnosed by a physician.

The legal basis for the use of devices for home testing is the *Clinical Laboratory Improvement Amendments Act of 1988* (CLIA). Its essential feature is the legal requirement that any error in testing be negligible and that there be a minimum risk of harm (accuracy and safety). Prior to the use of a home testing device for any medical reason, the patient should consult his/her physician for advice and guidance, and not act independently. The concept was not planned to eliminate the role of the physician.

BLOOD GLUCOSE MONITORS

Diabetic patients, especially those injecting themselves with insulin, require frequent monitoring of blood sugar in order to select accurate insulin dosage. They can avail themselves of a monitoring device (glucometer) to guide them with their insulin dosage and the physician's control of their diabetes. Physicians of diabetic patients would be pleased to be presented with readings at different times of the day in order to plan insulin dosage. The test requires a finger prick and a drop of blood. The standard technique has been modified to enable a visually impaired patient to perform the test.

A great effort has been made to determine the blood glucose level without actually drawing blood. The technique should be perfected in the near future. Warning: The results of the test may be affected by the patient's ingestion of acetaminophen (Tylenol) or ascorbic acid (Vitamin C). The patient's participation in the procedure of blood sugar testing should be under the guidance of the patient's physician.

BLOOD PRESSURE MONITORS are of great value to patients on drug therapy for hypertension. Physicians would be gratified to receive a diary of accurate readings taken at various times of the day in order to plan any changes in therapy.

Mechanical monitors with a gauge are generally more accurate than electronic ones (which are much easier to use). The standard mercury sphygmo-manometer is the most dependable, but one must be trained and skilled in its use. Others available include the spring gauge manometer, digital electronic units, and oscillometric units. All are generally sufficiently reliable for the purpose, and are valuable adjuncts to care under a physician's guidance.

BLOOD CHOLESTEROL TESTING

Testing for blood cholesterol is available for home use, but is relatively expensive and the results may not be accurate. More importantly, the other lipid determinations are not as easily available. A simple cholesterol reading is actually of little value to a patient for self-use. Besides, for a bit more in cost, the entire lipid profile can be obtained from the professional laboratory of the physician's choice. Therapy can then be planned using diet, exercise, and drugs.

TESTING FOR PROTHROMBIN TIME

Determining the exact dosage of an anticoagulant is too important for the physician to be dependent upon a patient's home device of testing for the prothrombin time. A high degree of accuracy with responsibility is essential and is better and more safely accomplished in a professional laboratory, again with the physician's awareness. The accuracy of the device is not questioned as much as is taking the responsibility from the physician.

OVULATION PREDICTORS are available to measure the urinary excretion of luteinizing hormone (LH) during ovulation. Anyone planning to use this technique as a home testing device would be well served by consulting her physician for an opinion and guidance.

FECAL OCCULT BLOOD TESTING is a valuable, inexpensive monitoring technique to be used at home in connection with a physician's supervision and available supplementary examinations. Otherwise, it would be dangerous for a person independently to test for occult blood in the stool and assume anything diagnostic on the basis of results (like the absence of colon cancer). Generally, the test may be part of a routine physical examination, which more importantly, would include a physician's digital rectal examination with or without colonoscopy and barium enema, depending upon the physician's findings and judgment. The performance of self-examinations at home on one's stool for occult blood is a very valuable consideration under medical *guidance* and supervision. The test is usually easy to perform and interpret (positive or negative). A major problem with the test is its poor specificity and predictive value of only 50 percent and its limited sensitivity of 50 percent.

PREGNANCY DETECTORS are available for home use by measuring human chorionic gonadotropin (HCG) in the urine. The test is convenient, inexpensive, qualitative, and not quantitative. Reliability improves after a missed period. False positives are noted after a recent miscarriage, use of fertility drugs, or in connection with an ovarian tumor. The test should never be assessed in the absence of a physician's input.

DETECTION OF URINARY TRACT INFECTIONS have indicators that are based upon the measurement of nitrate changes in the urine. A large problem is that ten percent of bacteria fail to react to the test. An even greater danger is that a positive result determined by self-diagnosis should not encourage one to proceed with self-treatment using antibiotics. The physician should certainly provide a professional opinion.

PEAK AIRFLOW METERS are used at home by many asthmatic patients. They measure the peak amount of air expelled, and the patient looks for the highest reading to exceed 50 percent of the maximal lung capacity. The test is useful in following the course of treatment under the guidance of a physician.

HIV TESTING DEVICES are available and require a blood sample. They do not test for other sexually transmitted diseases, which are essential to an examination. They should never be relied upon without the opinion of a physician.

DANGERS IN HOME TESTING

The dangers are quite apparent:

1) Granting patients the right of *self-diagnosis* disregards the corresponding responsibility for accuracy and medical supervision.

2) Failure by the patient to note that the results may be *false-positive* or *false-negative* on the basis of limited sensitivity and/or specificity of the test results. No test is 100 percent sensitive and also 100 percent specific.

3) Patients are likely to assume incorrectly that all results are accurate and conclusive 100 percent of the time—a dangerous assumption.

4) Being *magnetized by numbers* and taking every figure as 'carved in stone' without appreciating that there is always a *margin of error*.

5) Failure to observe a) FDA warnings on the label, e.g,, whether affected by heat, cold, humidity, expiration date; b) precautions in the directions, c) inaccuracies due to delays between steps in the procedure.

6) Failure to be responsible for and cautious in their taking the easy step from self-diagnosis to self-treatment without medical consultation—an essential part of the privilege of using a home-testing device.

7) Danger of falling into the *slippery-slope syndrome* of pursuing an easy, but false and dangerous path from self-diagnosis to self-treatment to self-destruction.

8) Evolution of ethical issues concerned primarily with a patient's incorrect assumption that the tests are accurate, when in fact there may be a significant margin of error as well as imperfect sensitivity and specificity factors. In other words, results may be falsely positive or falsely negative.

The ever-present cynics and naysayers have facetiously suggested that the ultimate in home testing devices based upon everyone's rights could be a do-it-yourself embalming kit.

CONCLUSIONS

Home testing devices show a remarkable advance in modern biotechnology. With caution, they can be invaluable both for diagnosis and in following the course of a medical problem. The key to their use, however, is that they should be part of the patient's monitoring, guidance, and approval by a physician. From the commercial standpoint, they are very popular and more will surely appear on the market. Caution in their use is well advised.

The key to the use of home testing devices is that the patient must not overlook the importance of responsibility to go hand-in-hand with the exercise of rights.

ROUTINE BLOOD CHEMISTRY

Our next consideration of ethical issues in modern diagnostic tests and therapeutic procedures is the common medical practice of *routine* blood chemistry screening of patients in the offices of their physicians and upon admission of patients to the hospital.

The *routine blood chemistry panel* has become a standard component of every complete physical examination. The expectation of its use is taken for granted without informed consent, of course, and is generally looked upon with great anticipation by the physician as well as the patient. It serves as an excellent model for the consideration of screening by laboratory methods. In its favor is that it comprises about twenty blood tests including glucose, urea nitrogen, creatinine, sodium, potassium, chloride, carbon dioxide combining power, protein, albumin, albumin/globulin ratio, calcium, bilirubin, alkaline phosphatase, lactose dehydrogenase, serum glutamic oxalacetic transaminase, cholesterol, uric acid, et al. The test and results vary somewhat in different laboratories.

Its purpose is to come upon a *chance* discovery of an abnormality. Hence, it is often referred to facetiously as a "fishing expedition." It is really an illogical "shot-gun" approach to diagnosis. If the physician were testing for some specific abnormality on the basis of his findings in the history and the physical examination he would expand his study into a given direction, and he would certainly not need many of the tests irrelevant to the problem. Although the test is actually not very expensive and is usually covered by insurance (properly) it is really not cost effective.

The results have standard deviations of error, and may show minor numerical aberrations with presumed inaccuracies. The information may therefore be misleading and difficult to interpret. The small variations may actually be normal for the patient.

The wise physician can make proper decisions about minor variations, or may, especially under patient pressure, be "magnetized by numbers" and follow every questionable abnormality down a path often of no return. Of course, following a lead may actually be occasionally rewarding. That is the issue.

The blood chemistry panel was never intended to be a substitute for 1) a thorough history and physical examination, and 2) specific tests relevant to the patient's problems.

Insurers are evidently aware of the non-specific nature of routine blood chemistry testing and some are questioning reimbursements for them in favor of specifically indicated tests based upon a specific diagnosis. The issue is a debatable one and deserving of discussion before reversal of the policy of reimbursement takes place.

In certain circumstances, there is no question regarding the justification of performing a battery of tests. These include a comatose patient in an emergency setting, especially without an available history.

A negotiated resolution of the ethical issue concerning routine diagnostic testing is the sensible recommendation that everyone should have a blood chemistry panel every two years on a routine basis as with the chest X-ray and electrocardiogram as part of a physical examination. More recently, discussion has arisen regarding the routine testing for colon cancer by colonoscopy and for prostate cancer by blood testing.

THE PROSTATE SPECIFIC ANTIGEN (PSA) TEST for cancer of the prostate has been heralded recently as a major advance in diagnostic testing. How effective is it?

PSA, a protein produced by the prostate is easily measured in the blood, and is regarded with value for its elevation in cancer of the prostate. It is also elevated, however, in the blood of patients with benign hypertrophy of the gland, infection and with certain drugs, e.g., saw palmetto. In fact only thirty percent of elevated levels are the result of cancer, and in twenty percent of cancers the levels are normal. The specificity-sensitivity factor regarding accuracy in screening is a serious concern.

Furthermore, the gold standard for diagnosis, the surgical biopsy, which is expensive and troublesome, is still required to establish the diagnosis and, even if positive, fails to reveal whether the lesion is the aggressive variety.

HAIR ANALYSIS

Last and definitely least among diagnostic testing procedures is the strange, unscientific analysis of hair for the diagnosis of a variety of medical disorders. It is a popular technique employed mainly by practitioners of alternative medicine. Several hundred thousand tests are performed annually in many laboratories. According to the Food and Drug Administration, the Bureau of Consumer Protection, the Federal Trade Commission and other prestigious organizations, hair analysis is regarded as unreliable and potentially hazardous in providing false results.

SCREENING FOR BREAST CANCER

Special consideration must be given to screening for breast cancer and its ethical issues. In diagnostic screening for breast cancer, the two standard studies are 1) the clinical examination, and 2) mammography. The average patient is over forty years of age, and the average frequency of the examination is bi-annually. Breast cancer serves as an excellent model to illustrate problems in screening.

POSITIVE REPORT: SIGNIFICANCE:

The average percentage of positive reports that turn out to be false is about 11.0 percent in the United States. A positive mammography report is based upon readings of "suspicion of cancer," and "indeterminate." A positive report that later turns out to be false has three immediate effects:

1) Indication of high factor of sensitivity (over-reading to err on the side of caution and safety)

2) Increased incidence of adverse psychologic effects: anxiety, depression

3) High costs of further studies: follow-up examinations, ultrasound, biopsy (gold standard for diagnosis)

ETHICAL ISSUES IN SCREENING

1) There is the hypothetical and unrealistic assumption of the likelihood of achieving a screening of 100 percent positive plus 100 percent negative *predicted values* (100 percent sensitivity plus 100 percent specificity).

2) Is *over-reading* and the resulting increase in false positive findings more desirable than *under-reading* and its resulting increase in false negative findings? Is lowering sensitivity preferable to raising specificity?

3) Should *cost* be a concern in a doctor's selection of tests and procedures he recommends to a patient? Should the doctor consider less costly, possibly second best tests and procedures? Should cost control be considered in selection of tests and procedures in the provision of quality care? a) to the individual patient and b) in overall health care?

4) Should a patient be made aware of the doctor's possible *conflict of interest* in recommending the location for tests and procedures (e.g., the physician's financial interest in a laboratory or other diagnostic facility?)

GENETIC TESTING FOR BREAST CANCER

Genetic testing has emerged as one of the remarkable advances in scientific medicine. As with any innovation, its benefits have been paralleled by a new set of problems and ethical issues (see Chapter 22). Breast cancer has been chosen as a model representative of the considerations in genetic testing.

Unlike most other forms of testing, the introduction of *genetics* as a new modality in testing creates an absolute need of counseling sessions and discussions prior to the decision to have genetic testing for the BRCA-1 and BRCA-2 genes observed in breast cancer. *Discussions* should include:

1) Reason for request of testing

2) Meaning, validity, and reliability of tests. The patient must be made aware that results will signify less than 100 percent positive predicted values plus 100 percent negative predicted values (100 percent sensitivity plus 100 percent specificity).

3) Significance of results as predictors of future disease

4) Plans for use of results in further actions

5) Psychologic, economic, and social implications of positive results (and, for that matter, of negative results)

ETHICAL ISSUES:

1) Does the patient have the assurance of privacy and confidentiality in the required respect for his ethical rights regarding the results? Are insurers and employers prevented from access to the patient's positive results, particularly when they may be paying for the costs? As indicated previously, the law is slow in adjudicating violations of ethical principles following the introduction of biotechnological innovations. Serious ethical issues involving discrimination by employers and insurers are in need of legal resolution and should surely be addressed by our Congress. The use of information obtained illegally regarding an employee's genetic screening resulting in an employer's hiring and firing practices or in an insurer's issuance of an insurance policy may be more than a question of

morality and really constitute criminal behavior (see Chapter 22).

2) Should the physician have the moral *responsibility* to inform the patient's mother, daughters, and sisters of the patient's positive results with possible breech of confidentiality? Is the patient's permission always required?

3) Should testing be conducted only in *research* with vigorous safeguards of the patient's confidentiality rights?

SURGERY AS A THERAPEUTIC MEASURE

A discussion of advances in biotechnology is incomplete without some reference to *surgery*. In general, surgery is second to non-surgical measures in the frequency of diagnostic testing and screening, as well as in the prevention, palliation and curative means taken in the management of disease. Our concern here is with the ethical issues that affect quality living and perfection of the semi-circle of life.

Besides the choice of surgical procedure, whether diagnostic or therapeutic, the most important concerns center about the choice of 1) the surgeon, and 2) the site of the procedure.

Assuming that every surgeon is properly educated, trained and qualified, there is no time for concern when the surgery represents an emergency or even when the procedure is a minor one. (It has been facetiously stated that the only minor operations are those done on someone else.) In reality, to every patient, a surgical procedure is a serious event, particularly if the anesthesia is *general* and the patient rendered comatose. There are indeed surgical procedures requiring local anesthesia that may be considered minor. The points we wish to address regarding ethical issues relate primarily to major surgical procedures.

ETHICAL ISSUES:

When a physician recommends a patient for consideration of

elective surgery, the surgeon may not but usually does give his approval of an operation. Under such circumstances, there is little need to question the surgeon's qualifications based upon his training, certification, experience and ability. The ethical issues involved, however, may be very subtle and are best illustrated in a reliable study performed in a nationwide survey and reported in a responsible and respected medical publication. The issues and the point of the discussion do not require that the surgery be identified. In the interest of protection of privacy, it need only be stated here that the reference is actual and correct and that the procedure is well known.

Several hundred thousand such operations are performed throughout the United States annually and at least an equal number elsewhere in the world, probably totaling a million such procedures each year.

The results of the study are as follows:

1) Fewer than 200 operations were performed per year in relatively small centers where less than fifty similar operations per surgeon were performed per year by a total of more than 3500 surgeons throughout the country. The overall morbidity rate (complications) was 6.8 percent and the overall mortality rate 3.9 percent.

2) More than 200 operations were performed per year in large centers where more than seventy-five operations per surgeon were performed per year by a total of fewer than 3500 surgeons throughout the country. The overall morbidity rate was 4.6 percent and the overall mortality rate 2.5 percent.

The details of the *complications* are not revealed here in order not to disclose the operation and to protect the privacy of all concerned. Suffice it to say, the complications were all serious and lifethreatening, not merely lengthening of the hospital stay and increase in the costs. In a number of instances, complications required the transfer of patients to another institution for additional care.

No one has questioned the validity of the study, although opposition has been raised regarding the significance of the findings. The differences in numbers are precisely the reason for the study's portending an ethical issue.

Lest the reader fails to notice, the complication rate of 6.8 percent in the small centers compared with that of 4.6 percent in the large centers is a difference of only 2.2 percent. What it of course means is that at least two persons in every hundred were more likely to have complications in the small center than in the large center. Furthermore, the mortality of 3.9 percent in the small center compared with 2.5 percent in the large center is a difference of only 1.4 percent. What it of course means is that at least one person in every hundred was more likely to die as a result of the operation in the small center than in the large center.

The results may not be sufficiently important for drastic changes in the performance of the surgery, but do raise questions about the need for *recommendations* that have been made to improve quality and safety in the best interest of health care:

1) Establishment of minimal criteria and standards that must be met to qualify for performance of any serious operation or care of any major illness.

2) Possible regionalization of facilities (e.g., in the illustration, all patients requiring the particular procedure should be referred to centers performing more than 200 operations per year by operators each performing more than 75 operations per year).

3) Requirements that the operation not be performed where expected complications would mandate the transfer of the patient to another institution.

The study was a valid, respected research project and it created much *controversy* and hence an ethical issue not easily resolved except by radical changes in the philosophy of health care.

CARDIAC DEFIBRILLATOR

Another outstanding example of a recent promotion of a highly biotechnological therapeutic procedure with enormous possible benefit as well as with immediate controversy and ethical considerations is the use of an established cardiac defibrillator in acute and sudden instances of ventricular fibrillation (not atrial fibrillation) caused by acute miyocardial infarction or by sudden cardiac arrest from other causes.

Ventricular fibrillation, if untreated, usually results in death within a few minutes. Successful defibrillation with restoration of normal sinus rhythm can result in 80 percent survival if treated within five minutes, whereas only two percent survival will occur if not treated within twenty minutes.

It is rationally estimated that at least fifty percent of the deaths due to ventricular fibrillation may be saved by a broad availability of a defibrillator.

The key question is to what extent should technical training, normally reserved for physicians, emergency medical technicians, and registered nurses in intensive coronary care units, be expanded to make defibrillators more available?

In support of the idea is that recently devised new *automatic* types are in the market for more general use. They are reported to be easy to operate by giving voice instructions, e.g.,"apply two (disposable) plastic leads to chest and push red button." The cost is on the order of about $3,000. Its lithium battery may last five years. A built-in safety mechanism prevents delivery of a shock if defibrillation is not indicated.

The plan is for increasing the availability of the defibrillator, for example, in commercial airplanes as part of their emergency kits, and for the flight attendants to be instructed in its use.

ETHICAL ISSUES

The ethical issues are many. In favor of expanding the availability of the defibrillator.

1) Its life saving opportunities are extended.

2) A reasonable number of personnel may be properly trained in its use.

In *opposition* to the extension of its use:

1) There are effective drugs, such as amiodarone, that could preclude the use of the defibrillator.

2) The indications for use are not always readily apparent, except to an expert.

3) The needed training can be complex.

4) Circumstances usually requiring defibrillation often intimidate hospital personnel (other than those specially trained) because of the gravity of the condition and the complexity of the problems.

5) Improper performance may do more harm than good.

6) There is a limited time factor for action. An absence of blood flow to the brain (a complication of ventricular fibrillation, the most serious of all cardiac arrhythmias) for longer than five minutes usually results in irreversible brain damage. (It is of interest that, on emergency call, a fire engine may take as long as five minutes and an ambulance up to 8-10 minutes to respond to a call.) Beyond five minutes, normal sinus rhythm may be restored but the patient may be brain-dead.

7) The safety and efficacy of the defibrillator in the hands of the general public has not been established or tested.

8) Technical failures of operation may be rare, but will inevitably lead to deaths and to lawsuits.

9) Amateur rescuers and occasional users of defibrillators will probably not be protected from liability (despite the protective application of the Good Samaritan Laws).

10) Facilities that neglect to follow the lead of airlines in installing defibrillators may risk liability for failure to have a

defibrillator in place ready for use. Such facilities may be health clubs, trains, office buildings, etc.

11) The function of the defibrillator may be affected by cellular phones (as are pacemakers). Interference does occur between a) implantable cardioverter defibrillators or cardiac pacemakers and b) electronic anti-theft surveillance systems or devices that emit magnetic fields. (Other types of surveillance systems pose no such problems.) The degree of interference correlates well with the proximity to the device and the duration of exposure to the magnetic field. The severity of the effects may be *deleterious* as follows:

a) by prolonged bradycardia or asystole due to inhibition of ventricular pacing,

b) by induction of ventricular arrhythmias due to inappropriate pauses or shocks,

c) by injury from falling, and

d) by physical and psychological discomfort due to multiple shocks.

RECOMMENDATIONS

Obvious recommendations that have been posed by concerned experts regarding these effects are:

a) avoidance of prolonged exposure, and b) the patient should be made aware of the presence of magnetic surveillance systems nearby.

ALTERNATIVE MEDICINE AND DIAGNOSTIC TESTS AND PROCEDURES

The many alternative medical practices are not inclined to make contributions to scientifically proved diagnostic testing and procedures. They borrow the entire diagnostic approach to health care from scientific medicine, however, they approach the therapy of disease with their own various unique alternative, non-scientific procedures.

Scientific medicine has never embraced any of the therapies of alternate medicine, including their herbal practices. Recently, however, in awareness of the enormous popularity of herbs and some alternative medical practices, most notably acupuncture, meditation, biofeedback, and psychosurgery, scientific medicine has become tolerant of their patients' indulgence outside of traditional health care. The opening of a budgeted office at the National Institute of Health for the study of alternative medicine, aided by assistance at several selected academic institutions, should possibly further a better understanding of alternative medicine by the allopathic medical profession.

An immediate objective is to learn what may be: 1) available that can be adjunctive to the practice of scientific medicine, 2) of little or no value, and 3) quackery and even fraud.

THE FUTURE OF DIAGNOSTIC TESTS AND
THERAPEUTIC PROCEDURES

In contemplating the future of diagnostic testing and of therapeutic procedures, there is little purpose in "crystal ball gazing" and in speculation other than to envision the direction of the path currently established.

It has taken several millennia to redirect a course of scientific medicine from an art form. The primary force has been the establishment of the *scientific method* in the assessment of any diagnostic or therapeutic biotechnologic innovation. Research testing, proving, and regulating are fundamental requirements, hence the absolute engagement of the Food and Drug Administration, the National Institutes of Health, and similar organizations devoted to the best interest of health care on a scientific basis.

Secondary factors, not less important, however, are the application of altruistic *ethical principles* of honesty, non-maleficence, beneficence, and respect for rights.

Thirdly, there must be constant reexamination, changes, and

improvements based upon *efficacy* and *safety* of all new biotechnological innovations.

Fourthly, the goal must be a *universal quality of living* combined with a perfected *heredity* and *environment* in the development of a *semicircle of life* resembling the perfect mathematical semicircular structure.

As a natural afterthought, one wonders if our diagnostic testing and therapeutic procedural efforts in the year 2000 will be abandoned as quackery in the year 2200 just as the blood-letting of imagined toxins in the year 1800 was judged and abandoned in the year 2000?

CHAPTER 19

INFERTILITY

The poorest man would not part with his health for money;
the richest man would part with his money for health.

— Anonymous

INTRODUCTION

Despite the fact that 1) the global human population has reached six billion in 2000 and doubles every thirty years, and 2) overpopulation may be the biggest threat to human survival, it is ironic that infertility has always been a serious impairment of quality living among many married couples since biblical times. Not until recently, however, has there been reason for optimism and joy with the emergence of an explosion of biotechnological advances in the correction or solution of the problem. As is inevitable with most innovations in health care, enormous controversies have arisen and have persisted as ethical issues. They have occurred mainly because certain elements in society have refused to accept some of the dramatic aspects of the innovative contributions to infertility, often for presumed religious reasons. Fortunately for sterile couples, many of the ethical issues have been adjudicated, resolved, and accepted, but those issues that remain are thorny. In vitro fertilization, for example, has been a remarkable innovation of great benefit to many infertile couples, but many people have raised strong objections to the discarding of unused fertilized eggs as destruction of human beings. A basic issue is whether or not a fertilized egg is a person.

This definition of a human being is in disagreement with the scientific definition of a human being. Another issue has been raised concerning the moral right of a sixty-year-old mother of an infertile daughter without a uterus to serve as a surrogate parent and carry a child for her unfortunate daughter. These and many ethical questions linger, not among infertile couples with a child of modern technology, but among people with inflexible opinions to the contrary, who are not infertile for the most part. Such disputations prevent successful quality living for all in society.

DEFINITION OF INFERTILITY
Infertility is defined as a failure to achieve pregnancy during a twelve-month period of unprotected sexual intercourse.

FREQUENCY OF INFERTILITY
The frequency with which infertility occurs is so common as to represent a serious societal concern, which weighs heavily upon an affected family's quality of living. In recent years, the remarkable advances in biotechnology, however, have been able to resolve the problem and have given happiness to many infertile persons.

Infertility occurs in about ten percent of couples anxious for a pregnancy. The cause of the problem lies with the female in sixty percent and with the male in forty percent of cases.

CAUSES OF INFERTILITY
Medical disorders responsible for infertility in both males and females may be infectious, obstructive, genetic, or there may be no detectable disease.

CAUSES IN THE FEMALE

In the female, the causes may be anovulatory, due to fallopian tubal disease, to cervical disease, or to endometriosis. In ten percent of the cases in the female there are no determinable causes.

CAUSES IN THE MALE

In the male, the causes may be due to testicular dysfunction, abnormal sperm transport, or to varicocele. In thirty percent of the cases in the male, there are no determinable causes.

SOLUTIONS TO INFERTILITY

The effect of this extensive problem is that the majority of infertile couples desire children and seek solutions. The pursuit of the diagnosis and treatment of the underlying medical cause of the disorder is the preferred solution, and is the only one without ethical concerns. Unfortunately, the approach is complex, costly, and low in success rate.

A number of solutions to infertility are now available to all infertile couples and have varying degrees of success as well as serious ethical concerns:

1) Adoption
2) Assisted reproductive technology
   a) Superovulation and intrauterine insemination
   b) Artificial insemination
   c) In vitro fertilization
   d) Surrogate parenting

ADOPTION

The adoption process has been available since antiquity with varying success. It is not a totally satisfying solution in that there is a scarcity of available children and there are complex social restraints. A simple solution would be that more women with unwanted pregnancies go to term instead of having abortions, thereby freeing the newborns for adoption.

Other unsatisfactory aspects to the adoption process include administrative problems, long waiting periods, high costs, racial issues, and lack of availability of babies for single parents or to couples with alternative life-styles. As a result of the deficiency, an enormous *black-market* has developed abroad for the benefit of childless American couples.

A serious concern that disturbs the household of a couple with a newly acquired adopted child of other parents is the presence of life-long psychologic problems in the child, especially regarding his or her *identity*, origin, and desire to communicate with the biologic parents and siblings. At times, the child may be so disturbed as to suffer from an *attachment disorder* and be responsible for violent and abusive behavior requiring psychiatric intervention and care.

An important factor in the aim for a solution to infertility is that many couples prefer children with fifty percent of their own genetic properties, so that the child has the genetic makeup of one of the parents. Such couples have no further interest in adoption and are ideally suited to newer trends. Recent advances in biotechnology have resolved this concern and have contributed greatly to the quality of living in many infertile situations by the application of *assisted reproductive technology*, now addressed in the text.

SUPEROVULATION AND INTRAUTERINE INSEMINATION

There are circumstances in which a couple's infertility has an unexplained cause, but can still be corrected. For example, the female has an unobstructed genital tract with evidence of ovarian function, and the male has motile sperm, even though they may be subfertile in quality. In such situations, *superovulation* may be induced with a *gonadotropin* or a follicle-stimulating hormone. The biologic father's sperm may then be used for intrauterine insemination.

The *risks* in this process include 1) ovarian hyper-stimulation and a thirty percent incidence of *multiple* pregnancies, 2) the questionable possibility of ovarian cancer, and 3) the risk of miscarriage. The costs of the procedure are very high, possibly on the order of several thousand dollars.

When successful, the overall improvement rate in quality living for an infertile couple is enormous. The high benefit to harm ratio justifies the use of the procedure, and is attractive in appropriate situations. A few ethical issues remain, however, but may not be too controversial.

ARTIFICIAL INSEMINATION BY A DONOR FOR MALE INFERTILITY

For many years, in order to keep a patriarchal family intact, male infertility has been managed by the use of sperm from an alien donor.

PROCEDURE

In this regard, there are suitable catalogues available with a listing of unidentifiable male donors. The donor is generally given a modest honorarium for his contribution. He is required to have a physical examination with emphasis upon his family's genetic history. He is then screened by a geneticist and two or more qualified physicians for such matters as potential fertility, general health, presence of infections including AIDS, and normal intelligence.

A chromosomal analysis is available upon request. The donor's semen is packed in vials, frozen, and stored in a *cryobank* for a maximum of about three days in dry ice or for a maximum of ten days in liquid nitrogen.

The semen is then thawed when ready for use. The insemination procedure requires a sperm count of about twenty million, a high percentage of motility, and a low percentage of structural abnormality. The recipient is an ovum and the uterus of the biologic mother.

SUCCESS RATE

The success rate of fertilization in this process is surprisingly high, perhaps eighty percent.

ETHICAL ISSUES

As with most other biotechnologic advances, a number of ethical issues arise, many resulting in legal action and adjudication:

1) The most obvious concern is the identity of the biologic father, generally considered *confidential*.

2) In actual cases, the newly adoptive stepfather, in a subsequent divorce from the biologic mother, has claimed that he is not responsible for child support because he is not the biological father.

3) In more troublesome divorce situations, the divorced husband (child's stepfather) has claimed that the child is a product of adultery, generally considered as a mean-spirited view.

4) Another significant ethical issue is a widow's demand for the extraction of living sperm from her recently deceased husband's testes in order to have the sperm implanted in her uterus, hopeful for a child. The family of the deceased has the ethical right to question such demand on the grounds that it lacks the approval of the deceased husband and that the estate should not be liable for child support.

5) In instances of presumed male infertility, sperm of dubious fertility has been injected directly into the cytoplasm of an egg (Intracytoplasmic Sperm Injection) with occasional success.

Artificial insemination is a popular solution to the male infertility problem in view of its great success in enhancing quality living despite its ethical issues.

IN VITRO FERTILIZATION AND EMBRYO TRANSFER IN FEMALE INFERTILITY

A recent advance in the biotechnologic solution of female infertility is the concept of in vitro fertilization and embryo transfer, a truly revolutionary development in human infertility and in quality living. It was introduced in England in 1978 and in the United States in 1984.

PROCEDURE

The steps in the complex technique are as follows:

1) An alien donor female is injected with hormones to stimulate her ovaries to produce one or more eggs in her next ovarian cycle. (Synchronization with the recipient is required.)

2) The hormone level is monitored to determine the time of ripening.

3) The eggs are harvested by laparoscopy under anesthesia.

4) The eggs are cultured in a Petri dish in the laboratory.

5) Sperm from the biologic father (or even from an alien donor) are placed by and inserted into the eggs by *micromanipulation*.

6) Fertilization occurs and succeeds in about eighty percent of the trials. The percentage may be even higher in the case of young egg donors.

7) A *test-tube baby* is produced, and is first called a *zygote* (union of male and female *gametes*).

8) The *zygote* is allowed to cleave (divide) several times over a period of two or three days.

9) The fertilized eggs, now zygotes, still microscopic in size, are transferred by vaginal route to the recipient's uterus.

10) Implantation is successful in only about twenty percent of the cases. Hence, in order to achieve success, several transplants are often introduced.

11) As a result, about twenty five percent of the successful births are twins or even triplets (and rarely more).

12) Unused fertilized eggs, now *embryos*, are stored up to

about one year by a process of freezing in liquid nitrogen known as *cryopreservation*.

13) During this time, they may be thawed as needed, and implanted into a recipient. The thawing process unfortunately reduces the success rate of implantation to less than twenty percent.

14) After about a year of preservation, unused fertilized eggs are discarded. An interesting determination has been the availability of unused fertilized eggs for adoption.

AVAILABILITY

A further disconsolate feature of the technique is its poor availability. Fewer then seventy-five medical centers are equipped for egg donation. A total of barely fifty percent of the centers have sufficient donors to meet the requests.

A modification of the standard technique includes the *intrafallopian transfer* of a zygote in order to achieve a better likelihood of uterine implantation.

POST-MENOPAUSAL PREGNANCY

An exciting consideration is the occasional demand for post-menopausal pregnancy, a previously regarded fantasy. The ability to freeze sperm and fertilized eggs now includes the ability to freeze the ova of young women for later use. It is well known that the eggs of older women are more difficult to fertilize than are the eggs of younger women, presumably because the more youthful eggs are of better quality.

Egg donations represent a groundbreaking advance in technology, especially in contemplation of possible post-menopausal pregnancy. Fertility clinics are reported to pay egg donors several thousand dollars, whereas sperm donors may be offered less than one hundred dollars per donation. (Ed: Three cheers for feminism!)

RISKS

In vitro fertilization is not without risks. There is little if any risk to the child. The recipient, however, may develop infection, have a miscarriage, or give birth to a stillborn child. Stillbirth, as a complication, occurs more frequently in recipients older than about forty years.

ETHICAL ISSUES

As with any biotechnologic innovation designed to improve quality living, a number of issues have arisen, many of which have ethical concerns:

1) Degradation of the magnificent process of child-bearing to the spectre of commercialization

2) Availability of the process to only a small percentage of infertile women

3) Inclination for detraction of the procedure from the normal, more desirable attention to correction of the underlying cause of the woman's infertility

4) Inevitable psychologic problems relating to the child, such as lineage, self esteem, and development of the attachment disorder, which consists of violent, abusive, and uncontrollable behavior by the child

5) Lack of knowledge regarding long term side effect of the drugs and hormones used to induce superovulation

6) The conception of children by artificial means in lieu of normal means

7) General restriction by law or common medical practice to married, heterosexual women

8) General exclusion of single women or couples with alternative life styles (couples of two women, and occasionally even couples of two men)

9) The occasional practice of *outcome-based pricing* by in vitro fertilization clinics, in which the clinic policy may guarantee a couple a partial or full refund if the procedure fails. This enticing attraction may, however, encourage exploitation. For example, the clinic may

implant as many as four or five embryos in order to assure success. A multiplicity of successful implants may be hazardous to the woman as well as to the fetuses.

10) A major concern is the answer to the question, "who is the mother?" Is she the donor of the egg or the carrier of the pregnancy? Generally, the donor is regarded as the biological mother and the carrier of the pregnancy as the surrogate mother.

11) Inevitable physical, psychological, and social problems of post-menopausal pregnancy via in vitro fertilization

12) Concern for a child who has lost a genetic parent (the biological mother) and the ensuing psychological problems

13) Unsettled dispute over the disposition of unused frozen embryos, which are usually discarded because of a lack of standard policy, is it ethical for the clinics to discard the embryos? Should the embryos be available for adoption?

14) Side effects and possible long term effects of the drugs used in the process (There are rare reports of renal failure.)

15) Need for counseling

16) Troublesome and costly need for ultrasonic monitoring, blood tests, surgical procedure, and office visits

17) Should ova be for sale? The sale of kidneys is illegal. The surrogate in surrogate parenting is paid only for medical expenses. Any other expense is illegal. Those willing to pay for ova insist that donors of ova would be unavailable unless compensated.

18) Should not a donor be altruistic rather than venal in providing a gift of life?

19) Fertility clinics offer generous payments to attract donors. Why would a donor refuse compensation?

20) Donors expect to be compensated as an established format

21) Is there an issue as long as there are willing buyers (the clinic and the recipient) and willing sellers (donors)?

22) Is procurement for a fee representative of:

a) Commercialization of reproduction with an egg as the commodity having monetary value?

b) Exploitation of women?

c) Sacrifice by women of their dignity?

23) Is society condoning the harvesting of eggs from poor women who put their health at risk for the benefit of the affluent?

24) Should high payments, e.g., $5,000, be permitted by law to entice poor women to be donors?

25) Do we need a commission to create a policy to set legal criteria concerning costs and procurement?

26) Range of costs are between $5,000 and $12,000. Two to three attempts are often required before success is realized. Are the poor deliberately excluded from consideration as recipients? Should the procedure be available only to the rich?

27) The procedure is rarely covered by insurance. Is this fair?

28) An overall low success rate requires more research.

29) The future consideration of a) the use of embryos for *spare parts* or for *organs*, as with aborted fetal tissue, b) genetic engineering to eliminate inherited defects.

30) Should a fertility clinic give frozen embryos of a couple killed in a car accident to a family member as property in a will? Is it not wasteful to discard unused embryos?

31) Should embryo-splitting (cloning) be used to help infertile couples?

32) Should fetal oocytes be used to help infertile women reproduce?

33) Is posthumous reproduction (by extraction of sperm from a deceased husband) ethical?

34) Does assisted reproduction with its high rate of multiple pregnancies (thirty percent):

a) Increase the burden on women?

b) Increase risks to the newborn?

c) Justify the high costs?

d) Justify selective reduction of the number of pregnancies?

35) Should sixty-year-old women have babies?

36) Should fertility clinics be helping post-menopausal women become pregnant? Should there be an age limit?

37) Should an infertile middle-aged woman with a serious medical problem, e.g., diabetes with associated kidney disease, be denied requested assisted reproduction? How about an HIV-infected infertile woman, who, when untreated, risks transmission of her infection to the child in twenty five percent of cases, but when treated with modern antiretroviral therapy, the rate of transmission is reduced to two percent? By the same token, a treated HIV-infected woman has a far better prognosis for life than an untreated patient, who would probably not live long enough to see her child reach adulthood.

38) The basic issue in the denial of assisted reproductive technology to any infertile couple is a challenge to the woman's right to (the principles of) autonomy and self-determination. Should anyone, including the law, have the right to deny a woman her right, provided she has the medical approval of her physician?

SURROGATE PARENTING FOR FEMALE INFERTILITY

Surrogate parenting is a successful and a suitable consideration for female infertility. It has been a common practice since ancient times. According to the Bible, Sarah engaged Hagar to bear a child for Abraham. The method used was of course the old-fashioned way. The current practice, however, is to obtain the sperm of the biological father and 1) artificially inseminate the ovum and uterus of a surrogate female, or 2) use in vitro fertilization of the ovum of the biologic mother or the ovum and uterus of the surrogate.

FACTORS FAVORING SURROGATE PARENTING

1) It may be looked upon as a form of adoption, provided there are no payments of fees other than medical expenses.

2) The right of privacy is preserved.

3) It is not a baby selling process. Man cannot buy what he already owns.

4) The process must continue to be kept legal; otherwise the procedure would be driven to the black market, as with the current status of adoption.

5) The matter can be satisfying as long as it is kept purely on an altruistic basis (as with the mother of the patient serving as the surrogate).

FACTORS OPPOSING SURROGATE PARENTING

1) Ethical issues are complex and controversial:

a) Who is the mother? Is it the donor of the egg and/or the uterus of the surrogate, or is it the adoptive parent?

b) The possibility of a multiplicity of parents is created—a real dilemma

c) Does the surrogate have any future rights to the child morally?

2) Psychosocial factors—Does not surrogacy

a) jeopardize family stability?

b) distort the mother-child relationship?

c) create problems for the child (and siblings) as in the adoption process?

d) violate human dignity by using the uterus for financial gain?

3) Age factors:

a) Multiple issues are raised by childbirth in post-menopausal women serving as surrogates via artificial insemination with fertilized donor eggs

b) Should there be a legal age limit for surrogacy?

4) Fee factors:

a) Is a surrogate selling her child as in the case of the (illegal) sale of a kidney or of the (legal) sale of blood?

b) Is the fee to a surrogate (average $10,000) for physical hardship, participation, and/or for medical expenses?

c) Is the legal fee valid (average $16,000) for preparation of a contract, which in itself may be invalid?

d) Is the father's fee valid for purchase of the child from the surrogate?

e) Can the father purchase what he already owns?

f) Is surrogacy a marketing device with a baby as a commodity?

5) Paternalistic factors: Does not the surrogate need protection:

a) from a choice she may later regret?

b) from underestimating a bond she created by gestation?

c) from the emotional trauma caused by giving up a child?

d) from potential coercion and exploitation?

6) Legal factors:

a) Pertinent laws are absent regarding

  i) parental rights,

  ii) qualifications for surrogacy,

  iii) standards as a sperm donor, and ·

  iv) handling of a child (that may be abnormal) as a gift from the mother may be a form of adoption and subject to adoption laws.

b) Does the surrogate have any future rights to the child legally?

c) Is a contract valid legally? Can it be appropriate for such sensitive arrangement?

d) Is the refusal by a court to honor a contract an interference with a woman's procreative liberty?

Court decisions have favored the following:

a) The gestational female (surrogate) should be established as the mother regardless of the source of the egg.

b) Surrogacy contracts must be illegal (as is the case in certain European countries). A good model is the New York State law, which forbids a contract with fees to a broker and the surrogate, except for medical expenses.

c) The sale of a baby is illegal.

d) The transfer of a baby as a gift may be legal.

CHAPTER 20

REPRODUCTION

Suffering is inherent in life and may be liberated by mental and moral self-purification.

— Buddha, 5th Century BC

INTRODUCTION

Among the many advances in biotechnology selected for discussion because of their intensity of ethical issues in relation to quality living, the topic of reproduction ranks foremost in *emotionalism* because of the volatile and divisive *abortion* issue.

Virtually everyone is either pro-life or pro-choice. Rarely is there anyone who is undecided or neutral in the matter of opposing abortion or favoring a woman's right of choice. As long as the issue remains unresolved, and emotions continue to run high, quality living is greatly impaired for everyone and there can be no peace in society.

ROE VS. WADE

From the standpoint of its societal significance as a social issue, the Roe vs. Wade trial concerning abortion in 1973 before the United States Supreme Court ranks among the best known and most controversial court cases in American jurisprudence over the past one hundred years. Perhaps of equal social significance historically are 1) the Scopes trial regarding the teaching of evolution in a public school in the 1920's and 2) the Nuremberg trial in which Nazi doctors were accused of performing outrageously brutal experiments on innocent victims who had been relegated to their death in concentration camps in the 1940's without having committed any crime.

The Roe vs Wade trial, which was finally settled by the United States Supreme Court in favor of a woman's *right to abortion* as a matter of choice, has remained to date as the center piece of emotionally charged discussions about abortion among pro-choice proponents and pro-life opponents. No issue in heath care has a sharper dividing line between the two groups (supporters and opponents).

The tragic significance of the issue is that neither side will bend away from its rigid, inflexible, and arbitrary position. The perpetuation of the dispute gives assurance that abortion may forever remain as an ethical issue and will thereby unfortunately and adversely affect and disrupt quality living in everyone's desire to exist compatibly in a utopian society and achieve a perfect semicircle of life.

A simplified outline of the position held by each side of the abortion issue is in order.

PRO-LIFE POSITION

1) The fertilized egg is a person and a human being.

2) Abortion is immoral and criminal, and constitutes the murder of a human being.

3) The embryo is a separate individual with a unique genetic code from the moment of conception.

4) The fetus is a helpless unborn child with the same right to life and independence as the mother.

5) A woman's right of privacy is not in the Constitution.

6) When a woman voluntarily indulges in sexual intercourse, knowing of the chance of pregnancy and becomes pregnant, is she not responsible for the presence and life of the unborn human being she carries?

7) Does not the living human being created and carried by the pregnant woman have the right to the use of the mother's body for food and shelter until the fetus is born?

8) Does a woman not have the same responsibility to the fetus if she is raped and pregnancy is not voluntary? (The answer is not a consistent one among pro-life supporters. Some feel that rape and incest may be valid reasons for termination of the pregnancy.)

9) Does not the unborn fetus have rights, and who in society is defending those rights?

PRO-CHOICE POSITION

1) Abortion is not wrongful killing, as no malice is intended.

2) The fetus has a right to life, but the right does not outweigh a woman's prior constitutional and moral right to life, liberty, and self-determination regarding her body.

3) Prior to viability at birth, the fetus is as much a part of the mother's body as is an organ or a limb, over which she has responsibility.

4) As to the genetic code argument, is it wrong to kill a live cancer cell, which also contains the mother's genetic code?

5) Is an acorn with its unique genetic code an oak tree?

6) A fetus has no brain-wave activity in the electroencephalogram until after eight weeks as an embryo—a similar finding as in an adult who is brain dead and judged scientifically as well as legally as dead.

7) In the first twelve weeks of gestation, the tiny fetus resembles and cannot be differentiated from a pig or a rabbit at the same age by gross inspection. (Their genetic codes are strikingly similar.)

8) The fetus cannot be considered as a person before the end

of the second trimester of gestation (twenty six weeks) because it lacks sentience (feeling, sensation, and the capacity for consciousness). In fact, the fetus cannot be considered a person until well after the second trimester (at about twenty eight weeks) when it may have a functional brain, be viable, and able to live outside the womb, no longer dependent upon the mother.

9) Is not a fetus with less than minimal criteria for a quality of living better off unborn, as in anencephaly (absence of a brain) or with spina bifida? (Some who favor pro-choice acknowledge that such decisions may open the door to the dangerous concept of a slippery slope.)

10) The pro-choice position is supported by a) a woman's constitutional right of privacy, autonomy, and self-determination (Roe vs. Wade pro-choice decision of the United States Supreme Court) and b) majority of people.

11) Should a woman with a medical disorder of sufficient magnitude to cause her death if she continues with her pregnancy (as with advanced heart disease) be asked to die in order to save the fetus? Abortion may then be regarded as killing in self-defense.

12) Is it morally right to ask a woman who is the victim of incest or rape to carry a fetus to term?

13) Is not the high mortality rate in women with illegally performed abortions a sufficient incentive to have abortions performed legally by properly qualified surgeons or by an abortifacient drug with a record of a negligible or absent mortality rate?

14) There are no records of violence and homicides among pro-choice advocates as compared with some pro-life fanatics, who defeat their own cause by outrageously unacceptable criminal behavior.

15) Does it make good sense to prevent the availability of a safe and approved abortion pill (mifepristone or RU-486) and simultaneously make abortion illegal?

SETTLEMENT OF ETHICAL ISSUE

In order to eliminate the fragmented quality of living in a hopelessly deadlocked community with a hostile antagonism between pro-life advocates and pro-choice supporters, every effort to mend the intolerable situation must be sought in the interest of quality living. Since negotiation is usually the best means by which enemies can come to a peaceful settlement, as is evident in labor-management disputes, serious efforts have been made to find a middle-ground solution to resolve the stand-off and restore a community to a desirable and expected quality living:

MIDDLE GROUND SOLUTION TO ABORTION ISSUE

1) Accept the Supreme Court ruling in Roe vs. Wade, but agree to avoid abortions after the fetus is twenty four weeks of age (except to preserve the life or health of the mother).

2) Conduct open discussions without emotionalism and consider that some abortions are reasonable, whereas others are unreasonable.

3) Positions of extremists may be modified toward a middle ground from a) total restrictiveness of pro-life advocates, and b) total permissiveness of pro-choice advocates.

4) Parental notification with involvement and assumption of responsibility concerning all pregnant minor women (with strong social service participation).

5) All couples planning a family should be educated to the fact that a high correlation exists between the sexual abuse of children and the incidence of teen-age pregnancy for the reason that a sexually abused child has a diminished capacity to say "no" later in life when confronted with inappropriate sexual advances.

The relationship between a parent and child must be built on love and support. Otherwise, when a teenager becomes pregnant, she cannot rely on her fragile dependence upon her parents for love and support in times of crisis. Parents must avoid creating a dysfunctional family, or a family in crisis.

6) Parental responsibility should seriously question bringing one's own children into existence under very adverse conditions that are unfair and even cruel to the child, as for example, in a family with Huntington's chorea, Tay-Sachs disease, dire poverty, the presence of HIV in a parent, especially the mother, alcoholism, and illicit drug addiction.

7) A specified waiting period (of days) should be established in order to engage in discussion and consultation regarding a final decision concerning one's pregnancy if termination is contemplated.

8) Education and counseling in schools and clinics regarding a) sexual behavior, b) contraception, c) abortion and d) responsibilities of pregnancy, including the burdens of child-bearing and child-rearing, the financial, vocational, social, and psychological burdens of motherhood including awareness that pregnancy constitutes a form of involuntary servitude, and awareness that pregnancy violates a woman's claim to a full sexual and social equality with males.

9) Improvement of social services regarding child support, day care, and employment for the mothers.

10) Establish limitations on the uses of federal facilities and funds.

11) All persons must be taught to avoid pregnancy unless they learn to establish minimal conditions that make life worth living (criteria for quality living).

12) Encourage women with unwanted pregnancies to carry their pregnancy to term and fulfill an assured legal arrangement with an infertile couple seeking a child. There must be an iron-clad pre-arranged legal agreement for adoption of the unwanted child at birth. Such commitment, if mutually advantageous and legally binding, could have an enormously favorable influence upon the resolution of 1) the infertility problem and 2) the abortion issue.

SPECIAL CIRCUMSTANCES REGARDING
THE ABORTION ISSUE

Since Jefferson wrote about *"Life, Liberty,* and the *Pursuit of Happiness,"* many interpretations have appeared regarding Jefferson's intent upon the use of those terms. Elsewhere in the text, without engaging in the pro-life, pro-choice issue, the author has taken the personal liberty of assigning 'to Jefferson's use of the word, *life,* the broadest possible concept of meaning health care for everyone. Is there a better way of giving life to everyone than providing one with life-long health care? In sharp contrast to the author's interpretation is the definition given to Jefferson's life by a prominent member of the religious community before millions of viewers on television, by referring to the pro-life view as forbidding abortion and thereby saving a life. The author questions such view as the narrowest possible one, and wonders what Jefferson really intended. Could he possibly have been thinking only of denouncing abortion and saving the life of an unwanted fetus, or did he have the life of all people in mind?

Patients who seek an abortion for an unwanted pregnancy must locate a physician who favors abortion and is qualified and willing to perform the procedure.

The physician who opposes abortion or cannot advise or prescribe contraceptive measures or an abortifacient drug on personal religious or moral grounds:

1) Need not become involved by giving advice or by doing the requested procedure

2) Must be familiar with federal and local laws governing the matter

3) Has the duty to assure that the patient is provided with the option of receiving competent medical advice and care from a qualified physician who does not have personal religious or moral opposition to the request

4) Should not impose his personal convictions upon the patient

If the patient is a minor and requests contraceptive measures or termination of her pregnancy without the knowledge of her parents, the physician (whether or not he favors the request), may have a conflict between his ethical duty to confidentiality and a responsibility to the parents or guardian. The physician should seek legal counsel or follow his conscience.

CHAPTER 21

ORGAN TRANSPLANTATION

No act of kindness, no matter how small, is ever wasted.

— Aesop, the Lion and the Mouse, 6th Century BC

BACKGROUND

An important area of health care that encompasses both a) *altruism* in its most exalted form by the donor and b) *egoism* in its most obeisant form by the recipient is organ transplantation, a truly remarkable advance in biotechnology.

There is little doubt regarding its enormously significant impact upon quality living when a diseased organ in a patient with a limited life span is replaced with a healthy organ that gives the patient the opportunity for a full life.

As with all other subjects in health care, there is, however, the concomitant introduction of new serious ethical issues, sufficiently important to be addressed in the hope that resolution will be found in order to make the matter free of concern forever.

Organ transplantation is a relatively new modality among the many recent biotechnological innovations that have been advanced in medical therapy. The treatment of disease was revolutionized (Murray, 1954) with the successful transplantation of a kidney in Boston. Many similar transplantations followed and some were attended by problems predominantly centering about organ rejection because of histo-incompatibility.

The public was again excited in 1967 when the first successful cardiac transplantation was performed by Barnard in Capetown, South Africa.

DEARTH OF AVAILABLE DONOR ORGANS

The rapid success of organ transplantation has demonstrated the enormous need of donor organs. Although thousands of patients have been fortunate to receive a variety of organs, especially a kidney or a liver, at least 60,000 very ill patients in dire need of a donor organ eagerly await a miracle of life. Of these, 6,000 (10 percent) die annually while waiting.

It is deeply regrettable that only 5,000 to 6,000 donors make their organs available each year. Interestingly, most people are in strong favor of serving as donors, yet only about ten percent of the population actually carry donor cards.

The breakdown in percentage figures among those awaiting organs is as follows: 70 percent seek a kidney, 14 percent a liver, 8 percent a heart, 4 percent a lung, and 4 percent a pancreas or bone marrow or organ combinations. One must realize that those who are eager recipients are in great suffering and pain physically as well as emotionally. They also endure great expense in order to survive. A typical example is the patient on a renal dialysis regimen three times a week while awaiting a donor kidney, an expectation which may never come.

REASONS FOR DEARTH OF ORGANS

The lack of availability of donor organs is due to many given reasons that become obstacles to what should be a well-intentioned desire to serve mankind.

These can be grouped as follows:

    I) Personal bias
    II) Ethical issues
    III) Religious considerations
    IV) Medical reasons
    V) Inequities in procurement
    VI) Inadequate means of allocation and distribution

I) PERSONAL BIAS: a) a sense of loss of identity, b) violation of one's dignity, and c) an impaired quality of life are cited ethical reasons. One wonders how trivial these reasons seem when compared with the enormous deterioration of quality living in a recipient desperately awaiting an organ and the awareness of a lack of likelihood of its arrival. When one considers that most organ donations are offered upon one's death, the problems seem insignificant for the donor.

II) ETHICAL ISSUES: Foremost among ethical issues is an apparent lack of altruism, a desperately needed virtue if everyone is expected to share in his and her compliance with the ethical principles that govern the ideal behavior of all in society. One can expect to hear the hesitant donor ask, "Am I my brother's keeper?" There is often an absence of voluntarism demonstrated in the preparation of an advance directive. This could be based upon the failed role of an aggressive personal physician who does not succeed in translating informed consent into an agreement to serve as an organ donor.

III) RELIGIOUS CONSIDERATIONS: Opposition to mutilation of the body, anatomic dissection, autopsy, and loss of an organ are inherent in some religions. Such objections must be respected and may not be contested. They should, however, be examined closely for accuracy, as they are often unverifiable.

IV) MEDICAL REASONS are too often the causes of failure of transplantation, more with some organs than with others. The best results are with the kidney. The anticipated rate of success with renal transplantation may be as high as 95 percent. Medical reasons are as follows:

a) Tendency to *immunologic rejection* of the donor's foreign tissue because of *histo-incompatibility* and the danger of graft-versus-host disease.

b) Danger of *infection* caused by either viral or bacterial agents. A clue in suspecting an etiologic diagnosis of infection is the identification of *antibodies* in the donor's serum.

c) Ten percent are medically unsuited for a variety of reasons, e.g., living donor kidneys are better accepted than cadaveric kidneys. The age of the organ is a significant concern.

d) Another major obstacle to medical success is the *shortage of transplant centers* (approximately 400) and too few skilled surgeons.

e) There are *exceptions* to the dearth of donor organs in the frequent need for adequate supply of corneas and heart valves (which include porcine). There is reasonable compliance with the need of perhaps 50,000 such organs per year. The reason for their availability is that everyone may be a donor at death because the tissues are avascular (lacking in blood supply), thereby causing no immunologic reaction, and creating no need for anti-rejection therapy.

Conventional corneal transplantation has been noted to fail in the repair of certain diseased corneal surfaces of the eye because of a depletion of needed limbal stem cells (at margin between cornea and sclera). In a recent major advance in ophthalmology, transplantation with *bio-engineered* autologous limbal epithelial cells, taken from the normal eye of the same patient and cultured on amniotic membrane, was shown to be effective in reconstructing the damaged corneal surface.

V) INEQUITIES IN PROCUREMENT Logistical inequities in procurement are responsible for a great deficiency in the number of organs that could be otherwise available, e.g.,

a) the need for rapid retrieval of an available organ poses a problem in transportation that is not easily met, and

b) there is a need for understanding modern concepts of unconsciousness in order to determine the optimal time for retrieval. Included are such states as reversible coma, persistent coma, irreversible coma, the vegetative state, brain death, and death (see Chapter 25).

IMPROVEMENT OF INEQUITIES IN PROCUREMENT

Recommendations have been offered to improve means of procurement:

a) By raising interest in voluntary contributions of organs—An effort should be made to attract living related donors, whose organs generally produce better results than cadaveric sources.

b) By providing a financial incentive, e.g., by trading an organ for free funeral expenses

c) By promoting the concept of offering an anatomic gift via the *Uniform Anatomic Gifts Act* which is legally available in all states.

d) By completing a *document of gift* form, insertion in a will or in a driver's license, etc.—Automatic gifts of the body or an organ may be made by a close relative or legal guardian of a decedent. Hospitals are required to ask patients on admission to the hospital regarding their wish to donate an anatomic gift or organ for transplantation.

e) By a uniquely designed concept known as *paired-kidney exchange program*, an arrangement is made between *two* donor recipient pairs (four people), in which the kidney of donor A-1 is offered to ABO-compatible recipient B-2 and the kidney of donor B-

1 is offered to ABO-compatible recipient A-2, instead of A-1 donor's kidney going to the intended A-2 recipient and B-1 donor's kidney going to the intended B-2 recipient, as follows:

The program is novel and may offer the benefit of saving the lives of two recipients. It is, however, not without risks of complications:

    i) A low mortality rate of 0.03%

    ii) Pulmonary embolism of less than 2%

    iii) Transient hypertension

    iv) Transient proteinuria

    v) Psychological effects: anger on the part of the donor if the outcome of transplantation fails, especially, as is usually the case, if the donor is unrelated to the recipient. Guilt may occur on the part of the recipient over a debt that cannot be repaid to a possible stranger.

The paired-kidney exchange program presents a number of ethical issues:

    i) Danger of one withdrawal of consent (the right of any individual)

    ii) Difficulty of preserving the rights of privacy and confidentiality

    iii) Technical and logistical hazards: the need to perform major urologic surgery upon four individuals in the same hospital at the same time

    iv) The ugly appearance of commercialization

    v) The frightful threat of exploitation

    vi) The dubious matter of public acceptance

    f) Finally, other means of procurement have been suggested on the basis of some success including the halving of a donor liver so that two recipients may benefit from the transplantation.

ETHICAL ISSUES ARISING FROM INEQUITIES
IN PROCUREMENT

Ethical issues abound when one considers the obstacles and the available solutions to the problem of dearth of organs due to inequities in procurement:

1) Exclusive of religious objection or when specifically forbidden in a written directive, should not all useful organs be made available for transplantation at the death of every individual as a civic duty of benevolence in compliance with the aim of everyone to maximize altruism in an effort to achieve quality living approaching the perfect semicircle of life?

2) Should not wastage of a precious human resource be prevented?

3) Should not the doctrine of *presumed consent* be applied, meaning that consent is presumed if it is not specifically discussed and negated by the potential donor? Is such consent a form of coercion?

4) Reports of accusations and counter-denials of the *hastening* of death of dying patients (not brain dead) who possess organ donor cards and are, by chance or design, in a transplantation center. The hastening of death is presumed to be due either to the a) administration of heparin intravenously to prevent blood clotting, but adding the risk of hemorrhage and death, or b) administration of an alpha-adrenergic blocker such as regitine to increase blood flow and improve the preservation of desired organs, thereby risking a drop in blood pressure, cardiac arrhythmias, and death.

5) Concern over the possible creation of headless human clones for transplantation from one's own cloned cells. The basis for this interesting and arcane concept is the known experimental creation of a headless frog embryo in Britain by suppressing the development of the frog's head.

Advantages of this esoteric idea include a) the elimination of the threat of immunologic rejection, b) relief of the shortage of organs, and c) bypassing legal restrictions: an organism without a brain may not qualify as an embryo in most medical and legal considerations.

As expected, there are opponents of this strange concept. The greatest objection is that it represents a science fiction fantasy and raises the frightening spectre of *eugenics*. Along these lines are expressed religious and moral objections.

It is evident that inequities in procurement elicit bizarre means of solution.

6) Increasing instances are appearing of the practice of invading the vas deferens of a recently deceased male and extracting live sperm without authorization or the patient's prior approval. The intent, of course, is the use of the sperm for artificial insemination.

7) Frequent efforts are made to buy or sell organs despite the *National Organ Transplantation Act (NOTA)*, which prohibits receipt or transfer of certain designated organs, including skin, for a *valuable consideration*.

VI) INADEQUATE ALLOCATION AND DISTRIBUTION The final obstacle to be considered that causes the dearth of donor organs is the inadequacy in the allocation and distribution of the donated organs. This is an especially troublesome matter in that only about 10 percent of urgently needed organs are available in the first place. The following are factors that magnify the inadequacy of allocating and distributing donor organs properly and fairly:

a) The severity of illness of the recipient and urgency of need

b) The position of the recipient on the waiting list in fulfillment of the first come, first served principle

c) Ability of the recipient to pay the costs, including the varying extent of insurance coverage

d) The age and general health of the recipient—Elderly

patients with other organ problems would be less desirable candidates for transplantation.

e) A pre-determined opinion of the recipient's anticipated length of survival thereby estimating the degree of benefit—a difficult assessment

f) Consideration of the improvement in quality living of the recipient, i.e., where it would do the greatest good from the utilitarian standpoint

g) A disturbing consideration is allocation on the basis of the recipient's social influence or celebrity status (the so-called mystique of the wealthy or the privileged)

h) The use of the lottery, an impersonal approach in which every potential recipient has an equal chance—a form of acceptable egalitarianism

i) Finally, allocation by organized committees—Regional review boards and community organ committees responsible to an organ procurement and transplantation network that is responsible to a united network for organ sharing that is, in turn, responsible to the Department of Health and Human Services where final authority resides and where, incidentally, consideration seems to be favoring patients in so-called Status I, who are most urgently in need of an organ wherever they may be located in the country. Giving such patients the highest priority seems rational, but raises its own *ethical issues:*

i) Those in Status I often need more than one organ and are at a very high risk for survival

ii) Some insurers refuse to pay for life-saving bone marrow transplantations in certain leukemias (Ed: Yet they pay readily for numerous manipulations in chronic disorders of the back in the absence of identifiable disease.) The insurer's rationale is that the former is experimental, whereas the latter is well established.

iii) There are many instances in which organ transplantations have been successful, yet the recipients cannot afford to pay for the expensive, lifetime need of immunosuppressive treatment essential to prevent rejection of the (foreign) donor organ. Inadequate insurance coverage has resulted in failure of the transplantation because of the recipient's inability to pay for the necessary drugs (a horrifying circumstance).

TREATMENT OF END-STAGE LIVER DISEASE (ESLD)

The treatment of ESLD is liver transplantation, which has several positive or favorable aspects:

a) It is lifesaving (utilitarian)

b) It is altruistic (beneficial to fellow man)

c) It is covered by Medicare

d) It is medically approved and feasible

Liver transplantation for ESLD has *negative* or unfavorable aspects:

a) About 8,000 patients are on a waiting list with an average waiting time of six months before availability of the organ

b) It is a scarce resource relative to the need

c) The cost is high and there is generally a low ability to pay for the expense

d) There is a high rate of recidivism

e) The results are variable—some poor, some good

ALCOHOL-RELATED END-STAGE
LIVER DISEASE (ARESLD)

A unique problem in organ transplantation concerns alcohol related (AR) end-stage liver disease (ESLD). Thousands of deaths due to ESLD occur annually. About fifty percent of these are alcohol related (ARESLD).

ARESLD is a disorder of *life-style* (as is hepatitis-B infection, a sexually transmitted disease). It is generally the result of 10-20 years of heavy alcohol abuse, and is totally preventable by abstinence and by early dedicated therapeutic attention.

ETHICAL ISSUES IN ARESLD

1) There is considerable societal bias against providing liver transplantation for alcohol-related ESLD.

2) Treatment centers are inclined to set rigorous standards with a low priority for ARESLD, including a period of sustained abstinence from alcohol prior to consideration and some kind of assurance of compliance with immunosuppressive drug treatment.

3) Failure of xenotransplantation with liver and other organs in trials with the baboon and pig. (Ed: This is a major area for continued research.)

4) Should not a child dying of congenital biliary atresia, a tragedy of birth, have a life saving liver available in preference to the needs of a patient with self-induced ARESLD?

5) Does a patient with ARESLD deserve a lower priority of surgical treatment with organ transplantation than does a patient with lung cancer due to self abused cigarette smoking, or possibly even a patient with coronary artery disease who knowingly abused a harmful diet, or even a patient with type-2 diabetes mellitus with a self-abusive life style of dietary misbehavior?

Some of these comparisons may seem outrageously far-fetched, but the question concerning punishment for abusive life style must be answered as an ethical issue. Another question of great concern is whether to consider different *grades* of life style abuses and assign them priority rankings.

It is readily apparent that resolution of the dearth of organs is the solution to many of the ethical issues raised in end-stage liver disease, especially when alcohol-related.

FUTURE ORGAN TRANSPLANTATION

The dearth of organs needed for transplantation will probably continue, especially since the population will grow and people will live longer en route to their full life span, thereby creating an increasing need for donor organs.

The expectation of increase in altruistic behavior in compliance with the major ethical principles (see Capter 8) does not extend so far as to include the donation of one's organs in the interest of beneficence as expressed in the Golden Rule. If asked, most people would agree to be potential donors, although factually only few carry donor cards—an anomalous and inexplicable situation.

In recognition and acceptance of this problem, attention must be given to the application of biotechnological advances in organ transplantation in the future. These means are presently experimental, although some are already successful. They include:

A) Xeno-transplantation

B) Human Auto-transplantation

C) Human Fetal Tissue Transplantation

D) Placental and Umbilical Cord Blood Transplantation

E) Human Embryonic Stem Cell Transplantation

F) Gene Transplantation

A) XENOTRANSPLANTATION OR CROSS-SPECIES TRANS-PLANTATION OR TRANSGENIC TRANSPLANTATION

Exploring and achieving the successful use of animal organs or tissues for human *cross-species* transplantation would be an enormous step in alleviating the severe donor shortage. Research in *transgenic* technology is rapidly advancing. Historically, the pig's heart valves have been used successfully in man. The pig's heart and kidney have been successfully transplanted in the baboon.

The adrenal medulla and the substantia nigra from the *midbrain* of a normal animal have been transplanted into the brain of an animal of another species with experimentally-induced *Parkinsonism*. Results have been promising.

The next step, of course, is the *Xeno-transplantation* from animal to man. In 1984, a surgical attempt was made to transplant the heart of a baboon into an infant named Baby Fae. The case made spectacular headlines in the media. Success was short-lived, however, the baby surviving only twenty days. The surgeon was rebuked severely for his innovative boldness, but commended by some for a possible break-through in new, uncharted territory.

Consideration for the use of the pig as an organ donor for man is a logical one in that the animal may be bred easily and is plentiful. It is not commonly appreciated that the pig's physiology is quite similar to that of man.

PROCEDURE IN CROSS-SPECIES TRANSPLANTATION

The procedure in cross-species transplantation is fascinating:

a) A sow is fertilized by artificial insemination.

b) Fertilized eggs are removed surgically from the surface of the sow's ovaries.

c) They are placed on a slide and microinjected with DNA of a human gene.

d) Cleaving eggs are then implanted into a foster mother sow.

e) A litter is delivered in approximately 114 days, yielding about 20 piglets from 100 piglet gene-altered eggs.

f) Tails are snipped for genetic analysis to see if they contain the crucial human genes.

g) Only one of every twenty (5 percent) is successfully transgenic. The remaining piglets are sacrificed.

The aim of the procedure is to create transgenic organs that will trick the human immune system into accepting pig organs.

ETHICAL ISSUES IN CROSS-SPECIES TRANSPLANTATION

1) Dangers and risks come readily into view, especially the possible unleashing of deadly porcine endogenous retrovirus into

human beings. This is a possibility reminiscent of the theoretical origin of HIV infection in apes and its spread to man.

2) High cost of transgenic organs in comparison with human donor organs

3) Sky-rocketing costs of anti-rejection drugs, e.g., cyclosporine, steroids, and newer experimental drugs

4) Vigorous opposition by animal rights activists regarding the use of pigs as factories making spare parts

5) Who would be offered human and who animal organs? Should the recipient be required to give approval?

CONCLUSION

If animal kidneys become readily available, a happy feature might be the end of renal dialysis in man except as an emergency or temporary measure. The end of the dearth of all organs needed for transplantation would be in sight and the attending problems eliminated.

In order to advance the concept of xenotransplantation and solve all of its problems, there is a great need to:

1) Develop a National Advisory Committee to consider the medical, social, financial, and ethical issues.

2) Develop a National Registry of participating patients.

3) Have a public debate and societal acceptance (as is required in every ethical issue).

B) HUMAN AUTO-TRANSPLANTATION
INTRODUCTION

An ideal model for experimental study has been human *paralysis agitans* (Parkinson's disease), a degenerative disease of the central nervous system involving primarily the *substantia nigra* of the brain stem, resulting in loss of *dopamine*, the chemical neurotransmitter needed to transmit messages across nerve cells.

A brief representation of the typical clinical picture is one with a) motor changes including tremors, reduced movement and debility, and b) cognitive changes with late intellectual deterioration. The course is a progressive one, with long-term disability. Treatment consists primarily of restoring the loss of dopamine with *L-DOPA*, a helpful, but less than curative drug.

EXPERIMENTAL BACKGROUND OF HUMAN AUTO TRANSPLANTATION

In the therapy of Parkinson's disease, it is of pertinent interest that the adrenal medulla of a patient with the disease has been transplanted into his own substantia nigra in the brain. There is obvious elimination of the need for immunosuppressive treatment. On the basis of limited research in this area, the benefits have been inconsistent. The transplanted tissue often fails to survive, as a result of which the procedure was forsaken in 1990 as a disappointing venture.

C) HUMAN FETAL TISSUE TRANSPLANTATION

Aborted human fetal tissue from the substantia nigra of the midbrain was transplanted into the mid-brain of a patient with Parkinson's disease for the first time in 1990.

Surprisingly, in several experiments, benefits varied from none to marked. When helpful, a graft placed unilaterally in the brain could produce a favorable effect bilaterally, as evident in the clinical picture.

Fetal tissue, consisting of immature nerve cells, is able to grow readily and is not too likely to be rejected by the host.

ETHICAL ISSUES IN HUMAN FETAL TISSUE TRANS PLANTATION

1) The best source of the graft is not definite, although tissue from the midbrain appeared to provide a longer effect than tissue

from the adrenal medulla. Tissue from the brain also seemed to be the best source for dopamine.

2) Multiple fetuses may be necessary to provide sufficient brain tissue to satisfy the need for a single transplantation.

3) The number of implants needed are unknown because of the unknown duration of effect, which may be short because of poor graft survival.

4) Little fetal tissue is available (mainly because of the national abortion issue).

5) Fetal tissue implantation corrects the motor changes (based in the striatum).

6) Fetal tissue does not correct the late cognitive changes which are based in nondopaminic systems over a wide area of the brain.

7) Too many unanswered questions demand much fetal tissue research.

8) Selection of the best fetal tissue source in the mesencephalon of the brain is unsettled.

9) Fresh tissue may be more effective than frozen tissue.

10) The optimal site for implantation is unsettled.

11) Immunosuppressive drugs needed to control rejection are still uncertain and could be improved upon; the main drugs used currently are cyclosporine and prednisone. Others are under study.

12) Risks of infection and/or malignancy occur in ten percent of the cases.

13) Long- term effects have not been evaluated.

14) Problems with procurement, allocation, and distribution are very much in evidence (as with organ transplantation).

15) There are high costs of approximately $10,000/year.

16) There is uncertain insurance coverage.

17) Does a woman have the right of freedom of choice
    a) to dispose of her fetal tissue?
    b) to donate fetal tissue as an organ donor?
    c) to recruit an unrelated donor of fetal tissue for herself or

for a relative (compare the current practice of recruiting kidneys or bone marrow from unrelated donors).

18) Should particular interest in fetal tissue justify the selection or prolongation of the time for abortion?

19) Would fetal tissue research encourage abortions?

20) Should the Federal Government fund fetal tissue research which is opposed by right-to-life groups as immoral and sinful?

21) Fetal tissue transplantation research was banned during the Reagan and Bush administrations because such research would encourage abortions. The ban was repealed by the Clinton administration in 1993 in full support by our National Institutes of Health (NIH) for the valuable advances in health offered by fetal tissue research.

22) On a local level, several states ban, whereas other states support, the experimental usage of aborted fetuses.

23) Opponents of the ban, such as the NIH, regard the ban as vague, irrational, and in violation of the right of privacy and of sound health care.

24) Does any factor in the procurement process raise the spectre of commercialization?

a) As in a fetal tissue retrieval fee by for-profit organizations.

b) As in payment of abortion expenses to obtain tissue for transplantation. (The sale of fetal tissue and organs was banned by the National Organ Transplantation Act of 1984, amended in 1988.)

25) Does the procurement process exploit the reproductive capacity of women, or denigrate human dignity?

FUTURE AREAS OF RESEARCH IN HUMAN FETAL TISSUE TRANSPLANTATION

Include the following disorders:

1) Alzheimer's disease

2) Huntington's chorea (neural tissue appears between the 6th and 11th weeks of the embryo's development)

3) Type 1 diabetes mellitus (pancreatic tissue develops between the 14th and 16th weeks of the embryo's growth)

4) Disorders of the blood and immune system (use of the fetal thymus gland)

5) Chronic pain disorders by fetal adrenal gland implantation (pain stimulates the release of enkephalins—endogenous peptides with opioid action—which compare favorably with morphine in efficacy)—They have no side effects and may be stored in the frozen state.

In order to seek a scientific explanation, it has been suggested that the benefits of acupuncture may be due to this phenomenon, resulting from pricking of the skin.

D) PLACENTAL AND UMBILICAL CORD BLOOD TRANS-PLANTATION offers the use of allogeneic (histocompatibly unrelated) hematopoietic stem cells and progenitor cells for reconstitution of bone marrow in patients who have no related histocompatible bone marrow donors. Its applications may be in genetic diseases of: 1) the lymphoid system, e.g., lymphoma; 2) the hematopoietic system, e.g., beta thalassemia, sickle cell anemia, hemoglobinopathies, and leukemias.

ADVANTAGES include 1) ease of procurement; 2) absence of risk to donor; 3) small likelihood of transmitting infection, e.g., cytomegalovirus, Epstein-Barr virus; 4) low risk of acute and chronic graft vs. host disease; 5) easily and rapidly available for shipment to transplantation centers. Problematic, however, are loss of privacy and identity, and sparsity of stem cells in any sample.

CONCLUSION

The advantages very much support continued experimental research in placental and umbilibal cord blood transplantation, particularly since early studies are favorable.

E) HUMAN EMBRYONIC STEM CELLS FOR TRANSPLANTATION

A few days after fertilization, *primitive, undifferentiated cells known as stem cells* develop. After the first eight weeks as an embryo, they become more mature fetal tissue, and eventually become the differentiated tissues of organs in the mature fetus. The undifferentiated cells are the same stem cells present normally in adult *bone marrow* and can be useful in transplantation in appropriate disorders of the hematopoietic system. Preliminary studies offer an optimistic view with potential benefits. Adult autologous stem cells do not pose an ethical issue in research.

ETHICAL ISSUES REGARDING HUMAN EMBRYONIC STEM CELL RESEARCH

a) Lack of universal agreement to use as a valuable source of stem cells: i) aborted fetuses, and ii) unused embryos discarded at in vitro fertilization clinics.

b) Legal prohibition and some religious opposition to embryonic research, despite the fact that our National Institutes of Health has approved embryonic stem cell research with stringent oversight, convinced that research will yield valuable contributions to better health and a better quality of living.

c) Resolution of these and other important questions in the interest of better health requires much needed public debate.

d) The major ethical issue concerning fetal stem cell research is based upon the legally forbidden availability of aborted fetal tissue. The issue is not likely to be resolved until there is settlement of the pro-life, pro-choice abortion issue.

FACTORS FAVORING AVAILABILITY OF HUMAN EMBRYONIC STEM CELLS FOR RESEARCH

1) Despite the ban on federal funding for human embryo research including stem cell research, private industry is permitted to engage in stem cell research. Their findings are not published, hence not available to the scientific community.

2) Stem cells are not an embryo and do not have the capacity to be born.

3) Stem cells are primitive cells and are too rudimentary to be assigned moral standing. According to the scientific community, an embryo is not a human being or a person at least until sentient.

4) Banning research is not supported by our Constitution, according to legal scholars.

5) Opponents do not offer to take any responsibility for their denial of benefits to those whose health could be improved.

FACTORS OPPOSING AVAILABILITY OF HUMAN EMBRYONIC STEM CELLS FOR RESEARCH

1) Stem cells are a part of a fertilized egg and therefore constitute a person or human being, according to a restricted religious view.

2) It is immoral to create embryos and then destroy them, whether by abortion or by discard at in vitro fertilization clinics.

3) The threat of misuse by cloning procedure is immoral.

4) It is grossly and offensively immoral to time abortions in order to retrieve tissue at various stages of their development and obtain tissue at specially designated times of maturity.

5) The ban on funding is proper, moral, and must be permanent.

6) Congress opposes human embryo research.

CHAPTER 22

GENE TRANSPLANTATION (GENE THERAPY)

The fault, dear Brutus, is not in our stars, but in ourselves.

— Cassius, in Shakespeare's Julius Caesar

GENE TRANSPLANTATION OR GENE THERAPY may be categorized under the general consideration of *genetic engineering*. It is probably the most intriguing and exciting exploration into transplantation advancement as a future biotechnological aim to improve man's quality living on a societal level.

An introductory background will first be addressed with brief references to molecular genetics, the human genome project, examples of gene disorders, and gene testing or screening before gene transplantation and its ethical issues are discussed.

As a basic reminder to the reader, the nucleus of every human cell has 46 chromosomes: 22-paired (44) *autosomal* (non-sexual) and two unpaired *sex-linked* chromosomes. Women have two X chromosomes and men have one X and one Y chromosome, for a total of 23 pairs of chromosomes in the nucleus of every cell.Among the 46 chromosomes are less than 100,000 genes, which are a) the chemical carriers of heredity and b) the directors of cell function.

In the 1950's, the research of several scientists led to the remarkable identification of *deoxyribonucleic acid (DNA)* as a *double helix* (Watson and Crick)—a molecular sequence of tightly coiled strands of DNA in each of the 23 pairs of chromosomes whose genes carry all inherited traits in every living cell. The DNA is microscopic in size, although it can be visualized in crystallized form by X-ray (Wilkins).

In the 1960's, the *genetic code* was broken and the DNA was shown to consist of millions of DNA base pairs of various combinations of copies of four protein units or bases: adenine (A) and guanine (G) (both are purines), cytosine (c) and thymine (T) (both are pyrimidines); thymine is 5-methyluracil. Each copy is attached to a sugar (deoxyribose) and a phosphate group strung together tightly coiled in a linear sequence in pairs. The molecules of DNA are arranged in a sequence of nucleotide bases (adenine pairing with thymine, and guanine with cytosine) that determine the sequence of their *amino acids*, which are the basic structural units of all proteins essential for all body functions. Every human being has about 3.1 billion base pairs in each cell, which together comprise a *genome*, unique for each person.

Genetic information encoded in the DNA of the chromosomes is transcribed into RNA (*ribonucleic acid*, or messenger RNA)—a nucleic acid in all living cells. The single-stranded RNA consists of adenine and guanine (both purines), cytosine and uracil (both pyrimidines), ribose (a sugar) and a phosphate. Whereas the DNA remains in the nucleus of every cell, the transcribed messenger

RNA leaves the cell nucleus and enters the cytoplasm to transfer information for making protein-forming systems or amino acids. In this manner, the genes regulate every life process.

Although every cell in the body contains the entire DNA code for making and maintaining a human being, many of the genes are not turned on (activated) or copied into RNA once embryonic development is complete. Various other genes are turned on or off, or not at all, according to the tissues they are in and their role in the body physiology.

In the 1970's, Sanger constructed the complete genetic code of a microorganism. Human genes were then successfully spliced into bacteria, effecting for the first time an important step in therapy. Such is the case, for example, with the modern production of insulin for the treatment of Type 1 diabetes mellitus.

Techniques were also created to clone multiple copies of specific DNA fragments. A genetic linkage map of 46 chromosomes could then be constructed.

The location was planned for the less than 100,000 genes responsible for disease by their mutations. The concept of the human *genome* project was thereby born.

In the 1980's, the first *transgenic* animal was created by insertion of a viral gene into the DNA of a mouse. Discovery was also made of the polymerase chain reaction, a new method of sequencing DNA. A remarkable advance in fingerprinting was created by the identification of individuals with bits of their DNA.

In the 1990's, two outstanding events excited the public:
1) The first mammal, a sheep named Dolly, was cloned from an adult cell. Since then, a raging battle has been on-going

regarding the ethical concerns over human cloning (see cloning later in this chapter).

2) *The Human Genome Project* was created by the National Institute of Health together with the Department of Energy. Its aim was to map and identify the codes of all genes, and to establish a deciphered blueprint of heredity and a complete set of all hereditary factors in every person.

In the early 2000's, completion of the human genome project was anticipated, consisting of the *mapping* of all of the 50,000-plus human genes among the 46 chromosomes in every human cell.

The drive toward accomplishing the Human Genome Project is primarily located at the National Center for Human Genome Research, but is also pursued, like the western gold rush of the nineteenth century, at a number of private research laboratories, all eager to be the first at the goal line.

On July 26, 2000, an important milestone was reached. Announced jointly by representatives of 1) Celera Genomics, 2) The National Center for Human Genome Research, and 3) The Department of Energy. As a result of a cooperative effort between industry and government, at least 97 percent of the first assembly of human genome sequencing involving 3.1 billion letters of the DNA code had finally been completed. A working draft of the human genome project then became available, a truly revolutionary advance in human genomics. As planned, the goal of deciphering the complete sequence of DNA nucleotides in all chromosomes—autosomal and sex—was finally in sight.

For some time, genomic sequencing already had been successfully accomplished in a number of species other than man, revealing surprising similarities. For example, the genes of the fruit fly, a model organism used in research, encode proteins closely resembling those of man. In the mouse, more than 90 percent of the proteins are similar to human proteins. (As stated elsewhere in the text, the chromosomal pattern of the chimpanzee is almost identical with that of human beings.)

It is not surprising that all normal human beings are *identical* insofar as their chromosomal structure is concerned, except for male and female sex distinction. Each human being, however, is uniquely *different* from every other one insofar as the genetic make-up is concerned. Although more than 99 percent of the genes are similar in all people, they differ from each other in less than one percent of the genes. The *uniqueness* of the genome in every person is due to 1) the fact that every person inherits one copy of the genome of each parent, and 2) the sequences of the DNA bases present in all genes vary from person to person.

With the accomplishment of the genome, the diagnosis and treatment of disease will be revolutionized. Thousands of mutated genes, which can be looked upon as the cause of disease, will be searching for a disease, which is currently without a known cause. This situation is the reverse of the current state of knowledge regarding disease, in which known diseases without a cause are searching among the mutations for the cause.

The imminent arrival of the completed genome at the brink of clinical application and the identity of all inherited diseases is not yet just around the corner. The next step in genomics will be the need to catalogue and analyze every protein, a process which may be more important in gene therapy than the genome itself. Therapy may be directed primarily toward the proteins.

MUTATION OF GENES

If Darwin, in his Origin of Species and The Descent of Man, had the anachronistic awareness of the modern scientific knowledge of genetic mutation one hundred and fifty years ago, he surely would have enjoyed less opposition and greater confidence in his magnificent concept of evolution, which he based upon natural selection and survival of the fittest.

A key factor in disease is genetic mutation—an abnormal change in the normal pattern of a gene. Genes may undergo two types of mutation: 1) inherited, and 2) acquired.

THE INHERITED TYPE OF GENETIC MUTATION originates with one or both parents, is present in all body cells, and can be passed on to their offspring. It actually accounts for a relatively small percentage of diseases due to genetic mutation.

THE ACQUIRED TYPE OF GENETIC MUTATION arises during the process of *cell division*. It is not inherited, and accounts for the *large* percentage of diseases due to genetic mutation.

Inherited diseases may be caused by a minor mutation in the DNA of a single gene or a major mutation of multiple genes.

A better understanding of gene mutations may be appreciated by a brief discussion of single gene disorders. In an *autosomal dominant* disorder, one copy of a defective gene, known as an *allele*, is present on one autosomal (non-sex) chromosome inherited from one parent. Examples include polycystic kidney disease and Huntington's chorea.

In an *autosomal recessive* disorder, one copy of a defective gene is present on an autosomal (non-sex) chromosome inherited from each parent, resulting in two abnormal genes (alleles). Examples include cystic fibrosis, phenylketonuria (PKU). and Tay-Sachs disease.

In certain *X-linked dominant or recessive* diseases, the defective gene (mutant allele) is present on an X-chromosome in one or both parents respectively. Males are more often affected than females.

Examples include the orofacial syndrome and Xg blood groups.

In certain X-linked recessive diseases, only males are affected. Included are Duchenne's muscular dystrophy, ocular albinism, and hemophilia-A.

GENETIC TESTING OR SCREENING

We now come to the matter of genetic testing or screening. There are currently at least 800 available genetic tests on the market and the number is rapidly increasing. Such procedures may be procured now and even more extensively with the completion of the Human Genome Project, at which time information can be obtained from the DNA of all genes. As a result, a total diagnostic picture can be secured by testing for all genetic mutations prior to the development of symptoms and the manifestations of disease. One is immediately struck by the numerous ethical issues that may arise (vide infra).

FACTORS IN SUPPORT OF GENETIC TESTING

1) Where the family history is strong, i.e., disease is present in at least two close relatives, genetic testing is appropriate.

2) Vigorous monitoring will be encouraged and deemed valuable, e.g., by colonoscopy for colon cancer and mammography for breast cancer.

3) Suggestive preventive treatment may be considered, e.g., mastectomy for positive testing for breast cancer.

4) A suspected diagnosis may be confirmed.

5) Planning long-term care is encouraged.

6) A person with the genetic mutation of colon cancer has an 80 percent risk of developing the disease and some added risk of developing breast cancer as well as ovarian cancer.

7) A person with any of four specific genetic mutations of the apolipoprotein-E gene has a statistically high risk for developing Alzheimer's disease, a common cause of dementia and death.

8) A woman with a positive BRCA 1 or BRCA 2 genetic mutation has a 50-80 percent risk of breast cancer and a 15-40 percent risk of ovarian cancer.

FACTORS IN OPPOSITION TO GENETIC TESTING

There are a number of factors tending to oppose genetic testing:

1) The interpretation of the results of testing are highly complex as far as the reference to statistical probability versus certainty is concerned. This matter is reflected in numerous examples of unsuccessful attempts to use results of DNA testing in order to a) establish or deny paternity in domestic disputes or b) claim guilt or innocence in criminal trials. As stated early in the text, the law is cautious and often slow in adjudicating unresolved issues arising in newly innovated biotechnological advances.

2) Predictive testing is available to identify only a small percentage (about five percent) of the roughly 4000 diseases caused by an inherited gene mutation: ten percent of colon cancers, five percent of breast cancers, forty percent of ovarian cancers, and five percent of patients with Alzheimer's disease. In other words, ninety percent of colon cancers, ninety-five percent of breast cancers, sixty percent of ovarian cancers, and ninety-five percent of patients with Alzheimer's disease may not yield positive results for inherited mutations. It is expected that these figures will change rapidly with advances in genetic screening technology.

3) Skilled counseling must be available and utilized for pretesting and post-testing procedures.

4) The cost of testing is high.

5) Negative test results do not eliminate risk.

6) Positive test results do not indicate that disease is inevitable.

7) Insurance coverage may be poor or absent.

8) A threat to a person's right to privacy is a real concern.

There is more than ample evidence of discrimination as well as violations of privacy by employers and insurers to warrant the need of urgent federal legislation to protect patients against criminal and uncivil acts. There is no moral justification for an employee to lose his job or be denied health insurance because a genetic defect revealed by screening indicates the employee has some chance for disease. The information should be a part of his confidential medical record (or possibly not in the record at all).

SCREENING PRIOR TO PREGNANCY

Planning is a judicious consideration in young adults who are offspring of members of a family affected by the heritable diseases previously outlined.

Deliberation and resolve are essential in the consideration of pregnancy as well as screening. Expert genetic counseling should be sought for consultation.

GENETIC DISEASE SCREENING DURING PREGNANCY

Many women, particularly those with family histories of genetic disorders, and especially somewhat older pregnant women, are aware of serious diseases that they and / or their mate can cause via transmission of appropriate mutated genes to their offspring:

1) Down's syndrome, determined by amniocentesis or by chorionic villus sampling.

2) Neural tube defects, learned by testing the maternal blood for alpha-fetoprotein.

3) Testing for carrier states of heterozygous traits, e.g., Tay-Sachs disease, thalassemia major, and sickle cell anemia.

4) Late onset diseases such as hemochromatosis, Huntington's disease, and polycystic kidney disease.

SCREENING IN THE NEONATAL PERIOD

Screening may be performed for the following:

1) Treatable diseases causing mental retardation:

    a) Phenylketonuria (PKU) occurs in one in 12,000 pregnancies. Treatment consisting of a protein-poor diet, which restricts the intake of phenylalanine, is effective.

b) Hypothyroidism (cretinism) occurs in one in 7000 pregnancies. Treatment with thyroid hormone is effective.

2) Several non-treatable diseases such as sickle cell anemia, cystic fibrosis, and Duchenne's muscular dystrophy.

SCREENING FOR HERITABLE FORMS OF BREAST CANCER

Positive results in screening for heritable forms of breast cancer occur in roughly five to ten percent of examinations.

PROCEDURE

In testing for breast cancer, genetic material (DNA) is extracted from the patient's blood and examined for BRCA genes for a correct or a mutated version. Either or both of two genes, BRCA 1 *and* BRCA 2, may be involved. Two copies of each gene are present normally for cell growth and cell division.

The disease occurs ten times more frequently in Ashkenazi Jews of Eastern European origin than elsewhere in the population.

Whereas it is estimated that as many as fifty percent of the genes may be active in a variety of cancers, about five percent occur in breast cancer alone. This information offers a clue to future cancer therapy.

APPROACHES TO BE CONSIDERED IF TESTING RESULTS ARE POSITIVE

1) Close surveillance: frequent breast examinations and mammography regularly after age twenty-five years

2) Prophylactic mastectomy. Removal of normal breasts is a challenging concept, but may be a potentially rewarding one.

3) Maintaining a high quality life style: tobacco and alcohol restriction; control of blood pressure, weight and saturated fat in

diet; and a regular exercise program.

4) Testing all close relatives: fifty percent are at increased risk for cancer.

5) Genetic counseling

6) Checking with insurance company, which often covers a screening procedure. The problem of disclosure, possible loss of privacy, and discrimination are serious risks.

GENOTYPE SCREENING IN ALZHEIMER'S DISEASE

The DNA of the blood or saliva may be analyzed for the *apolipoprotein E gene,* two of which are present in every person normally in forms named *apolipoprotein 2, 3, or 4.* The presence of two copies of apolipoprotein 4 are associated with an increased risk for Alzheimer's disease. The overall results are inconclusive at present, however, but active, on-going research will certainly clarify any doubts regarding the subject.

ETHICAL ISSUES IN GENETIC SCREENING

The ethical issues in genetic screening may be grouped in the following classes:

1) Confidentiality and legality Issues

2) Significance issues

3) Technical issues

4) Psychological issues

5) Financial issues

1) CONFIDENTIALITY AND LEGALITY ISSUES:

a) Does the patient's physician have the legal or moral duty to disclose positive predictive results to family members, to insurers, to employers, or to anyone paying for the service?

b) What constitutes adequate informed consent for testing and for post-testing counseling?

c) Should a positive test result be kept out of the medical record to assure confidentiality and avoid discriminatory activities by employers and insurers?

d) Can a doctor be liable for not recommending the test in an appropriate situation?

e) Regulations of genetic testing by state and federal law are in progress to prohibit insurers and employers: i) from gaining access to genetic testing results without written permission by the patient; ii) from retaliation if the patient refuses to give permission; iii) from discriminatory actions upon learning about a genetic testing abnormality; iv) from compelling the patient to take specified testing; v) from searching for the identification of applicants for testing; vi) from misuse of positive testing results in hiring practices and in seeking or obtaining insurance; vii) from denying coverage for the cost of testing and for disability based upon the use of the testing procedure as a pre-existing condition.

f) Federal actions have been taken by a Presidential Commission for Study of Ethical Problems in Biomedical Research, including the legality of human cloning research (see later in chapter).

An extreme example of violation of one's privacy is the ability of industry to discover a genetic mutation, obtain a patent, and legally own all rights to that mutated gene in everyone. You may then have a specific, mutated gene in your genome that does not belong to you. That is really so.

Laws protecting the consumer are urgently needed.

2) SIGNIFICANCE ISSUES

What do testing results actually signify? Does predisposed mean predestined? How often does a genetic mutation result in serious disease? Testing positive for a genetic mutation should not be confused with inevitability of the disease. This fact argues against routine genetic testing.

3) TECHNICAL ISSUES

a) The general lack of 100 percent accuracy in the form of false positives and false negatives may have adverse consequences.

b) There is need for caution in the interpretation of results, either positive or negative.

c) During pregnancy, there is often a decision to determine the sex of the fetus (by amniocentesis or chorionic villus sampling). Suppose a genetic abnormality is found?

d) Should carriers of a dominant disease avoid marriage?

e) Should two carriers of the same recessive disease: avoid marrying each other, risk pregnancy, risk in vitro fertilization and artificial insemination, terminate the pregnancy if the fetus has inherited the disease, consider the ultimate benefits of screening (in an altruistic frame of mind) in order possibly to eliminate sickle cell anemia, thalassemia major, Tay-sachs disease, cystic fibrosis?

4) PSYCHOLOGICAL ISSUES

a) A stigmatization factor may be the effect of learning one is a carrier of an autosomal disease or a sex-linked disease.

b) A reactive mental depression may have serious consequences.

c) A feeling of futility in acquiring information for which no therapy exists.

d) Burdening expenditure of time, effort and expense in pre-testing and post-testing counseling and planning regarding one's future, career, child bearing concerns, near end-of-life decisions, et al.

e) Danger of arousing fanatical concepts of eugenics and that of a masterrace (in the Hitler sense).

5) FINANCIAL ISSUES

The high cost of testing ($600) and other expenses, including counseling and legal fees may be justified on the basis of the answer to the key question: are the benefits worth the cost?

CONVENTIONAL WISDOM REGARDING GENETIC SCREENING

1) It is inappropriate for a physician

    a) to impose his personal views on a patient,

    b) to be paternalistic or maternalistic,

    c) to dispense information indiscriminately (on the basis of the patient's right to know),

d) to withhold information and practice a physician's therapeutic privilege on the basis of the patient's best interest, or of not harming the patient.

2) It is often forgotten that some patients actually do not wish to be informed of their risk status.

GENE THERAPY

Not long ago, the concept of gene therapy was a vague and distant future consideration, likened to the planning of the first space ship to the moon—unbelievable and imaginative, but presumably technologically attainable.

The key to the future of gene therapy lies with the human *proteins*, against which new therapy will be directed. On the ready alert in this regard is the pharmaceutical industry, eagerly awaiting the manufacture of treatments tailored to specific gene proteins in a process probably called *pharmacogenomics*

BACKGROUND OF GENE THERAPY

The reader is reminded that the nucleus of each cell in the human body carries an identical set of less than one hundred thousand genes located among the 46 chromosomes in each cell. Every cell copies only selected genes into individual molecules of messenger RNA from which specific proteins derived from DNA are constructed to perform specific functions.

PATH-BREAKING GENE TRANSFER EXPERIMENT AS A PRELUDE TO GENE THERAPY

In a path-breaking gene transfer experiment (Mulligan, 1979), a monkey was infected with a benign virus. Infected cells were removed from the monkey. A rabbit gene for hemoglobin was spliced into the monkey cells infected with the viruses. The monkey cells now made hemoglobin protein, and not viruses. The new cells were implanted into the monkey's kidney. The kidney cells began to make hemoglobin.

This astounding work readily offered potential therapy in common hemoglobin-related diseases with missing or broken genes pertaining to hemoglobin, e.g., sickle cell anemia, thalassemia, and hemophilia.

FOLLOW-UP TECHNIQUE OF GENE THERAPY:

1) Cells with a damaged gene are removed by the research geneticist from selected tissue in a patient with a specific disease.

2) The cells are exposed to gene transfer vectors in the laboratory.

3) The vectors with genetically corrected cells are introduced (in vivo) into tissues of the patient needing treatment.

4) Any missing, broken, or mutated gene is replaced with the virus (vector) carrying the normal gene. The vectors must be able to serve as safe and efficient gene delivery vehicles.

Tamed viruses are ideal as vectors for transfer of beneficial genes to cells. They presumably and hopefully do not multiply, cause disease, or destroy cells they infect. In fact, prevention of the hazards must be assured.

Any drawbacks held by viral agents of gene delivery may be overcome by new non-viral systems, such as lipoplexes, naked DNA, polyplexes, et al.

CURRENT APPLICATION OF GENE THERAPY:

An outstanding example of the successful and forward-looking application of gene therapy is in *cystic fibrosis*, among the most common hereditary diseases in the United States. It affects over 30,000 children, and is a splendid model for gene therapy. The aim, simply stated, is to replace the defective genes in the lung with normal genes by the following technical *procedure in gene transfer*: Normal genes from the lung are inserted into the common cold virus, which is then introduced into the patient's nose. The virus then spreads the new (normal) genetic material throughout the lungs, thereby replacing defective genes with normal genes.

SOMATIC VERSUS GERM CELL LINES IN GENE TRANSPLANTATION:

The transplantation of genes may be conducted 1) with somatic (non-sex) cell lines, the safety of which has already been established in human beings or 2) with germ (sexual) cell lines (XX: female; XY: male), the safety of which has not yet been established.

The safety and efficacy in the use of *animal* models for germ cell transplantation has already been established. The involvement of human beings, however, needs much research, including public discussion regarding the matter of human cloning.

In order to satisfy the predominant ethical issues revolving about transplantation of genetically engineered sex cells, a number of requirements have been recommended including: 1) that all proposals have prior public consideration and 2) needless to say, that all interventions have the informed consent of the persons for transplantation.

FUTURE APPLICATION OF GENE TRANSPLANTATION:

Diseases that would be most desirable as targets for gene transplantation are the neurological disorders and malignancies.

Among the most common neurological disorders that would benefit from successful transplantation are Alzheimer's disease, amyotrophic lateral sclerosis, and Parkinson's disease. The insertion of normal genes into brain cells of patients may hopefully induce slowing of damage due to the disease. Other considerations include the replacement of lost cells in damaged tissue by transplanting neurons or by delivering growth factors. In the case of tumors, normal genes could be inserted in order to arrest growth of the neoplasm.

DANGERS IN GENE TRANSPLANTATION

There are unpredictable and unprecedented dangers in gene transplantation. The frightening concept of *'playing God in a cell'* sums up the issue in a few colorful words. Some *risk factors* include the following:

1) Malfunction: the promotion of activity in the wrong cells is a terrifying thought.

2) Uncontrolled growth can be imagined.

3) The development of cancer in benign tissue could be a possibility.

4) Overwhelming viral infection with increase in pathogenicity is a conceivable hazard.

5) Alterations in the germ-line may affect future generations.

6) Alterations in somatic cells die with the patient. An exception is that viral vectors may infect germ cells by a mechanism called *viral escape.*

7) The unsettling spectre of eugenics and the design of a master race are the most unnerving dangers.

The conceivable benefits of genetic transplantation are so enormous that the discomforting issues must be addressed individually and overcome one by one until all are safely harnessed and under complete control. Not until then can gene transplantation be envisioned and fully accepted as a future therapeutic modality in the drive toward the highest quality of living for all in society.

THERAPY WITH HUMAN FETAL TISSUE AND EMBRYONIC STEM CELLS, like gene transplantation, has far-reaching potential qualities as curative of diseases currently regarded to be incurable. The National Institutes of Health and other prestigious scientific institutions have expressed their favor in strong terms in the pursuit of research in these uncharted areas of health care. They recognize the need for the establishment of criteria addressing limited research opportunity with strict monitoring.

As expected, there is some very strong opposition in society, particularly by certain religious elements, to even think about possible research with human fetal tissue and human embryonic stem cells.

The subject matter, as a potential in the cure of disease, is too vast and too important to be cast aside without the benefit of public discussion and particularly with Congressional hearings. A governmental approach to the possible resolution of the ethical issues would be welcome and most essential.

The fundamental ethical considerations are 1) whether or not a fertilized egg is a human being (a religious, not a scientific consideration), and 2) whether or not abortion would be encouraged by approval of human fetal tissue and embryonic stem cell research.

EUGENICS

Some explanation must be given to the subject of eugenics, which would appear superficially to be a beneficial concept. Altruistically, eugenics pertains to the study and control of influences that improve hereditary characteristics in the human race, an obviously highly desirable consideration.

In its *negative* form, eugenics would be defined in terms of prevention of mating of individuals possessing inferior or undesirable traits. In its *positive* form, it would encourage the promotion of the optimal mating of individuals possessing superior or desirable traits.

What comes to mind is the frightening concept of the master race conceived by a fanatic with numerous followers in Nazi Germany in the 1930's and 1940's. To a lesser degree, but no less frightening, are sterilization programs conducted in recent years in Sweden (1935-1976) involving 60,000 people, in Finland (1935-

1970) upon 11,000 people, and in France upon 15,000 women. The *ethical issues* are obvious and concern *violations* of:

1) The *sanctity of life ethic*

2) The ethical *principles*

3) The basic rights of *informed consent*, privacy, autonomy, and self-determination

4) Benevolence and the *Golden Rule*

5) The *primum non nocere* principle expressed in the physician's Hippocratic Oath.

PUBLIC REACTION TO EUGENICS

Public reaction to large scale eugenics is very strong and hostile in its regard that the concept is the ultimate in *fanaticism*, barbarism, and man's inhumanity to man; that it would inevitably lead to a *slippery slope* involving more and more people with fewer and lesser undesirable traits; that it arouses a demand for governmental apology and compensation; and it should be banned forever.

CLONING (SOMATIC CELL NUCLEAR TRANSFER)

The subject of gene transplantation is not complete without some consideration regarding the recent innovation of cloning and its place in the advancement of health care and improvement of quality living in society. (Never mind that it represents a scientific innovation beyond our capacity to comprehend it fully.)

DEFINITION

Technically known as *somatic cell nuclear transfer*, cloning is a branch of *transgenics*. Scientifically, it is the *asexual* production of progeny from a single cell of an individual animal or human being.

HISTORICAL BACKGROUND:

Cloning has been achieved successfully with little public notice by use of mice, frogs, and monkeys from embryonic cells of the animals as donors. Not until 1997 has there been a scientific explosion as great as the cloning of a female sheep named Dolly at the Roslyn Institute in Scotland. Little notice had been given to their prior failures in 277 unsuccessful similar attempts at cloning.

The procedure in cloning Dolly is presented in the following algorithm on the next page:

CLONING OF DOLLY

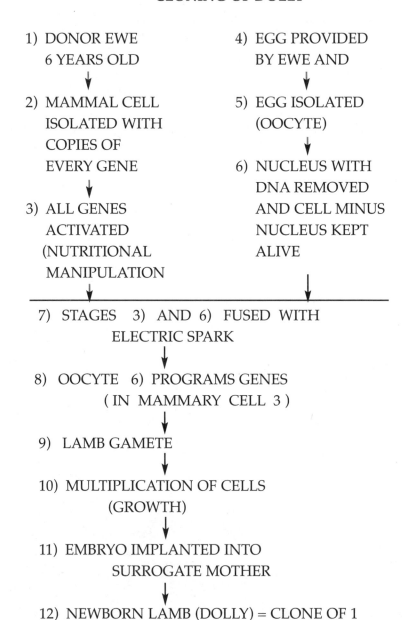

1) DONOR EWE
   6 YEARS OLD

2) MAMMAL CELL
   ISOLATED WITH
   COPIES OF
   EVERY GENE

3) ALL GENES
   ACTIVATED
   (NUTRITIONAL
   MANIPULATION

4) EGG PROVIDED
   BY EWE AND

5) EGG ISOLATED
   (OOCYTE)

6) NUCLEUS WITH
   DNA REMOVED
   AND CELL MINUS
   NUCLEUS KEPT
   ALIVE

7) STAGES 3) AND 6) FUSED WITH
            ELECTRIC SPARK

8) OOCYTE 6) PROGRAMS GENES
         (IN MAMMARY CELL 3)

9) LAMB GAMETE

10) MULTIPLICATION OF CELLS
    (GROWTH)

11) EMBRYO IMPLANTED INTO
            SURROGATE MOTHER

12) NEWBORN LAMB (DOLLY) = CLONE OF 1

PUBLIC REACTION TO HUMAN CLONING FOLLOWING
THE CLONING OF DOLLY

Cloning is generally regarded by the public as 1) an offensive idea for human beings and 2) should be *banned* forever. The scientific community, however, especially the National Institutes of Health, gave its full support to human cloning and outlined the valuable advantages of cloning research. They pointed to its particular value in advancing our knowledge of 1) cell regulation, 2) disease therapy 3) programming human cells to treat disease, 4) generating compatible skin cells and bone marrow to avoid rejection in grafting, and 5) generating nerve cells in patients with incurable neurologic disorders, just to cite a few examples of the value of cloning research.

The Clinton administration promptly placed a ban on federal funding and a moratorium on cloning research, but appointed a National Bioethics Advisory Committee to review the subject and submit a report with its recommendations.

The scientific community accepted the Clinton administration's ban on cloning research, but offered a broadly worded recommendation that would permit basic and applied research with strict guidelines, regulations, and carefully considered limitations. Research scientists remind us that there was vociferous opposition to in vitro fertilization when it was first introduced, only to accept and utilize the technique subsequently as highly valuable in resolving female infertility.

ETHICAL ISSUES IN CLONING

1) "Playing God" by genetic manipulation
2) The terrifying threat of eugenics
3) Will Dolly age like a normal newborn lamb, or will she be old like the six year old lamb from which she was cloned? If old, then at birth she may have aging related genetic mutations and a possible predisposition to cancer and other age related diseases.

MEDICAL ISSUES OF CLONING
High risk of genetic and developmental abnormalities.

TRANSGENICS
Transgenics is the science of crossing genes from an animal of one species to an animal of a different species, one of which may be human. The sources of genes for crossing include 1) tissues, 2) serum proteins (albumin or fibrinogen fractions), and 3) vaccines. The techniques utilized in transgenics include 1) microinjection and 2) cloning.

TECHNIQUE OF MICROINJECTION:
Eggs are harvested from ovaries of cows marked for slaughter. The eggs are fertilized with bull sperm, allowed to divide and become an embryo. Each embryo is injected with the DNA of human genes. Only a small number of embryos take up the DNA. All embryos are implanted in surrogate mothers.

The procedure is laborious and costly. Certain facts are unknown until after birth, including the newborn's sex and which took up the human DNA.

TECHNIQUE OF CLONING
Female fetal cow cells are enucleated and incubated with human genetic DNA from serum albumin and are made antibiotic resistant. An electric current opens cell membranes and admits human DNA. The cells are placed in a Petri dish containing an antibiotic. Only cells that took up the antibiotic resistant human DNA survive. The injected nuclei fuse with the surviving egg cell. The eggs are implanted in a surrogate mother cow, whose resulting calves are the clones of the original fetus.

REGULATION OF HUMAN CLONING AND
ITS RESTRICTION TO MEDICAL RESEARCH

SUPPORTIVE FACTORS

1) The success of somatic cell nuclear transfer in a wide range of animal species bodes well for successful cloning of human embryos and the production of viable human embryonic cell lines.

2) Immunologic histocompatibility and elimination of immuno-suppressive therapy may be expected.

3) Innumerable medical benefits may be anticipated. Their denial is a devaluation of human life.

4) To those who believe that an embryo is not a human being until sentient, its destruction, except for retention and cultivation of stem cells, is feasible in light of the advantages.

5) A high percentage of embryos, if allowed to mature, a) do not develop into normal human beings, or b) do not survive.

6) Private research is not illegal and is not harmed by the lack of federal funding. Besides, their findings do not become a part of the public domain, as do the results of federal funding.

7) Organized medicine and the National Institutes of Health favor the process for its potential health benefits to everyone.

OPPOSING FACTORS

1) To many, an embryo is a human being at conception. It is immoral to create and then destroy it.

2) Cloning of a human embryo opens the door to cloning a human being and the hazardous slippery slope path to the spectre of eugenics.

3) The process is too close to the availability of abortion, hence unacceptable.

4) The danger exists of overproduction of embryos for sacrificial purposes.

5) Immunosuppressive therapy may not be eliminated entirely.

6) The likelihood of Congressional funding is remote in the present political climate.

7) Embryonic stem cell research can be accomplished as well with adult stem cells from bone marrow—a moral, legal and valid process.

8) Animal cloning is fraught with a high rate of fetal and neonatal mortality and congenital abnormalities—a frightening thought for human cloning.

SECTION D

SUBJECT V:

MEDICAL RESEARCH

If I can stop one heart from breaking,
    I shall not live in vain;
If I can ease one life the aching,
    Or cool one pain,
Or help one lonely person
    Into happiness again,
I shall not live in vain.

— Emily Dickenson, 1830-1886

MEDICAL RESEARCH

The false does not live so long, but the truth is ethical to the end of time.
— Anonymous

INTRODUCTION

Medical research is the fifth of the seven major subjects in health care the author selected because it is as rife as the other subjects with ethical issues adversely affecting quality living. The subject is also the backbone of medical progress and is the leading contributor to basic advances in the constant effort to extend everyone's life to its full and natural life span, which is genetically encoded in the newborn infant.

Although health care has been practiced unscientifically as folk medicine since the origin of man, modern medical research based upon the application of the scientific method is barely fifty years old. It took the added incorporation of human and animal rights to place research on a sound ethical footing as well as on a scientific foundation.

GOALS OF MEDICAL RESEARCH

The goals of medical research are clearly established as follows:

1) To advance medical science by the pursuit of truth in order to create systematic, rational, organized, ethical knowledge.

2) To improve the health of mankind and increase quality living and the length of everyone's life to its natural encoded life span.

3) To make the results of the research available to educated, trained, and licensed graduates of medicine, its specialties, and its allied professions including veterinary medicine, nursing, dentistry, histopathology, microbiology, pharmacy, biochemistry, psychotherapy, radiology, physical therapy, occupational therapy, speech therapy, dietetics, social services, medical technology, et al., in order that they can serve to eradicate disease.

4) To make the results ultimately available for a supportive, receptive society, whose quality of living and attainment of a more perfect semicircle of life can be realized.

Medical research that does not involve human beings or animals as experimental subjects has been given its consideration elsewhere in the text as, for example, in the use of the patient's medical record in Chapter 24. The thrust of this chapter will be on the specific involvement of human beings and animals as experimental subjects because of the uniqueness and enormity of the ethical issues that emerge therefrom. There is a crying demand for resolution in order to achieve universal quality living.

STAGES IN PLANNING MEDICAL RESEARCH
Medical research is a complex process that must comply with a variety of criteria both ethical and scientific, essential for statistically significant and valid results.

In the planning of any research project, the research scientist must involve himself thoroughly in several considerations or stages in order to complete the research project:

1) The source of funding, if any, must be revealed, and there must be no conflict of interest on the part of any of the research team.

2) The project must be planned with a high benefit (efficacy) to low risk (safety) ratio; otherwise the project is not acceptable.

3) The project must be approved by the a) Institutional Review Board in the facility where the study is to be conducted and by the b) funding agency or any other grantor of funds.

4) Voluntary, unbiased, uncoerced, informed consent must be given by and obtained from the subjects participating in the study.

5) The rights of the subjects must be respected, especially those pertaining to freedom from harm and protection of their confidentiality and privacy. The identity of subjects is generally deleted by use of coded identifiers.

6) Adherence to the principles of the scientific method, which consists of the following components:

a) A planned proposal with an ethical hypothesis.

b) A sufficient number of randomly selected subjects for proper statistical analysis and significance known as a power calculation.

c) Application of the double-blind technique with or without placebo control (its use depending upon the absence or presence of prior treatment). The need for continuation of treatment must be a considered factor in determining whether or not the control subject may be given a placebo.

d) A testing phase with clinical trials according to a clearly designed protocol.

e) Identified length of study including a follow-up period (the longer the study, the more reliable are the factors of efficacy and safety).

f) Accurate, objective, unbiased observations and findings.

g) Statistical analysis of results, conclusions, and their significance.

h) Correlative listing of authors, associates, and participants in the study.

i) Acknowledgments and references.

j) Acceptance and approval of findings by the Food and Drug Administration and any other concerned agencies.

k) Acceptance of the submitted findings by a valid scientific publication.

l) Published study available for peer review, critique, replication, modification, or refutation of findings—a dynamic, ongoing, never ending process.

The scientific method in research is the primary feature that separates a proven, valid, reliable study from a non-scientific, unproven, invalid, unreliable presentation to the public of any product for health care, whether it be a drug, test, or procedure. The reader is urged to rely upon this information before giving credence to the recommendations made in connection with any product, old or new. A helpful aid in this regard is the clearly stated presence or absence of approval by the Food and Drug Administration.

CHAPTER 23

HUMAN BEINGS AND ANIMALS AS EXPERIMENTAL SUBJECTS, THE SCIENTIFIC METHOD , THE PLACEBO

The best thing to give to your enemy is forgiveness; to an opponent, tolerance; to a friend, your heart; to your child, a good example; to a father. deference; to your mother, conduct that will make her proud of you; to yourself, respect; to all men, charity.
> — Lord Arthur Balfour, 1848-1930

In order to have a comprehensive appreciation and understanding of the modern principles of using human beings as experimental subjects in medical research, it is imperative that we first review the egregious violations of human rights and mistreatment of human subjects in past research projects.

HISTORICAL BACKGROUND

Two landmark cases of extreme violations of rights have left a blight on the research records involving human beings by the record's reduction of human beings to an ignominious level of degradation.

In the 1930's, our Public Health Service sponsored an experiment currently referred to as the Tuskegee Incident. The subjects were 412 poor, uneducated, black male sharecroppers, who were afflicted with untreated late-stage syphilis. (Until that time, there had been no satisfactory specific treatment for long-standing disease.)

The subjects were used as controls without benefit of any treatment. On the other hand, 204 white males with early syphilis received the new drug, penicillin, as treatment, and, as expected, became free of the disease.

In the 1940's, in Nazi concentration camps, experiments were performed by cruel, sadistic German Nazi doctors on thousands of captive Jews, gypsies, and other 'undesirable' human beings. The studies were atrocious, pointless, shoddily designed, and the results were meaningless.

In both the Tuskegee and Nazi studies, there were many shameful violations of the rights of all patients. The subjects were all coerced, deceived, and there was no informed consent. There was, of course, no adherence to the required stages of the scientific method, described earlier in this chapter. The subjects and their families had no recourse or compensation for the deliberate injuries and deaths following the experiments. In short, there was no respect for human rights, and the studies illustrate the extreme extent of man's inhumanity to man.

RESPECT FOR HUMAN RIGHTS

The worldwide notoriety given to these horrendous acts has led to modern, universally accepted criteria for ethical behavior and respect for human rights in the conduct of quality medical research and quality care in pursuit of everyone's desire for quality living.

CRITERIA FOR ETHICAL CONDUCT in the interest of human rights have appeared in various forms (see Chapter 11) in the Nuremberg Code, 1947; the Universal Declaration of Human Rights, 1948; the Declaration of Helsinki, 1964, which establishes guidelines and standards for ethical conduct in research involving human subjects; the Patient's Bill of Rights, 1973, in which a patient has the right to advice regarding his role in human experimentation and his right of refusal (based upon the principle of right of self-determination); and in federal regulations, 1970's.

FEDERAL REGULATIONS IN SUPPORT OF RIGHTS OF HUMAN BEINGS SERVING AS EXPERIMENTAL SUBJECTS IN MEDICAL RESEARCH

Federal regulations pertaining to the principle of ethical conduct and respect for human rights have emerged since the 1970's. A series of federal policies have been introduced to protect human subjects used in research. Also included are references to women, children, and prisoners as subjects, heretofore excluded as subjects.

Federal agencies such as the National Institutes of Health and the Food and Drug Administration have regulatory roles in government-funded projects to oversee protocols submitted by applicants following approval by the researcher's Institutional Review Board. Emphasis is placed on 1) informed consent, 2) evidence of benefits with minimal risks (basic human rights), and 3) ethical conduct in the research.

In 1997, the Clinton administration made a public apology for our government's misconduct in the Tuskegee experiment, regrettably too little too late, but commendable in its performance and good intentions.

In the year 2000, Congress was struggling with an attempt to advance the patient's position regarding rights, but was unable to come to a unanimous agreement.

Fortified 1) with the knowledge of these egregious violations of human rights in the misuse of human subjects in medical research, and 2) with the references to the many protective measures now in operation, we may proceed with a better understanding of our aims in the current practices of medical research involving human subjects than we ever experienced in the past—not before addressing many of the ethical issues that have arisen along the way.

ETHICAL ISSUES REGARDING HUMAN SUBJECTS IN MEDICAL RESEARCH

The remainder of this chapter is devoted to the many ethical issues that materialize from the current status of medical research involving human subjects. They all require a) resolution with the help of legal adjudication and b) eventual societal acceptance. The following ten issues will be addressed:

1) Discrimination and bias
2) Paternalism and maternalism
3) Randomization
4) Informed consent
5) The scientific method
6) The placebo
7) Sham surgery
8) Authorship
9) Advertising
10) Use of animals as experimental subjects

1) ETHICAL ISSUES REGARDING DISCRIMINATION AND BIAS

The research scientist requires the evaluation and approval by his Institutional Review Board (IRB) in its review of his application for a research project. In determining its approval, the IRB may be unintentionally biased because of its familiarity with the researcher, and/or its members may be advocates for, or against, the subject to be investigated. A neutral, disinterested opinion from a consultant may be required.

Bias may rear its ugly head again in the peer reviewing process after completion and publication of the findings in the research project. In this situation, the problem may be resolved by withholding the identity of both the author (by a process called masking) and the reviewer (by a process called blinding).

2) ETHICAL ISSUES REGARDING
A) MEDICAL PATERNALISM

Is it ethical for the physician i) to be the sole determiner of the risks to which the subject will be exposed, and ii) to downplay the risks with flawed informed consent?

B) MEDICAL MATERNALISM

Is it ethical for the physician to protect the subject i) from all risks, ii) from the subject's autonomous right to choose and act in accordance with the information offered for consent, and iii) from the subject's right of self-determination leading to the subject's right of refusal to participate in the study?

3) ETHICAL ISSUES REGARDING RANDOMIZATION

In the scientific method, the matter of randomization requires particular attention. Its principle is that human subjects should be assigned randomly by chance, and not by a deliberate selection process. Women and children, heretofore excluded from voluntarism, are now included with FDA approval. Bias and deception may thereby be eliminated. It deserves a statement of emphasis that those subjects who serve as controls sacrifice their best personal care in the interest of science and in the interest of the many in the community, thereby performing a commendable act of altruism.

Their decision, however, may conflict with the best available care for themselves personally. They are illustrating the major ethical principle of the greatest good for the greatest number (utilitarianism, or benevolence).

In considering randomization further, certain problems may arise in the selection process that should be avoided, namely a) overly aggressive recruitment, b) exclusion of women, children, and racial minorities, and c) coercion; the selection process must have only volunteers.

Although long known, it has become increasingly apparent that the exclusion of children as experimental subjects in research with application of the scientific method has created an enormous void as well as an array of ethical problems:

a) In at least eighty percent of drug use in pediatrics, dosage has required extrapolation on the basis of age and weight, using adult dosage (scientifically determined) as the reference.

b) Accurate standardization of drug dosage has been difficult to determine.

c) Children differ significantly from adults in their pharmacokinetics, therby raising another question of reliability of dosage.

d) In a sense, the determination of drug dosage in children can be likened to the description of off label drugs (see Chapter 15) despite their FDA approval.

As a result of these concerns, the introduction of the random selection of children as volunteers in medical research has changed the research scene dramatically in recent years, there now emerging an increased number of studies in pediatric research. The FDA has been in the forefront of this drive.

The increase has created new ethical issues:

a) Awareness of exposure of children to risks.

b) Placebo control in sick children may be hazardous.

c) Compared with the vast drug market in adults, the drug

needs in children are relatively small, and the number of available children for study may be quite limited.

d) As with adults, the unresolved question of reimbursement for the subjects may be raised, especially in view of the fact that many subjects may be poor, and costs may be an issue for their parents. Since investigators are often compensated, should not the subjects too be party to the financial arrangements? Investigators do not agree among themselves regarding this ethical issue.

4) ETHICAL ISSUES REGARDING INFORMED CONSENT

The matter of informed consent requires some additional discussion in the description of the details of the scientific method. The researcher must make an unbiased presentation to the subjects of all the information in the study that is pertinent to the randomized selection of patients. In offering the potential subject the appropriate information to enable informed consent, the researcher must avoid an overly enthusiastic presentation with strong opinions, although he may of course have personal hunches that actually led to his planned research. In addition, the documentation and disclosure presented to the subject in order to obtain informed consent must not be too bland, or unbalanced and misleading. Exaggeration of the potential benefits must also be avoided by the researcher in his disclosure. Risks and side effects, however, must be explained to the fullest extent known to the researcher and must not be minimized. (Additional unforeseen risks and side effects will inevitably emerge later.)

The researcher is required to obtain the patient-subject's signed approval to participate in the study, although the patient should be made aware that he may withdraw at any time in accordance with his rights—a decision that should be made by the subject with responsibility and good reason, and not frivolously.

5) ETHICAL ISSUES REGARDING THE SCIENTIFIC METHOD

The scientific method is generally accepted as sacrosanct and inflexible in medical research and is rarely opposed, altered, or reduced.

OPPONENTS OF THE SCIENTIFIC METHOD

A small group of outspoken, hostile, often fanatical rights-oriented activists, however, have emerged and claim their desire to protect the interests of fetuses, children, elderly, retarded, disabled, and especially animals against the use of the scientific method:

1) As part of their beliefs, they favor non-randomization in their opposition to a fundamental step in the scientific method of research. (Ed: Randomization is basic in that it prevents bias, although it does sacrifice the best interest of the subject in favoring the interest of scientific advancement and the many in society who would benefit from the studies—an altruistic principle.)

2) They insist that all patients should have immediate access to experimental, scientifically unstudied drugs that may improve their health, especially those patients with AIDS or with metastatic cancer.

3) A sick patient should not be part of any scientific study. (Ed: Is there any alternative to the use of patients with similar health conditions in doing a scientific study?)

4) Patients' rights supercede any concern for scientific interest. (Ed: Egoistic view; how else can we all learn what does and what does not have merit? Should not concerned patients have sufficient interest in the common good to make a personal sacrifice for the general good as an act of altruism?)

(Ed: Furthermore, is it wrong to sacrifice the health or life of a few for the advancement of the health or life of the many? Few believe this to be valid.)

5) The opponents also claim that medical scientific research caters to gender and racial bias. (Ed: It is true that scientific studies

have dealt mostly with white, young, or middle-aged males as a matter of convenience.)

6) Opponents are not concerned with physiologic or biologic differences among sexes and races.

In contemplating the identification of the opponents of the scientific method, it becomes very puzzling to wonder why anyone would oppose an entity as basic as the scientific method in its importance in scientific research. Close examination reveals that these opponents are generally supporters of various alternative medical practices, where the scientific method is generally disregarded altogether in their treatment of disease. They are antagonistic to scientific medical practices except that they do accept the diagnostic advances made in scientific medical research. They then often reject or supplement standard therapy and rely instead upon non-scientific, unproved anecdotal and testimonial benefits in their selection of treatments.

PROPONENTS OF THE SCIENTIFIC METHOD

Research medical scientists offer as a rebuttal to the posture of the opponents of the scientific method the following opinions:

1) The opponents are self-serving and totally remote from any altruistic philosophy which favors the greatest good for all people.

2) The opponents are actually impeding the advancement of health care because the sincere endeavor of research medical scientists is to improve quality living for all mankind.

6) ETHICAL ISSUES REGARDING THE PLACEBO IN MEDICAL RESEARCH

The reader is referred to Chapter 15 for a detailed discussion of the placebo as it was prescribed therapeutically in the past, and is under consideration for occasional therapeutic use again today.

The current role of the placebo is solely in medical research. Its use is based on: 1) the subject's moral right to know and on 2) the legal requirement of informed consent. It is therefore used exclusively as a control in selected scientific research studies that are designed to determine the efficacy and safety of medicinal substances, tests and procedures. Accordingly, in the process of obtaining informed consent, the patient agrees or disagrees to serve a) as a control with or without a placebo, or b) as the subject receiving the experimental substance being tested in a double-blind study.

The placebo serves as the most ideal control in view of the following:

1) It is inert and has no side effects.

2) It has no delayed or long-term adverse reactions.

3) It is in compliance with the primary aim in research, i.e., non-maleficence.

4) It may be as effective as a) all existing treatments and b) the research preparation being tested.

A number of ethical issues arise regarding the use of the placebo:

1) Should a placebo be used as a control in research only when effective treatment is not available?

2) Should a placebo be used as a control in research even though effective treatment of the patient's underlying condition may already be available as a control, or already in use by the patient?

In recent HIV studies in South African women, placebos were used as controls instead of anti-retroviral drugs currently available and effective as therapy. The subjects were not offered the benefit of informed consent. Our government contributed to the funding. (Ed: Is this reminiscent of the Tuskegee Incident?)

3) Would it be ethical to support proposals to revise (downgrade) the fifth revision of the Declaration of Helsinki by a) weakening the strength of the informed consent component and b) allowing placebo control in the research studies conducted in developing countries instead of using the best current treatment

(because of the high cost of drugs as controls)? Supporters of the proposal claim greater efficiency of the studies. Opponents of the proposal claim that quality research would be undermined and they raise the question of immoral conduct.

4) Should not the placebo be used only if an effective treatment of proved value does not exist? Should not the subjects in the control group receive the best known existing treatment, particularly if the patient has a serious illness, e.g., AIDS or cancer? In addition, if a drug is used, will it be a standardized dose to fit the protocol, or will it be tailored to fit the patient's need?

5) If a subject is already on beneficial treatment, should it ever be discontinued in order to establish placebo control?

6) Should a patient with a serious illness ever be given a placebo (no treatment) instead of an unknown, possibly hazardous experimental substance? Would such action be in violation of the modern ethical principles of non-maleficence, beneficence, and patient's rights?

7) ETHICAL ISSUES REGARDING SHAM SURGERY

The reader is referred to Chapter 15 in the discussion about the power of the placebo by the author's relating the example here of sham surgery. In a study regarding the treatment of angina pectoris, the chest was split and no surgery was performed in the control group, whereas, in the treated group the chest was split and the internal mammary artery was ligated (to determine if it would relieve the chest pain). Better results were observed in the improvement of angina pectoris in the control group (untreated) than in the surgically-treated group! The improvement was purely subjective (not measurable) and clearly demonstrated the power of the placebo.

The ethical question is whether sham-surgery as a control is justifiable. The question is clear in the use of a single example, and the answer to the question does not require other available illustrations, of which there are ample studies. Some research surgeons defend their support of sham surgery as follows:

a) Sham-surgery as a control is the only way to prove the validity of a surgical procedure.

b) Absolute risk from any harm is not an ethical or legal requirement in any research involving human beings.

c) Surgical procedures in research should not be held to a more stringent standard than is required for a non-surgical procedure.

d) Patients who agree to serve as controls are brave pioneers helping to advance the frontiers of research and to benefit themselves and also society (altruism).

e) Sham-surgery is generally acceptable with certain conditions:

i) That there be at least a more than reasonable balance between expectedly low potential risks and high potential benefits.

ii) It is unreasonable to expect the subject to be assured that there are no risks as long as the subject is informed of and agrees to potential risks in relation to benefits.

f) The research plan has the approval of the grantor of the funding and of the Institutional Review Board, thereby reducing the concern of risk to a minimum.

g) The principle of informed consent is fully respected and followed.

h) Animal models serve as a valuable resource in surgical research. Human beings are rarely exploited de novo with surgical innovations in the absence of prior experimental animal investigation, hence the application of the common term guinea-pig for human beings in research studies.

8) ETHICAL ISSUES REGARDING AUTHORSHIP OF RESEARCH PAPERS

In the past, ninety-five percent of research publications had a single author who submitted a research paper for acceptance and publication in a medical journal. More recently, however, ninety-five percent of research studies have multiple authors because of 1)

increased complexity of the studies, 2) need for many interdiscipli-
nary specialties in collaboration, and 3) subtle factors pertaining to
pursuit of academic or company promotion, tenure, etc.

Ethical issues that arise in connection with authorship derive
from the following:

a) Applications for funding and grants often require multiple
participants because of the highly competitive nature of the project.
Conflicts may result.

b) There is a lack of standards and minimal criteria regarding
the significant order of listing contributing participants after the
lead author.

c) The extent of a co-author's contribution may vary from substantial to minimal according to the listing from first to last.

d) There is always the rare and undesirable aspect of non-par-
ticipating guests and ghosts as co-authors.

e) It is not unusual for co-authors to be listed for political reasons or for reasons of possible influence. Although such identities
can be questioned, they are not necessarily without justification as
far as the publication is concerned. To be sure, it is very rare indeed
that a name is listed among the authors of a publication, whose
contribution is entirely irrelevant or nil. The lead author, generally
the primary researcher, should be given the benefit of doubt in his
choice of listing of authors.

9) ETHICAL ISSUES REGARDING ADVERTISING

The research process in medical science makes every effort to
achieve the highest ethical standard in its drive toward a) improving the wellbeing and length of life of everyone and b) fulfilling
everyone's goal of attaining a full and natural life span. In this
regard, we are quick to point to the questionable ethical practices in
advertising as they pertain to wellbeing and quality living.

What comes to mind is the pharmaceutical industry's popular

engagement of a movie celebrity or a famous sports figure to endorse a product and thereby create a purchasing bias. It is also pointed out that the herbal marketing technique is guilty of the same behavior as well as their additional use of anecdotes and testimonials by prominent people in lieu of evidence by scientific research. Is the public presumed to be so naive as to be impressed that, if a movie star or a sports hero recommends the company's product, then he or she uses it, and ordinary people should also use the advertised item? To be sure, the advertisement does not say beyond a doubt that the celebrity actually uses the product. From the company's standpoint, the illusion is created that the endorser will help promote the sale of the product, which after all is presumed to be in the best interest of the health of the ad reader. Does not that indicate that more people will have better health than if there were no advertisement? The company's reasoning may take a convoluted route. Should advertising a health product be equated in every respect with borderline ethical and tasteless advertising of many non-medical products in the commercial world?

When it comes to health care, should anyone other than a patient's physician be the determining factor in what is best for anyone's health? Such reasoning is direct and uncontestable.

10) ETHICAL ISSUES REGARDING USE OF ANIMALS AS EXPERIMENTAL SUBJECTS IN MEDICAL RESEARCH

Despite enormous advances in health care that have been made with the extensive help of animals as experimental subjects, continued friction exists between a) scientists who cannot make any progress without the aid of animals and b) many outspoken activists deeply concerned with animal rights, who do not even agree to the use of animals as experimental subjects in the same harmless manner as are human beings with the same respect for their rights. After all, human beings volunteer for participation in studies as altruistic benefactors for the health of animals as well as for people. Evidently, animal rights activists do not share this consideration.

POSITION OF OPPONENTS OF THE USE OF ANIMALS IN MEDICAL RESEARCH

Opponents of the use of animals for medical research have been given a number of names that identify them, such as animal rights activists, animal liberators, animal sympathizers and antivivisectionists.

Their philosophy is as follows:

1) Animals have ethical rights and require people to represent them in those rights.

2) All species have a unique biology, and animal research findings cannot be applied to man—hence the failure of xenotransplantation and frequent conflicting results.

3) Animals for research are often procured and treated in an inhumane manner.

4) Researchers are cruel, cause pain and suffering and even death of animals.

5) Animal research is often wasteful and unnecessary.

6) Better methods than use of animals for research are available:

    a) Epidemiologic studies

    b) Clinical observation

    c) Laboratory tests

    d) Cell cultures

    e) Imaging

    f) Tissue biopsy

    g) Endoscopy

    h) Autopsy

7) Dissection of animals in school anatomy courses is brutalizing and unnecessary.

8) Drug studies are better learned in human beings.

POSITION OF ADVOCATES OF THE USE OF ANIMALS IN MEDICAL RESEARCH

1) Animals are vital to medical research and often cannot be replaced by any other modality.

2) There is little or no difference between human and animal physiology, pathology, chemistry, endocrine and hormonal function, reaction to infection, tissue injury, etc.

3) The chromosomal make-up of the chimpanzee is almost identical to that of man; the genetic make-up of many animals have significant similarities with man, including the commonly used mouse in medical research.

4) Elimination of animal dissection in schools and in research laboratories would cripple medical education.

5) Advanced modern surgical skills could not be learned by the old apprentice method at the operating table, to say little of the risks to patients.

6) There has been no outstanding progress in the treatment of disease until biomedical science was placed on a sound basis by way of animal experimentation. This point is especially exemplified in the advances in drug therapy.

7) A few specific illustrations of the advances in medical science via animal experimentation are as follows:

a) Pasteur, et al

i) Infection, immunity

ii) Bacterial causes of diphtheria, tetanus, rabies, pertussis, tuberculosis, poliomyelitis, measles, mumps, rubella

iii) Vaccines

b) Lister: Sterilization, asepsis

c) Harvey: Blood circulation

d) Florey and Chain: Penicillin as an antibiotic (via the mouse protection test)

e) Gibbon: heart-lung machine for open-heart surgery

f) Replacement of diseased heart valves (The pig's heart valves are in current use.)

g) Advances in renal dialysis

h) Development of heparin as an anticoagulant by extraction from animal tissues (pig) and testing for safety

i) Insulin: Extracted from animal pancreas (pig)

j) Recent vaccine against H. Influenza meningitis

k) Advances in drug treatment, e.g., in development of anti-hypertensive agents

l) Research in xenotransplantation is essential in view of dearth of organs for human transplantation

m) If animal activists had a greater knowledge of science, they would be more impressed with the need of animals in research

n) Cruelty to animals is far greater in nature among animals and in legal hunting as a sport than in research laboratories designed to improve the health of man. For example: lions kill zebras, cats kill mice, etc.

o) Some animal activists are not vegetarian in their eating habits, and eat beef, pork, chicken, etc.

p) Techniques other than animal experimentation are used extensively in research by in vitro techniques, statistical methods, and a constant search for alternatives to animals.

q) There is little hope, however, in eliminating animals altogether for research as long as there is a high priority for improving the health of human beings, extending their lives, and endeavoring to improve their quality of living.

r) Supporters of animals for research are in agreement that an ethical issue exists regarding animal rights, but ask: If animal research were discontinued, who would stop the real killers of people? If there are lingering doubts about animal research, opponents of animals for research should close their eyes and think about children with terminal illnesses, especially cancer, and the need to find a cure.

s) Everyone should acknowledge that society owes a debt to both human beings and animals who (altruistically) support medical science.

t) The advances made in the interest of health care by the use of human beings as experimental subjects are all utilized in veterinary medicine for the health benefits of animals. Is it not reasonable that animals too should offer themselves as subjects in their own interest?

FINAL THOUGHTS IN USE OF HUMAN BEINGS AND ANIMALS AS EXPERIMENTAL SUBJECTS IN MEDICAL RESEARCH

Quality research can be optimal only if the investigator is mindful of the burdens he assumes:

a) Trust of the subjects, particularly regarding their safety.

b) Total disclosure in the informed consent process.

c) Absence of bias and conflicts of interest, especially financial conflicts.

Pursuit of the truth, the whole truth, and nothing but the truth (inherent in the definition of science).

CHAPTER 24

THE MEDICAL RECORD, PUBLICATION OF RESEARCH, MEDIA REPORTING, THE CORPORATE COMMUNITY, CONFLICTS OF INTEREST

Kind words can be short and easy to speak, but their echoes are truly endless.

— Mother Theresa, 1910-1997

THE MEDICAL RECORD

In addition to the use of human beings as experimental subjects in medical research, the patient's MEDICAL RECORD is often a valuable resource as well. It has many important purposes among which are the following:

1) To monitor the health of populations in epidemiologic studies for trends in major chronic diseases, such as coronary heart disease, stroke, cancer, diabetes, et al

2) To identify populations at high risk for disease

3) To assess the usefulness of diagnostic tests and screening programs

4) To determine the efficacy of treatment

5) To quantify the prognosis of diseases

6) To influence policy by use of cost effective analysis

7) To support administrative functions

8) To monitor the adequacy of care

9) For epidemiologic and clinical research, and for publication

10) For observational outcome studies to improve health care and medical education

ETHICAL ISSUES

1) It is not *generally* appreciated that a patient's medical record is the *property* of the providers (doctor, hospital, laboratory, radiology department), who are the preparers and keepers of their records, to which only the concerned patient has full rights of *access* upon written request. Release of any information from one's record requires the patient's *written* approval.

2) A patient has the *right* to make a written request of a copy of all or any part of his own medical record.

3) The patient may expect respect for his or her *privacy* and the exercise of confidentiality in any use of the medical record.

4) Violation of confidentiality, thereby causing ethical conflicts, has been made easy by the ready availability of the medical record in the newly increasing electronic environment. More and more, patients are fearful of loss of *privacy*, especially in sensitive areas of illness, including sexually transmitted diseases, psychiatric disorders, reproductive problems, genetic testing results, etc.

5) There is an increase in *distrust* by patients of the release of personal health data known to a) the federal government via Medicare and Medicaid, b) private insurers, c) employers; d) in general, to those who may be paying the costs or contributing to the coverage of the costs.

Safeguards have evolved against the misuse of the medical record and especially of violation of confidentiality:

1) Access to the medical record is protected by the *Patient Rights and Privacy Act of 1976*, by the federal *Department of Health and*

Human Services, and by state laws:

a) Requiring the patient's approval for release of information

b) Written request by the patient for release of information, even when the patient wishes the information for personal reasons

2) The use of one's medical record for research requires, a) deletion of direct identity, b) the indirect use of coded identifiers, and c) the assurance of use of the record for clinical research and not for the private gain of an employer or insurer.

PUBLICATION REQUIREMENTS BY MEDICAL JOURNALS REGARDING RESEARCH PAPERS

1) Release of research data to media and to the public is forbidden prior to publication (*Ingelfinger Rule,* New England Journal of Medicine). The rule may be waived when the findings of the research have immediate implications regarding health, for example, the startling report that the drug combination, Fen-phen, was a cause of serious heart disease.

2) Mandatory approval of the study by the researcher's Institutional Review Board

3) Adherence to a standard ethical code, e.g., The Declaration of Helsinki

4) Explicit delineation of sources of the funding for the study

5) Possible conflicts of interest, e.g., payment to the author by a supporter of the study

The only problem with this excellent array of requirements is that they are not uniform among all the medical journals.

PRINCIPLES IN MEDIA REPORTING OF MEDICAL RESEARCH

1) The issue of *timeliness*: researchers are anxious to expose their work by acceptance in a prestigious publication or by presentation at a scientific meeting, but there is a generally accepted rule that the

work may not be aired or given to the press before the scientific community learns about it.

2) In media reporting, the *identity* of the source must be accurate, e.g., a named, peer-reviewed medical journal, a specific press conference, etc. The identity should not be a 'reliable source.'

3) An important matter in reporting to the media is that of *accuracy*. The wording must be precise, not oversimplified, exaggerated, or sensationalized. The often reported wording as 'preliminary findings' are not a 'breakthrough' according to the media.

4) A single study is usually regarded as proof that it is not definitive, needs confirmation, and remains *tentative* until a body of evidence points in the same direction as the single study. Individual case studies, frequently published in the past, are now rarely reported.

MEDICAL RESEARCH AND THE CORPORATE COMMUNITY

Research in biotechnology and drugs is closely watched by those concerned with the stock market. Any innovation may trigger a major change in stock values, i.e., a favorable finding can cause a surge in the purchase of the stock pertaining to the pharmaceutical company that manufactures the product. Similarly, an unfavorable report may inspire an increase in sale of the stock and a corresponding fall in its stock value. A key guide, known to the corporate community, is *FDA* approval or disapproval of a product.

A governmental safeguard against civil and criminal liability and against defrauding investors is the *Securities and Exchange Act of 1934*.

ETHICAL ISSUES

Ethical issues pertaining to scientific research and the corporate community are the following:

1) The aforementioned matter of availability of research information prior to publication in a medical journal may result in a

violation of the Securities and Exchange Act known as *insider trading* (trading on advanced non-public knowledge). This is a sufficiently serious *violation* to result in incarceration of the offender.

2) A highly unethical practice is that of *corporate pressure,* consisting of suppression of research findings because of high corporate costs and a vested interest in the outcome. A striking example is the discovery of the tobacco industry's long history of *deception* in the *denial* by some of its leaders that the nicotine in cigarettes is addictive and carcinogenic.

3) Another form of corporate pressure by a manufacturer of drugs is in the practice of blocking the manufacture of cheaper generic equivalent versions of products of another company by charging *flawed studies.*

4) There is also evidence of corporate pressure in blocking the publication of the *negative* effects of a product, the preparation of which was a costly venture.

5) Medical scientists, who are fulltime corporate employees a) have a fiduciary *duty* to the corporation, b) must refrain from personal use of its confidential non-public research, and c) may not trade on any findings.

6) Academic medical scientists employed temporarily by a corporation are subject to the same *restraints* as fulltime employees. If the source of the funding does not require confidentiality, the scientist may trade on advance knowledge of research findings.

7) Employees of a medical journal have a primary duty to their employer, not to any corporation, and must therefore refrain from using non-public information obtained from material submitted to the publication for personal gain. Such action would be in violation of journal regulations.

CONFLICTS OF INTEREST IN MEDICAL RESEARCH

(See Chapter 12, sub-section pertaining to the physician and conflict of interest.) Busy practitioners of medicine with large practices are often engaged by pharmaceutical manufacturers to perform *clinical trials* (required by the FDA for the approval of new drugs) in order that the physicians may be able to use their own patients.

Financial arrangements are often made by the company with the physician who receives a specified honorarium for each patient used. It would then seem reasonable to expect that the physician might be biased and more cooperative than normal, and less likely to criticize the safety or efficacy of agents.

In addition, the ethical question arises regarding informed consent and the extent of the patient's awareness that he is taking a drug as a free sample for some appropriate condition. An interesting question has arisen concerning the patient's *sharing* of the fee the physician receives for his participation in the clinical trial.

The overall result of the evident conflict of interest on the physician's part is a probable diminution in the quality and accuracy of the medical research by bias and positive influences. Furthermore, on a longterm basis, the public may show skepticism and uncertainty in company-sponsored medical research and in the public's respect for their physicians.

SAFEGUARDS

Safeguards are inherent in the policy structure of a medical journal in that an author's disclosure of financial interest gives aid and comfort to public *trust*, but does not resolve the *bias* issue.

Recommendations made for correction of some of the ethical issues are obvious. There should be:

a) Strict adherence to the scientific method with the double blind technique and placebo control wherever indicated and applicable.

b) Investigators must be unbiased.

c) Should not patients share in any financial benefits on the part of the physicians? Actually, neither physician nor patient should benefit financially, thereby eliminating bias altogether.

SECTION D

SUBJECT VI:

DECISION MAKING
IN THE MATURE YEARS

A careless word may kindle strife

A cruel word may wreck a life

A bitter word may hate instill

A brutal word may smite and kill

A gracious word may smooth the way

A joyous word may light the day

A timely word may lessen stress

A loving word may heal and bless

— Anonymous

CHAPTER 25

DECISION MAKING REGARDING LATE LIFE CARE

Blessed is the man who, having nothing to say, abstains from giving in words evidence of the fact.

— George Eliot, 1819–1880

The sixth and penultimate major medical subject with an abundance of ethical issues that relate to quality living is the vital matter of decision-making during one's mature years about the direction of one's late-life health care.

The process has been called the *long good-bye,* a regrettable term in that the discussion really tends to bring an unknown entity and mysterious future into a clearly acceptable and satisfying dynamic. There is little reason for a mournful and frightening session to take place in the presence of one's family, physician, and attorney. In its concept of a will regarding one's health care, it is akin to a will regarding one's financial affairs.

THE PLANNING PROCESS
The preparations for the decisions may actually be made at any time in life. Young people, however, are not psychologically

prepared to accept the responsibility or the need for late-life decision making, just as they are not prone to prepare a *living will* or
other advance directive. In middle-life, on the other hand, they
are generally more likely to be interested in, and concerned with,
the necessary considerations. In late life, the likelihood of chronic
illness, debilitating disease, and the beginning of mental impairment may raise questions concerning one's required mental
capacity, although they may be best able to express what they
really believe.

COMPETENCE

First and foremost, all decisions pertaining to the long-term
planning process must be made within the medico-legal concept of
one's mental *competence*. The patient's state of mind must unques-
tionably be one capable of making sound decisions. In late life, the
surrounding members of the family must be alert to the patient's
early changes suggestive, for example, of Alzheimer's disease or
senility due to cerebral arteriosclerosis, neither of which may be
suspected by the patient himself.

The essential components of competence need further elucida-
tion. The patient must have the ability to

a) understand his or her medical situation fully upon thorough
explanation by the physician,

b) comprehend the nature of recommended medical treatments
and procedures,

c) assess information regarding risks and benefits of the various
aspects of treatment,

d) make a decision based upon full disclosure that is stable over
time, consistent with the patient's values and goals, rational, not
delusional, and is demonstrative of the patient's trust in the integrity of his physician.

A problem with the specificity of competence is that it may have varying standards for different medical conditions. Competence is rarely questioned when the patient agrees to the recommendations of the physician because acceptance demonstrates that the patient understands that a doctor's recommendation is offered in the patient's best interest.

When the patient refuses to accept the recommendations of his physician, the patient's competence may then come into question because the patient's failure to appreciate the recommendations is presumed to be contrary to his own best interest.

TOTAL DISCLOSURE

An important factor in decision making is that of disclosure. Whereas the physician's extent of disclosure of information needed for informed consent is only to a *reasonable* degree (see Chapter 11), the amount of disclosure for decisions in mature years regarding end-of-life care is *total*. Nothing can be withheld when the patient is expected to decide his course of action concerning his terminal care.

Full disclosure by the physician must a) never be perfunctory, b) be presented with minimal distress to the patient, c) be offered in understandable terminology, d) reflect the physician's sensitivity to the patient's reactions and responses, especially if the patient, by chance, is suffering from a serious illness, and (e) be empathetic and reassuring.

In the provision of full disclosure, a physician may resort to the use of a legitimate principle known as *therapeutic privilege*. On the basis of discretion, he may *withhold information*

a) if he considers that total disclosure may be psychologically harmful to the patient,

b) if the physician makes a judgmental or procedural error provided that the information does not affect or alter the care of the patient, and the physician is not negligent,

c) if the future is uncertain,

d) if full disclosure is in striking conflict with *hope* (total candor has been called *the rape of hope*). Under such circumstances, an extra amount of serious discussion may be required regarding a patient's decision-making in the mature years of life, when he is preparing a living will, an advance directive, a durable *power of attorney*, and considering whether or not to withhold life-sustaining treatment, etc.

Needless to say, the physician is expected to be fully competent in the entire process. It is not unusual for him to engage legal aid in the matter.

Following the full disclosure, the patient may exercise the right of refusal (unless compelled by law) on the bases of the Self-Determination Act of 1991, liberty under the Constitution, right of autonomy, right of religious beliefs, and the right to die principle.

In accordance with the author's emphasis upon the mandate of responsibility that must accompany every right, a patient's refusal of a physician's recommendations that accompany disclosure implies that the patient is prepared to accept the physician's reluctant decision to depart from the further care of the patient. The patient, in exercising his right of refusal, may be fully prepared to dissolve his relationship with his physician—a privilege within his rights. The patient's primary concern will be the uninterrupted continuation of medical care.

PATIENT'S CHOICE OF DIRECTION OF CARE

Early in the discussion between the physician and the patient, the patient should be guided toward a consideration of the direction of his health care in late life. The physician must enable the patient to make a choice between two categories of care, I) The Sanctity of Life Ethic, and II) The Quality of Life Ethic.

I) THE SANCTITY OF LIFE ETHIC is a religious, orthodox, dogmatic and quantitative philosophy. Its basic concept is that a) every life is intrinsically good, b) no one life is less valuable than any other, and c) all lives are sacred and should be preserved at all costs. There is considerable disagreement among the followers of this view regarding the quantitative amount and extent of the phrase "at all costs." The circumstance of the patient, whether elderly and terminal, newborn, or even a fetus or embryo, does not reduce the value of the patient's life or justify termination of living.

The obvious approach to medical care by patients in pursuit of the sanctity of life ethic is in favor of receiving *aggressive* care with the full use of advanced medical technology, even though they may not ultimately be completely opposed to the withdrawal of life-sustaining measures at some appropriate point in care when the end is imminent. A favorite outcry is, "I'll spend everything to live another day." Cynics may consider that the patient is actually not living another day, but rather *prolonging* the dying process another day.

II) THE QUALITY OF LIFE ETHIC, on the other hand, is philosophically a more laic, temporal, secular, and clearly *qualitative* view. It is concerned more with the quality of one's living rather than the duration of one's life. It is the *antithesis* of the sanctity of life ethic. Its approach is favored by the majority of people, although there are frequent instances of changing one's mind when circumstances are terminal, and death may be anticipated within a brief period of weeks or months.

The decision regarding the desire for the prolongation of life is generally considered as discretionary and judgmental. A simple way of understanding the quality of life ethic is by the application of the expression, *death with dignity*, and by the tendency to withhold life-supportive measures, including cardio-pulmonary resuscitation, as a part of the patient's hospital *do-not-resuscitate* (DNR) orders, which must be placed in writing by the physician in charge of the patient's care.

PHYSICIAN'S RESPONSIBILITY

The physician bears a number of responsibilities in his provision of professional opinions and advice to the patient making end-of-life decisions.

His primary responsibility is to offer and discuss information regarding all available avenues of treatment clearly with skill and without *bias*.

The physician must be knowledgeable in, and be guided by 1) federal and state laws, and 2) the patient's written wishes following the physician's provision of full disclosure of all pertinent information. He must then place into the patient's medical record notes regarding his discussion with the patient and family as well as copies of the patient's *advance directive* and any other related documents.

If the patient's values and preferences have not been made known to the physician, the physician is expected to confer with the family and/or the *surrogate*, where applicable, and arrive at an agreed-upon decision in the patient's best interest. Included should be notes reflecting the patient's specific wishes regarding the choice of quality of life versus sanctity of life.

The physician is responsible for the provision of treatment reflecting the patient's expressed wishes and best interest, which does not depend upon the patient's competence.

PHYSICIAN'S RIGHTS

In addition to responsibilities, the physician has rights just as does the patient:

1) He may reject the request of the surrogate or proxy, especially if it represents a *substituted judgment* and not the patient's known wishes.

2) He retains the right not to offer or comply with any treatment he believes to be futile, contraindicated, or in violation of his own professional or ethical principles.

3) In taking an adverse position, the physician is obligated to a) refer the matter to an Ethics Committee or b) a court, c) consider withdrawing from the care of the patient, or d) seek legal counsel.

RESPONSIBILITY OF OTHERS

Hospitals and other *health care facilities* also have responsibilities relating to a patient's decision-making in late life. They are required by law *(Patient Self-Determination Act of 1991)* to offer patients receiving Medicare or Medicaid information regarding the right of the patients to provide a Living Will, an Advance Directive, a Durable Power of Attorney, a Surrogate or Health Care Proxy

The patient's designated *Health Care Proxy* has responsibilities in connection with the patient's decision making to the extent that the proxy's decisions and actions must be made in accordance with the patient's expressed *preferences*. The proxy's judgments must be the same as those the patient would have made. A proxy's personal judgment regarding the patient's quality of life risks bias.

LIMITATION OF RESPONSIBILITIES

The delineation of responsibilities of the various participants in the patient's decisions regarding late-life wishes is limited by counteractions from multiple sources. These include third party insurers, government regulations, institutional policies and national standards of practice that: 1) mandate cost controls, 2) create conflicts with the wishes, preferences, values, decisions, and differences among the patient's health care *proxy*, physician, or patient's family, and 3) create conflicts with the autonomy of the physician as well as the patient.

THE PATIENT'S CHOICE

In decision making, the patient has a broad gamut of choices concerning his terminal care. The patient should address his choices in his living will. They are based upon the patient's *right* to decide about the details of his living and dying.

At the moment of making his *decisions in writing*, the patient has considered his choice of pursuing a sanctity of life ethic or a quality of life ethic, which actually relate to the degree and intensity of his terminal care.

One cautionary responsibility should be considered by the patient in that he should avoid abuse of his autonomy in taking action by deferring to his family's rights. He should make certain compromises and concessions. For example, living another day at all costs may be the patient's egoistic and legal right, but certainly not an altruistic or moral approach to a consideration of the needs of a spouse or children.

THE PATIENT'S DECISION IN WRITING

Decision making must then be made by the patient in *writing* so that there is no ambiguity in a complex process. The patient's physician and/or attorney will offer him the choices of a Living Will, an Advance Directive, a Durable Power of Attorney, and the designation of a Surrogate of Health Care Proxy.

THE LIVING WILL

The Living Will, a term coined by Kutner in 1969, specifies in advance, within the context of the patient's mental competence, the nature and duration of the medical care preferred by the patient when there is no expectation of recovery from illness. The basis for this decision is the patient's right to die, a valid medicolegal point of law. The guiding considerations include the quality of life, the quantity or sanctity of life, the desire for dignity at death, the extent of suffering, and concern over costs.

The *Living Will* should include a declaration of *choices* regarding:

a) Hydration, oral vs. parenteral (intravenous)

b) Nutrition, oral vs. nasogastric or via gastrostomy

c) Life-sustaining measures, mechanical ventilator, renal dialysis, cardio-pulmonary resuscitation, blood transfusion, et al

d) Tests and procedures

e) Medication, antibiotics, chemotherapy

f) Control of pain

g) Radiation

h) Surgery, including emergency, palliative, curative

i) Do-not-resuscitate orders

j) Donation of organs for transplantation

k) Disposition of remains, e.g., availability for medical teaching

PREPARATION of the Living Will Forms:

a) Standard forms are available.

b) Signature and date of execution by the patient are required.

c) Witness by the physician, a notary, or attorney is essential.

d) The document must be made known to, and copies provided for, the family and physician.

e) If hospitalization is required, as is usually the case, it is essential that the Living Will be attached to or be a part of , the hospital record of the patient by his physician. Furthermore, it is mandatory that the physician place an appropriate notice on the patient's order sheet in order to avoid unnecessary therapy by an enthusiastic hospital staff, always eager to save lives as is its devoted aim and expectation.

The Living Will has certain *shortcomings*:

a) In general, only about ten percent of the adult population takes the trouble to prepare it.

b) The document as presented, is not recognized as valid in all states.

c) State laws often limit its application, which may be available only for the terminally ill.

d) Its interpretation may have a narrow range in its lack of flexibility.

e) Its presentation as a laundry list limits the type of treatment that can be refused by the patient.

f) The document usually does not provide for a proxy

g) It lacks a penalty if the health care provider fails to honor the document

h) The patient may change his mind at anytime, but the physician must make a corresponding change in the patient's order sheet.

Ethical Question regarding the Living Will: Can one compel others to carry out an action without regard 1) for its social or legal impact, or 2) for the family's objection to the mandate?

ADVANCE DIRECTIVE

The Advance Directive primarily addresses the limitations of the Living Will. A good example is the Medical Directive of the Harvard Medical School.

DURABLE POWER OF ATTORNEY

The Durable Power of Attorney, a legal document in every state, establishes a surrogate or proxy to act in behalf of the patient when he/she becomes incapacitated. Standard forms are available.

SURROGATE

The surrogate, also known as a *conservator* or *protector* may be the Durable Power of Attorney or a proxy. He may be designated in the Advance Directive. His role is to perform a duty in the patient's best interest without bias. He is expected to know the patient's preferences and choices. A close family member is among those best suited to the task.

PROXY OR PROCURATOR

The proxy is a person chosen by a competent adult patient to make decisions for the patient when or if the patient becomes incompetent and is unable to decide for himself. The decisions made by the proxy must be consistent with the patient's wishes (if known) or best interest (if the patient's wishes are not known). Some states require a signed Power of Attorney by the patient as part of a proxy.

Proxy laws do not apply to minors or to mentally impaired, who are not eligible to serve in a proxy capacity. In addition, the proxy laws do not recognize assisted suicide as a valid consideration. An excellent example of a proxy that can serve as a model is the Massachusetts Health Care Proxy (1990).

The choice of a Health Care Proxy should be determined by the thoughtful consideration of the one most knowledgeable in the faithful reflection of the patient's wishes, his right to autonomy, and best interest in the application of a *substituted judgment*. The proxy must not be tainted by any concerns questioning his own conflict of interest.

Finally, the proxy should show concerns regarding the time spent, the energy expended, and the costs sustained by the patient's family members, whose own opinions and wishes may be in conflict with a) the patient's autonomy as well as b) the physician's obligation to comply with the patient's written wishes and best interest, in addition to the physician's own principles.

SUBSTITUTED JUDGMENT

A Substituted Judgment is made by the *Surrogate* or *Health Care Proxy* in the absence of an Advance Directive by the patient. The same guiding principles apply in the making of decisions for an incompetent patient with the same rights as the competent patient, to wit, the right of self-determination and the right of refusal of treatment, based upon the elements of total disclosure as expected in the matter of informed consent.

In the Substituted Judgment, the surrogate or proxy must of course consider the patient's 1) preferences and choices during his era of competence, 2) quality of living, and 3) best interest. A fundamental need in the exercise of a substituted judgment are *safeguards* against bias.

Historically, the Substituted Judgment was first enunciated in the landmark Quinlan case before the New Jersey Supreme Court in 1976. A new medical concept of unconsciousness, namely, the vegetative state, arose requiring a universal definition.

DEFINITIONS OF TERMS

In order for the physicians to be able to approach the care of patients near the end of life, they and the patient's family and caretakers must understand fully the modern medical definitions of the following terms:

a) Terminal illness
b) Consciousness
c) Unconsciousness or coma
d) Vegetative state
e) Brain death
f) Death

TERMINAL ILLNESS

Terminal Illness does not have a specific definition in medical terminology. It is actually a legal term coined in 1959. It implies that the patient is in an *irreversible state of illness* with or without treatment, and that death is likely within *six* months or thereabouts.

In view of its accepted requirement of irreversibility, the aim in treatment is primarily directed at maintenance of the patient's *comfort*, especially the elimination of pain and suffering, both physical and psychological. Aggressive therapy is inappropriate and futile, hence abandoned. Treatment of terminal illness, however, must never be abandoned. Added support and comfort may be needed for close family members as well.

The course of action should be guided by the pre-determined near-end-of-life wishes of the patient in the Advance Directive.

CONSCIOUSNESS

Consciousness is a term coined by William James, eminent philosopher and psychologist, in 1890. Consciousness has *two dimensions*:

1) Wakefulness plus arousal (first dimension) plus sleep-wake cycles (circadian rhythm)

2) Awareness of self and environment (second dimension) plus presence of first dimension

UNCONSCIOUSNESS OR COMA

In unconsciousness or coma, there is *total absence* of the first and second dimensions of consciousness.

CAUSES

The causes are numerous and include hemorrhage, trauma, drugs, anoxia, mass lesions, end-stage degenerative neurologic disease, et al.

CLINICAL MANIFESTATIONS:

The clinical manifestations consist of

a) no purposeful movements,

b) absence of pain or suffering,

c) heart beat is present and respirations may or may not be present, and

d) electroencephalographic (EEG) activity is polymorphic.

PATHOPHYSIOLOGY

a) Reduction in blood flow *(ischemia)* to brain resulting in b) reduced oxygen supply to brain *(hypoxemia)* and c) reduced blood sugar *(hypoglycemia)* to brain. Total absence of blood flow to the brain for about four to six minutes results in *destruction* of cerebral cortex while usually *sparing* the brain stem (lower portion of brain).

PROGNOSIS

The prognosis depends upon the cause, extent of the reduction in blood flow, and the patient's response to appropriate therapeutic measures. The net result may vary: 1) recovery, 2) the vegetative state, or 3) death.

THE VEGETATIVE STATE

The Vegetative State is a relatively new concept. The diagnostic term was coined in 1972, and is not to be confused with a vegetating state—an unkind reference to some patients in domiciliary care.

COMPONENTS

Its major components are as follows:

a) Total unconsciousness

b) Absent awareness of self and the environment (second dimension of consciousness)

c) Presence of intermittent wakefulness and sleep-wake cycles without the presence of arousal (The presence of arousal is expected in the first dimension of consciousness.)

d) Central nervous system involvement

    1) Absent cortical function

    2) Preserved autonomic functions (completely or partially) in the hypothalamus and brain stem

    3) Extent of involvement determines the patient's capacity for survival

e) Variously preserved cranial nerve reflexes: pupillary, corneal, vestibulo-ocular, and gag

f) Variously preserved spinal reflexes

g) EEG activity is polymorphic

h) Reduced cerebral metabolism of both sugar and oxygen, measurable by the PET scan

CLINICAL MANIFESTATIONS OF THE VEGETATIVE STATE:

a) Absence of higher brain function: cognition, language, expression, comprehension

b) Incontinence of bowel and bladder

c) Absence of sustained, purposeful, voluntary responses to visual, auditory, noxious, or tactile (pain) stimuli

d) Heart beat present

e) Spontaneous respirations present

CAUSE OF THE VEGETATIVE STATE: Severe brain damage.

TREATMENT OF THE VEGETATIVE STATE

Treatment includes the following:

1) Artificial nutrition and hydration

2) Artificial respiration (usually not necessary)

3) Patient or Surrogate (by the Living Will) may withhold treatment—an approach held by most physicians and laity as valid.

PROGNOSIS OF THE VEGETATIVE STATE

The outlook of the Vegetative State depends upon the cause. The condition may be 1) temporary, 2) persistent, or 3) permanent (irreversible usually after three months). Life expectancy is generally from 2-5 years. Survival rates longer than ten years are rare.

The vegetative state launched the right–to-die movement following the course of the Quinlan Case in the *Right to Privacy Act, 1976*.

BRAIN DEATH

The disorder known as *brain death* was defined in 1968 as a *permanent absence of all brain functions* including the cortex, brain stem, and cranial nerves in a patient with a beating heart and breathing with the aid of a ventilator. It is a form of *irreversible coma* and is currently acceptable as *death*.

CLINICAL MANIFESTATIONS

The manifestations of brain death consist of:

1) Unconsciousness with total and permanent absence of the first and second dimensions of consciousness

2) Absent pain sensation

3) Absent purposeful motor function

4) Absent respiratory function, which may be restored with a ventilator

5) Cardiac function is intact with restored respiratory function

6) Spinal reflexes may be present or absent

7) EEG activity is absent (isoelectric)

DEATH

Prior to the description of brain death in 1968, death was simply diagnosed when there was absent functioning of the heart (circulation) and lung (respiration).

A Presidential Commission was set up that led to the *Uniform Determination of Death Act of 1981*.

The *diagnosis* of death was established on the basis of scientific criteria including all of the following:

1) Permanent unconsciousness

2) Irreversible cessation of circulatory and respiratory function (although both may be active temporarily by supportive measures; such activity must not be misinterpreted as temporary restoration of life)

3) Irreversible cessation of all functions of the entire brain (which coordinates and integrates all body functions) including

a) higher (neocortical and subcortical) functions of awareness, cognition, reasoning,

b) lower (brain stem) functions of eye movements, pupillary reaction, gag reflex,

c) absence of all signs of receptivity and responsiveness, and

d) isoelectric electroencephalogram,

4) A diagnostic religious criterion: the spirit leaves the body

QUINLAN AND CRUZAN CASES

Pertinent events arose as an outgrowth of the landmark Karen Ann Quinlan case (1975-1984):

1) Right to Privacy Act, 1976

2) Right to die movement

3) Right to withdraw life supportive treatment

4) Need for a Living Will and Durable Power of Attorney

Similarly, following the landmark Nancy Cruzan case (1983-1990), emphasis was placed on the following:

1) Need for a Living Will

2) Designation of a Surrogate or Health Care Proxy

3) Right-to-die movement

4) Formulation of the federal Patient Self-Determination Act of 1991

Following both the Quinlan and Cruzan cases, the form of unconsciousness known as the vegetative state became better appreciated medically as well as legally.

Pertinent ethical issues arose which to date have not been answered to everyone's satisfaction, and remain unclear and controversial:

a) Are nourishment (food) and hydration (water) part of extraordinary life-support systems?

b) Does a surgical gastrostomy differ from a spoon and straw or from naso-gastric tube feeding?

THE PATIENT SELF-DETERMINATION ACT OF 1991 requires that *providers* of health care:

1) Ask patients to consider and choose the manner of their dying.

2) Inform patients that they have the right to forego or to discontinue life-prolonging medical interventions including CPR, ventilators, tube feeding.

3) Invite patients to prepare an Advance Directive regarding their care when, or if, they are unable to speak for themselves.

4) Encourage patients to designate a surrogate or proxy with authority to make the same decisions regarding treatment as would the patient.

A number of *therapeutic measures* pertaining to life support should be given consideration in the preparation of a patient's Advance Directive. These include the following:

a) Cardiopulmonary resuscitation (CPR)

b) Do not resuscitate orders (DNR)

c) Parenteral hydration (intravenous fluid therapy)

d) Artificial nutrition (nasogastric, gastrostomy)

e) Mechanical ventilator

CARDIO-PULMONARY RESUSCITATION (CPR)

AIM

The aim of cardio-pulmonary resuscitation (CPR) is to *reverse* sudden, unexpected, imminent death. It is an *emergency* consideration and allows no time for deliberation.

DECISION

The decision should be made in *prior* discussions between the doctor and the patient or surrogate whenever possible in order to prepare a comprehensive plan of care when the critical time arrives for immediate action.

At the time of need, the physician's action must then depend upon the patient's expressed choice. *Under any* circumstances, CPR is not appropriate for a moribund patient and death seems imminent. The physician is then expected to place a DNR (do-not-resuscitate) order on the patient's order sheet. If such order has not been placed, the application of CPR is valid and will be pursued by an aggressive medical staff.

In a patient with a terminal and irreversible illness, and death is not expected for some weeks or months, the physician must rely on 1) a patient's written directive, 2) the advice of a surrogate or 3) a discussion with a responsible member of the family. The physician's personal judgment in the matter raises ethical questions, and he should not act upon unilateral decisions.

A repugnant and clearly unethical practice is the rarely (hopefully never) employed *slow code* (also known as the *light blue code*, or the *show* code) in contrast with the standard *code blue*. Its use, which should be condemned, is for the purpose of pretension only, without complete sincerity or good intent. The impropriety of the slow code is that it requires a deliberate decision not to bring the patient back to life by applying less than full CPR. It represents a known futile and truly harmful intervention and it violates the fundamental principle of *primum non nocere*.

The slow code must not be confused with a *failed code*, wherein a patient dies despite all effort to revive him.

A common setting for the unethical consideration of a slow code is:

1) A patient in a terminal or persistent vegetative state, and the presumption that the patient will not survive. Death is regarded as a foregone conclusion.

2) Absence of a DNR order.

3) Absence of informed consent (via prior discussion with the patient or his family).

4) The patient's preference is not clearly known.

Finally, in addition to constituting unethical conduct, the slow code compromises the patient's right to autonomy.

DO-NOT-RESUSCITATE (DNR) ORDER

The standards for the do-not-resuscitate decision were set by the *American Heart Association* in 1974.

The DNR order is appropriate:

When the circulation and respiration are not likely to be restored in a patient with multi-system organ failure. In this regard, the most common setting concerns an elderly patient in failing health admitted to the hospital with one of the following: metastatic cancer, advanced congestive heart failure, cardiac arrest, intracranial hemorrhage, or any other catastrophic illness.

The physician, in the doctor-patient relationship, should encourage all patients in their middle age, surely before their late years, to address this issue among all others to be considered in end-of-life decisions in their preparation of an *advance directive*.

In keeping with the general popularity of the quality of life ethic and the withholding of life-sustaining biotechnologic measures, patients and physicians, as well as the families of patients, are inclined to set limits earlier than previously in situations that are likely to have a poor outcome. There is certainly an extensive amount of dialogue and discussion these days among the public and the medical profession. There is also an increasing amount of *legislation* pertaining to: a) the patient's rights to autonomy and self-determination based upon the right to full disclosure and informed consent, and b) professional and hospital guidelines and policies.

A serious ethical concern is a DNR order based upon a physician's unilateral action without the patient's or the surrogate's participation in the decision. Physicians are usually aware that unilateral action constitutes legal battery. Likewise, there is an equally serious concern if the hospital caretakers of the patient ignore a DNR order in their enthusiasm to save a life. Such action, too, constitutes legal battery, a violation of the law.

To be sure, a DNR order does not indicate that the patient is to be abandoned. In fact, the alternatives, to which the patient's caretakers are committed, may be even more challenging in the decision-making process with the maintenance of quality living as a primary aim.

PARENTERAL HYDRATION AND ARTIFICIAL NUTRITION

To most physicians, intravenous fluid therapy and feeding via artificial means (naso-gastric tube feeding or gastrostomy) are considered as extraordinary. measures, and as interventions with risks as well as benefits. These measures may be withheld when consideration is being given to the withholding or withdrawing of other life-sustaining measures that are actually extraordinary.

To some physicians, however, intravenous fluids represent *ordinary water and sugar*, and should never be withheld, as with water and sugar given by teaspoon or straw. The denial of water to a patient is certain to result in dehydration and rapid death.

The *legal status* of these therapies is very much in dispute, varying from state to state. The obvious question is whether or not *nourishment* and *hydration* are part of *extraordinary* life supportive or life-sustaining measures. Also, does a surgical gastrostomy or naso-gastric intubation differ from a teaspoon or straw as the tools of nourishment and water? Clarification is needed because of the frequent decision to withhold or withdraw life-sustaining measures.

An interesting thought concerning this matter is the ethical and legal status of the deliberate *refusal* by a patient for nourishment and hydration or even for the teaspoon and straw in a determination to commit *suicide* as a legally acceptable right to die. Suicide is never a recommended form of therapy, but in this case it is indeed a solution of the ethical issue regarding nourishment and hydration, as long as there are no religious contradictions.

THE MECHANICAL VENTILATOR

The use of the mechanical ventilator is the most visible form of life support and is useful in conscious patients with various pulmonary problems associated with respiratory failure. It is generally applied in most cases of unconsciousness in association with the establishment of an airway and the delivery of oxygen. There is little need of its use in the vegetative state wherein respirations are spontaneous. In the case of brain death, however, respiratory function is usually absent and may be restored with a ventilator. Cardiac function is then restored in tandem. Even in early death, respiration may be activated temporarily by mechanical means for a very brief duration.

Mechanical ventilation is a complex modality and should be under the control of specially trained personnel in its operation and discontinuation.

WITHDRAWAL OF LIFE SUPPORT

The patient and the physician both have basic rights to request or to accept the decision to withhold or to withdraw life-sustaining, extraordinary treatment. It is legal in all states and is approved in all religions, providing that the criteria are proper. The *patient's rights* to a positive decision are based on the following:

1) The common-law right based upon the federal *Self-Determination Act, 1991*

2) Prior documentation with creation of a Durable Power of Attorney and, in addition, a surrogate or health care proxy (to be available when or if the patient is mentally incompetent)

3) The patient's choice of the quality of life ethic in preference to the sanctity of life ethic, which is considered by many as more burdensome

4) Choice of comfort and freedom from suffering

5) Concern regarding dignity: assurance that others remember the patient as he wishes them to

6) Concern over costs

7) Consideration of not serving as a burden to the family

THE PHYSICIAN'S RIGHTS regarding withdrawal of the patient's life supports are based on the following:

1) Protection by the patient's documentation in the Advance Directive

2) Support by the Durable Power of Attorney, surrogate or proxy

3) The patient's condition warrants the decision by being seriously ill in a) a terminal state, b) a permanent vegetative state, c) a permanent unconscious state, or d) brain dead

4) The prognosis is considered *hopeless* and treatment has been and remains *futile* —not always an easy judgment

OPPOSITION BY PHYSICIAN TO WITHDRAWAL OF LIFE SUPPORT

There are *bases* upon which the physician has the right to *oppose* any request to withhold or withdraw life-sustaining treatment:

1) He is not compelled to act against his own moral or professional values, if such are present.

2) He believes there is a possible or reasonable chance for the patient to recover.

3) He feels that the family or surrogate are not acting in the patient's best interest (should there be an absence of valid documentation).

4) He has a premonition of a possible malpractice litigation on the part of the family of the patient.

5) The physician may have some question about the legality of the matter in the state where treatment is conducted.

6) The physician has concern about ethical issues pertaining to the request.

7) There is opposition by the family to the patient's request, which the physician may be obligated to respect.

8) Questions are raised about the inconsistency of the situation with local practices, which set the legally approved standards for management.

IN CASE OF DISAGREEMENT by the physician and opposition to the request for withdrawal of life support, he must follow definitive measures:

1) Appreciate and be sensitive to the reluctance of the family to accept withholding or withdrawing extraordinary therapy.

2) Engage in explicit discussion with the family or surrogate regarding his views.

3) Offer the option of a second opinion.

4) Consult the hospital's Ethics Committee, the Chief of his Service or hospital counsel.

5) Consider transfer of care of the patient to another physician.

6) Seek a supportive court order.

REMOVAL OF LIFE SUPPORT IF PREFERENCE OF PATIENT IS UNKNOWN

If the preference of the patient is *unknown* and the patient is in a

1) persistent and irreversible unconscious state, unaware of surroundings and unable to respond purposely, or is in a,

2) persistent vegetative state, but is not terminally ill or brain-dead, and does not experience benefits of treatment and does not suffer discomfort, then removal of life support is *controversial* and requires both a legal and an ethical consensus for decision (as with an incompetent patient).

In 1) and 2) above, since the preference of the patient is unknown, an interesting ethical question may be raised: Is removal of life support akin to assisted suicide? Some say yes, although most say no.

REMOVAL OF LIFE SUPPORT IF PREFERENCE OF PATIENT IS KNOWN

Under such circumstance, attention must be directed to the presence or absence of an Advance Directive:

1) The patient has provided an Advance Directive that life-sustaining treatment be withheld. The patient's directive must then be obeyed.

2) The patient has not provided an Advance Directive; then the doctor and the surrogate may by mutual agreement withhold life-sustaining treatment via a Substituted Judgment or an assessment of the patient's best interest.

In this regard, an interesting ethical question asks: Are DNR orders and withholding or withdrawing life support consistent with the primum non nocere principle or the Golden Rule?

Let us now consider the circumstance of a patient who is *brain-*

dead. Regardless of the patient's known preference, the discontinuation of life support is generally approved.

There are valid circumstances in which the physician may order
temporary continuation of life support to body function:
1) To give the surrogate a privileged opportunity to prepare to
donate selected organs of the patient for transplantation
2) To give the surrogate an opportunity to preserve organs for a
previously arranged transplantation
3) To bide time for counseling and comforting the bereaved
4) To sustain a viable fetus in a pregnant patient

ABUSE OF A PATIENT'S RIGHT-TO-DIE DIRECTIVE
ETHICAL ISSUE
It is not infrequent that a patient's right-to-die directive is not
executed in the precise manner described by the patient's wishes. A
contrary action by a hospital staff that is generally anxious to resort
to aggressive therapy in any critical situation is always due to
faulty communication or misunderstanding and never intended to
be deliberately antagonistic. It is essential that the patient's mandate must be clearly written and in place on the order sheet.

If the family or representative of the family consider the action
of the hospital staff as contrary to wishes or as abusive, they may
bring action against the hospital and claim *assault and battery* upon
the patient In such matters, the positions of the I) accusers or plaintiffs and of II) the defendants require some clarification.

I) POSITION OF PLAINTIFF IN AN ASSAULT AND
BATTERY CLAIM
The patient's family, who are the accusers or plaintiffs in a legal
action suit against the doctors and hospital (the defendants), make
the following claim:
a) Negligence by the defendants in ignoring the patient's right

of refusal of treatment, previously expressed in an Advance Directive

b) Infliction of physical, emotional, and financial distress upon the patient

c) Committing medical and legal assault and battery upon the patient

Verdicts generally favor the position of the plaintiff in these circumstances.

II) POSITION OF THE DEFENDANTS

(Physicians and Hospital):

a) Medically, the patient is receiving the best possible treatment.

b) Saving a life can never be judged as against the law.

c) Sometimes patients and/or the family change their minds regarding the patient's directive when death is imminent.

d) The providers of care are not acting out of malice.

e) It is occasionally difficult to predict the quality-of-living outcome when treatment is initiated.

f) The directive is often unclear and lacking specificity.

g) The patient's situation may seem to require emergency intervention and there is no time to check the presence of directives, insurance, etc.

These positions are generally regarded as legally weak. Verdicts usually do not favor the defendants.

USE OF ADVANCED MEDICAL TECHNOLOGY IN END-OF-LIFE CARE

In making decisions regarding preferential care in end-of-life situations, a series of ethical considerations must be given to the justification for the fullest possible use of advanced medical technology, which every institution, by offering acute care, makes every effort to have completely available. As a result, advanced biotechnology is an essential component of an aggressive approach to modern critical care. There is little doubt of its life-extending virtues, but the use of advanced medical technology in end-of-life care raises the following questions:

1) Occasionally excessive?

2) Always appropriate?

3) Extending the patient's quality of living? Is the dying process being prolonged?

4) Unnecessarily expensive? There is ample evidence of excessive costs in the application of advanced medical technology in the relatively common situation of a dying elderly patient. As an illustration, approximately one-third of Part 1 Medicare (hospital) costs are for care during the last year of the patient's life. Contributors to the cost include intensive care involving high technologic laboratory and radiologic tests and procedures, drugs, twenty-four hour nursing care, multiple specialty physicians, etc.

A low estimate of costs for a patient in an intensive care unit is $2,000 per day compared with an average hospital cost of $1,000 per patient per day. Needless to say, the costs are greater in the United States than in any other country in the world. An added factor in this financial burden is that coverage by private health insurance may be very limited.

5) Encouraging the hospital staffs unwittingly to devote more attention to acutely ill patients with a more favorable prognosis? This is not surprising when one considers that the caretakers cannot be in two places at the same time.

6) Causing a prolongation of excessive pain and suffering? Such unsatisfactory effect is responsible for the reference to advanced medical technology as a good servant, but a cruel master.

7) Having an adverse effect upon the public generally in that the unfavorable features of advanced medical care have made many people fearful of an extended dying and a *technological death* despite all of its benefits?

Answers to these questions cannot be generalized, but must be considered individually.

As a result of the many questions, there has occurred a significant rise in popularity of:

a) The right-to-die movement

b) Passive (as well as active) euthanasia

c) Palliative and hospice care

These are obviously trends in opposite directions away from the technological extension of the dying process.

As a reflection of this trend, statistics relative to the location or facilities where elderly patients have recently chosen to die are as follows: fifty-five percent in hospitals (with a significant percentage of Do Not Resuscitate orders in accordance with the patient's prior written directive), twenty percent in nursing homes, and five percent at home. (See later in this chapter regarding the twenty percent of patients who die in hospice care.)

QUALITY LIVING VS. QUALITY DYING

In considering quality living, equal time must be devoted to a discussion about quality dying.

Let us therefore now clarify the current status of *euthanasia* (which literally means *easy death*).

We must first recall that the normal, expected role of the physician is always to bear in mind that all human beings have a moral claim to humane treatment. The physician is obligated to relieve pain and suffering without harm (primum non nocere). He must also comply, however, with the written requests of patients. The physician is subject to the restrictive laws and to established professional and personal mandates.

PASSIVE EUTHANASIA

The term euthanasia is generally reserved for assisted suicide, or active euthanasia The concept of the term passive euthanasia would therefore be an oxymoron, or even non-existent or forbidden in usage. The author prefers the term of passive euthanasia, however, based upon a patient's constitutional right to die and to the universal right to suicide legally and morally, although forbidden in certain religious beliefs. It is reflected in 1) do-not-resuscitate (DNR) orders and 2) the withholding or withdrawing of life-sustaining treatment under valid circumstances. To those who oppose withdrawing life-sustaining measures as an act of killing, supporters feel, as do most concerned, that in the withdrawing of treatment, only the dying will die of their disease, and therefore the procedure is not an act of killing.

In the application of passive euthanasia, death is considered to be imminent and impending. It has been documented by the patient in an Advance Directive as desirable treatment in order to avoid the prolongation of the process of dying and to *die with dignity*.

ETHICAL ISSUES

1) To hasten the outcome in the expectation of a more imminent death by withdrawing life-sustaining measures does not always assure early death. Is this an ethical concern?

2) To hasten the outcome by withdrawing nutrition and hydration in an act of denying the patient bread and water is a moral question. Is not life being terminated by avoidable starvation? It would not have ethical concern if the patient *chose* to refuse to take nutrition and hydration, and thereby commit *suicide*, a perfectly legal right of the patient, although as a moral consideration, some religions oppose suicide.

INDICATIONS FOR PASSIVE EUTHANASIA

The patient, in a prior competent mental state, has given written approval and documentation that he wishes to have life-supportive measures withdrawn or withheld by DNR orders when he is 1) terminally and irreversibly ill (dying is expected within six months), or 2) in an irreversible coma, or 3) in a persistent vegetative state, or 4) brain-dead.

CONTRAINDICATIONS TO PASSIVE EUTHANASIA

Two circumstances are generally agreed upon as contraindicating the application of passive euthanasia: 1) prolonged *mental depression*, which is usually treatable satisfactorily, and 2) chronic *uncontrollable pain*, which is presumed to be treatable—a situation which is controversial and not always certain. The legality of prescribing unusual amounts of narcotics by well-meaning doctors for the relief of pain varies in different states. Unfortunately, some physicians have been punished legally, whereas others have been commended for their dedicated approach to pain relief.

The principle of *double effect* becomes pertinent here. The patient may require sufficient narcotics to relieve pain (*good effect*), but is given an excessive amount of narcotic *inadvertently* in order to accomplish the analgesic effect, thereby causing death (*bad effect*). If sufficient narcotic is given to cause death knowingly in a deliberate endeavor to relieve pain, the bad effect outweighs the benefit, or good effect. The process is then illegal.

When the good effect predominates as the intent, the treatment is valid generally, but debatable in some state legalities.

The management of chronic pain is of enormous medical, ethical, and legal concern. It is desperately in need of public discussion and a universally accepted legal resolution. In the meantime, patients and doctors suffer over its confused status.

ACTIVE EUTHANASIA
DEFINITION
The rigid definition considers that active euthanasia is the act or practice of painlessly putting to death by lethal agents persons suffering from incurable, debilitating, and distressing disease as an act of *mercy*.

FORMS
There are two forms of active euthanasia:

1) Assisted Suicide (Mero, Humphry)

2) Physician-assisted suicide (Kevorkian, Netherlands System, Oregon Death with Dignity Act) (Ed: Would a better or another term for assisted suicide be *Assisted Dying*?)

ASSISTED SUICIDE OR ASSISTED DYING
DEFINITION
The legal definition of assisted suicide and physician-assisted suicide is the causing or aiding another person to accomplish requested suicide or requested death.

ETHICAL ISSUES
There are a number of ethical dilemmas inherent in this process:

1) The definition is unclear. For example, is advocating, counseling, or providing the means of suicide actually causing or aiding?

2) Is it a crime to aid another person in attempting suicide (his legal right) or to complete his wish to die?

3) There has been a surprising increase in the number of patients requesting the assisted means of death.

4) State laws vary widely, although there is general opposition.

OPPOSITION TO LEGALIZATION
There is considerable opposition to current efforts at legalization of active euthanasia on the grounds that:

1) It represents homicide.

2) It is prohibited in the Hippocratic Oath, other codes, and in Judeo-Christian biblical teaching.

3) Its acceptance would easily become broadened and abused, leading by way of the *slippery slope* to include the elderly, disabled, demented, criminals, et al. Fortunately, legal restrictions now assure protection of the most vulnerable candidates for obliteration.

4) It is opposed by all religious groups, the American Medical Association, and other respected organizations as an act of homicide.

5) The question is raised repeatedly: Is there a moral difference between withdrawing life-sustaining treatment and assisted suicide? Most feel there is, but there are differences of opinion.

SUPPORT OF ASSISTED SUICIDE

Although there is much organizational and religious opposition, there is considerable evidence of *covert* support of assisted suicide.

1) Two-thirds of the population favors it (secretly, not openly).

2) Among physicians, in a survey of 5000 doctors in one of our largest states, sixty percent secretly expressed support of a law allowing voluntary euthanasia. Fourteen percent of the physicians admitted that they had each helped at least one terminally ill patient to die, although the means of death was not specified. To be sure, few if any physicians would acknowledge publicly their private actions.

3) Doing everything possible to prevent dying frequently causes more suffering than providing comfort. There is often inadequate relief of depression or of pain.

4) Should people who manage their affairs in life be prevented from managing or controlling the conditions of their death?

5) In families where a terminally ill patient is begging for relief from suffering, the observing close relatives invariably become supporters of assistance in dying.

6) Physician-assisted suicide is not killing or murder. In murder, a victim's life is terminated against his will. In physician-

assisted suicide, the patient is assisted in dying at his own request and will. Opponents are either unable to grasp the difference, or unwilling to be moved by the difference.

In instances where assisted suicide has been accomplished, the most common means of death has been 1) by the administration of lethal drugs that are legal, such as sodium pentobarbital, morphine, potassium chloride, curare, et al., or 2) by carbon monoxide inhalation.

ASSISTED SUICIDE PROGRAMS

A number of programs pertaining to assisted suicide have been popularized. All are controversial from the ethical standpoint. They will be addressed in the following.

Reverend Ralph Mero has headed group supporting assisted suicide. They are strong believers in compassion *in dying*. They operate rather secretively, making no public announcements. The group does not provide or administer lethal drugs, but it does offer advice on the dosage of lethal drugs they recommend. The patient is provided with guidelines, and compassion is emphasized in the belief that religion should assist in alleviating suffering. Their aim is to avoid violent suicide, which is regarded as an unacceptable end. (Ed: In this regard, the tragic history of failure and suffering in personal amateur attempts at suicide would justify professional advice.)

Another group involved with assisted suicide is the *Hemlock Society*, founded by Derek Humphry in 1980. It supports the option of voluntary euthanasia for terminal illness. Its basis is the frequent circumstance that many patients with advanced illness are in great suffering and wish to die. The group recommends the legal methods of suicide. Humphry's book, 'Final Exit,' is a good source for their philosophy.

PHYSICIAN-ASSISTED SUICIDE

As far as physician-assisted suicide is concerned, the best known reference is to the physician, Jack *Kevorkian*, a retired pathologist, who has been variously called an angel of mercy and the patron saint of medicine on the one hand, and simultaneously a serial mercy killer, and the death doctor on the other hand. Kevorkian, a self-designated obitiatrist considers his motto as a rational policy of planned death. He does personify the debate over whether or when a physician can help a patient terminate an incurable, unbearably suffering, deteriorating illness. In his favor is that, as a physician, he evaluates each request for his aid carefully, and he attempts to dissuade the patient from ending life. He offers, but does not apply, his so-called suicide machine, which provides a lethal amount of carbon monoxide.

From the legal point of view, Kevorkian is looked upon as conducting active euthanasia, which is illegal. He has, therefore, been charged with first degree murder. Repeated efforts to condemn him to prison failed because of the success of his defense that he has not broken any laws. Charges have been dropped repeatedly, but his medical license was suspended. After numerous legal efforts, he was finally found guilty of murder, as charged.

ETHICAL ISSUES

Ethical issues arising from the Kevorkian experience concern primarily the *slippery slope*. If approved, where can assisted suicide lead? When is aiding suicide, an act of mercy, and when is it an act of murder? Does Kevorkian's passive role make him less culpable than if his role were active?

Kevorkian's bold attempt to legalize assisted suicide remains as a major ethical issue. Everyone is either for or against the concept, and no one is neutral or unconcerned about it. All were either saddened or elated when, after several court appearances, he was finally sentenced to jail. He succeeded, however, in raising the level of interest supporting assisted suicide to a national fervor.

On a legislative basis, the United States Supreme Court in 1999 ruled that there is no constitutional right to assisted suicide and that states could individually either ban it or permit it. Congress has endeavored to prevent it by considering the Pain Relief Promotion Act of 1999.

States have responded by a) the majority prohibiting assisted suicide, b) some still considering it, and 3) only Oregon legalizing it by referendum in the *Oregon Death with Dignity Act* in 1995 and enacted in 1997. The state has published a guidebook for health care providers, which explains the requirements for both patients and physicians, who wish to consider it.

Essentially, in the Oregon plan of approval, the patient must be terminally ill, mentally competent, and has made several oral and written requests within a certain period of time. The physician must have approval by psychiatric consultation.

The patient receives a prescription for about ninety 100 mg. secobarbital capsules. Their contents are emptied into a dessert such as applesauce. The patient takes an antiemetic one hour before ingestion to prevent vomiting and aspiration. The contents are consumed within an hour. The presence of the physician is optional. In the first year of its implementation in 1998, fifteen of the twenty-three patients died following the suicidal attempt.

Another highly publicized experience with physician-assisted suicide is the *Netherlands System*. It is an open system of tolerance of assisted suicide. The procedure is permitted by practice, not by statute. There is very little government control. Although there are at least 10,000 patient requests per year in the Netherlands, physicians actually provide the means in less than two percent of the requests and actually perform the life-ending means in less than one percent of the requests.

The method used is induction of sleep with barbiturates followed by a lethal injection of curare.

There are strict *guidelines* in place as safeguards in the Netherlands System of assisted suicide:

1) The patient must be mentally competent.

2) The patient must document a request for euthanasia voluntarily, repeatedly over a reasonable time.

3) The patient must be suffering intolerably from a serious medical illness with no prospect of relief, although he need not be terminal.

The physician must consult with another physician who is not involved in the case, and be joined in approval or disapproval.

LEGALIZATION OF ASSISTED SUICIDE

Almost everyone is either strongly in favor of the legalization of assisted suicide or strongly opposed to the process. It is interesting that those who have a close family member in prolonged suffering from a debilitating illness favor assisted suicide with rare, if any, exceptions. Each group presents a number of factors that favor or oppose legalization.

Those in *support* of the legalization of assisted suicide cite a number of factors that tend to favor assisted suicide as follows:

1) The right -to-die laws

2) The tragedy of the Quinlan case, 1976

3) The patient's bill of rights

4) The Patient Self-Determination Act of 1991

5) Respect for the patient's right of autonomy based upon the concept of informed consent

6) Repeated acquittals of Dr. Jack Kevorkian

7) The Oregon Death with Dignity Act of 1995

8) Legalization of Assisted Suicide in Oregon, 1997

9) The Right to Die Declaration in a Living Will, Durable Power of Attorney, or Advance Directive available to everyone who in a state of mental competence is considering his end-of-life preferences

10) Legality of suicide

11) The Quality of Life Ethic pertaining to the withdrawal of life-supportive measures in a philosophy of dying with dignity

12) The fact that very few sanctity of life proponents favor sustaining life at all costs

13) Many individuals in private surveys are in favor of assisted suicide

14) Relief is offered from the:

　　　a) futile perpetuation of a poor quality of living,

　　　b) prolonged suffering without relief in a terminal illness,

　　　c) prohibitive, wasteful costs in the prolongation of the dying process due entirely to advanced biotechnology.

15) Not a clear deviation from withholding or withdrawing life-sustaining treatment in a patient in a) a vegetative state, or in b) a brain-dead state

16) Many personal suicide attempts are botched, some repeatedly, as a result of the patient's inability to obtain the means or the ability to perform the act despite good intentions.

17) Numerous *safeguards* are in place ensuring that the patient's desire for assisted suicide is a function of the following:

　　　a) Self-determination—the decision is voluntary and is not coerced,

　　　b) Competent state of mind

　　　c) Receipt of full disclosure by the physician in providing the patient with all relevant information regarding the medical condition of the patient, including prognosis

　　　d) Informed consent of the patient after reliably considered evaluation,

e) Not a manifestation of treatable depression or treatable pain (despite their lack of total adequacy)

f) stable and durable request

18) Question: Is it rational for an eighty-five year old man wracked with pain and suffering from extensive metastatic cancer, facing certain death, to lack the legal right to be assisted in his desire for suicide? (Some opponents offer the admittedly more cruel option for the patient to withhold his own food and water.)

19) Question: Should a hopelessly ill patient on treatment that offers minimal, if any, benefit, who is in prolonged suffering, and who even refuses food and water as well as life-sustaining measures, not be allowed to receive assistance in his desire for suicide that he is physically unable to accomplish by himself? (Opponents say the patient should be kept as comfortable as possible whether or not comfort is totally adequate.)

Those who *oppose* the legalization of assisted suicide cite a number of *factors* that support their position as follows:

1) The Hippocratic Oath: 'First do no harm' (primum non nocere)

2) The Ethics Manual of the American College of Physicians

3) The American Medical Association Council on Ethical and Judicial Affairs

4) Successful hospice care

5) The classical image of the physician as healer and comforter, not as an agent of death

6) Compromise of the patient's trust in the physician

7) The sanctity of human life as projected in all religious views

8) Possible harm in the rare instance of a faulty diagnosis and a basically good prognosis

9) Opposition by all religious, legal and medical organizations (despite the many private and covert opinions of individuals)

10) Danger of the slippery slope phenomenon and opportunities

for abuse, especially if regulated on a case-by-case basis in lieu of general law

11) Legal consideration of assisted suicide as active euthanasia, hence as homicide—There are legal variations among the states in this regard.

12) Question: If legalized, would the physician have a natural and innate lessening of an incentive to optimize supportive care?

13) In opposition to assisted suicide, Congress has proposed *The Pain Relief Promotion Act of 1999*, designed to protect citizens against assisted suicide. There are convincing arguments for and against the proposal, depending upon pro and con points of view.

Assisted suicide remains an ethical issue because of popular pro and con opinions, despite overt legal and organizational opposition.

In view of strong opposition, it is not surprising that in sharp contrast to the concept of assisted suicide there is a 180-degree turn by many in the direction of hospice or palliative care, nursing home care, or home health care. Such patients are primarily followers of the sanctity of life ethic as opposed to the quality of life ethic and its policy of death with dignity. Occasionally, patients in hospice or nursing home care turn to aggressive technologic care in hospitals when death seems imminent.

HOSPICE CARE

Hospice Care, also known as *Palliative* Care, has reemerged in popularity over the past thirty years in reaction to various unsatisfactory and unacceptable aspects of the following:

1) Death following prolonged, advanced technological therapies (often a manifestation of compliance with the sanctity of life ethic)

2) Passive euthanasia including assisted suicide (for those favoring a quality of life ethic)

3) Vegetating existence, awaiting death in a nursing home, and occasionally in one's own home

First established in 1967 by Dame Cicely Saunders, St. Christopher's Hospice, Sydenham, England, hospice care offers *palliative* and humane care on the basis of acceptance of impending death as a *natural* and biological part of life. The patients are assisted in a transition from dying to death with support and *comfort*. The families of patients are also helped during the patient's dying process and also after the patient's death.

The delivery of care is conducted by physicians, nurses, social workers, and pastoral bereavement counselors.

Approximately 500,000 patients utilize about 3000 hospices throughout the United States where each patient spends an average period of thirty-six days. Twenty percent of patients end their lives in hospice care, compared with fifty five percent in hospitals, twenty percent in nursing homes, and five percent in care at home.

Medicare and private insurance coverage are generally adequate, but more resources are often required in hospice care.

Hospice care is more widely used in Great Britain, Canada, and Australia than in the United States, where it is underused and somewhat undervalued, but gaining in popularity.

Opponents of hospice care are few, but outspoken in the consideration that the hospice philosophy is one of *defeatism* and of giving up hope. Instead, opponents favor the extremes of high-technologic aggressive therapy or else euthanasia.

NURSING HOME CARE
Nursing home care accommodates about twenty percent of dying elderly patients and serves as a choice for those who are:
a) not interested in aggressive care, b) not aiming for euthanasia, c) not favoring hospice care, and d) not suitable for home care.

Typically, the patients in nursing home care resemble the fewer number of patients in a home care setting: elderly, disabled, in an irreversible, vegetating condition, and requiring twenty-four hour daily nursing care.

Despite the costly care, an adequate number of beds in approved and desirable facilities is not easily available. Generally, when patients become too ill to manage in nursing homes, as is the case with home care, they are often referred to hospitals for emergency treatment, often with advanced medical technology, which usually proves futile. Benefits are more often satisfying to the patient's family than to the patient. In such circumstances, an advance directive of the patient is essential.

HOME HEALTH CARE

Agencies, including visiting nurse facilities, are available to offer home health care. They can provide nursing care and therapies at all levels, generally under the supervision of a physician, who may be available for consultation, but is usually not able to undertake the responsibility of on-going care requiring home visits. Such situations, when necessary, are more likely to favor hospital care or hospice care. In addition, the administrative and financial burdens of around-the-clock quality nursing care rarely enables home health care to be totally adequate.

CONVENTIONAL WISDOM REGARDING DECISION-MAKING NEAR THE END OF LIFE

1) Everyone expects and deserves the highest quality of health care throughout life.

2) The goal in health care is to prevent and cure disease, provide comfort, and prolong life to one's natural life span of 85 to 115 years by correction of all genetic defects, environmental hazards, and by improving quality living to its highest level.

3) The goal is not to abolish death and seek immortality, or even to prevent the aging process.

4) All patients should be kept free of pain and suffering even if life incidentally—not deliberately—is thereby shortened.

5) As a primary consideration, everyone should decide for himself whether to follow the quality of life ethic or the sanctity of life ethic.

6) Every person's dignity, privacy, personhood, and autonomy must be respected.

7) Every competent patient's legal and ethical right to refuse any treatment (self-determination based upon informed consent) should be respected and honored.

8) Every competent adult should prepare an Advance Directive and appoint a Durable Power of Attorney and a Surrogate or a health care Proxy to make health care decisions consistent with the patient's wishes, should the patient become incompetent.

9) It is strangely ironic that, in the United States, the richest country with the best available health care in the world, there are millions of poor children and elderly people who are inadequately insured or are uninsured, and are unable to obtain adequate health care that may be needed desperately.

10) It is equally ironic that many ill people are compelled to endure, often against their will, expensive and invasive biotechnological measures that are often futile and not even in the patient's best interest in that they prolong dying, not quality living.

11) Should not the burden of living be balanced against the benefit of living and consideration be given to quality living?

SUMMARY OF HIGHLIGHTS IN DECISION-MAKING

In a carefully planned written decree, each person should determine whether he wishes to have one of the following as life nears its end:

I) Aggressive, *life-sustaining* care known as medicalization, or

II) Aggressive, *life-ending* care, or

III) *Palliative*, alleviative care

I) MEDICALIZATION (AGGRESSIVE LIFE SUSTAINING CARE)

The basis for medicalization, or the use of heroic and intensive measures, is the *prolongation of life* and the *delay of death* (notwithstanding the contention by opponents that the process is too often *prolongation of dying*).

The need for use of medicalization has no opponents in *acute* emergency situations where cardio-pulmonary resuscitation and advanced biotechnology are indicated and life-saving. It becomes a debatable issue, however, in *chronic* disorders with no emergency components and there is time for consideration whether or not to apply costly high technological, multi-specialty, procedure-oriented, tertiary medical care.

In the application of medicalization, the *diagnosis* and its complications are generally well known, and there is total concentration upon the *treatment*, which then involves extensive, costly, advanced biotechnology; mechanical ventilation; excessive laboratory, and complex radiologic procedures; medical specialty supervision; new drugs including antibiotics, analgesics, and chemotherapy; intravenous fluids; naso-gastric feedings; Foley catheter bladder drainage; surgery; around the clock nursing and monitoring.

SUPPORT OF MEDICALIZATION:

In support of medicalization are the following:

a) More patients die in hospitals than in all other facilities combined (hospice, nursing home, patient's home).

b) Hospital facilities are generally available for emergencies. Medicalization is the expected form of treatment in all seriously ill hospitalized patients.

c) Attending physicians are willing, able, enthusiastic, and available.

d) Medicalization has a valuable role in purposefully delaying death in patients in coma with irreversible brain damage or in a vegetative state, in order to be prepared for the timely transfer of organs in planned transplantation.

e) Prognosticating recovery may be difficult, and is often ill-advised.

The common biomedical philosophy in the application of medicalization is that extension of life is available and theoretically unlimited. "It is better to do something than to do nothing, even with little expectation of benefit"—an interesting, highly controversial and common ethical consideration.

OPPOSITION TO MEDICALIZATION is as outspoken as is its support:

a) Care can be painful.

b) There may be a high cost to low benefit ratio, hence, wasteful.

c) There may be little or no prolongation of life.

d) There may be prolongation of the dying process.

e) The dying patient may be deprived of autonomy and dignity.

ETHICAL ISSUES PERTAINING TO MEDICALIZATION:

a) Are life-sustaining measures in use as a result of the patient's expressed written wishes in an available Advance Directive?

b) Are they in the best interest of the patient?

c) Are the physician's views consistent with the patient's and/or the family's wishes?

d) Are DNR orders indicated and authorized?

e) Are there legal mandates, such as an Advance Directive, in place, particularly to authenticate the physician's orders in the patient's medical record?

II) AGGRESSIVE LIFE-ENDING CARE

In a patient's choice of an aggressive life-ending interventional decision such as passive euthanasia and the withdrawal of life-sustaining measures, the principle, *first do no harm,* is raised. Those who favor the withdrawal of life-support claim that continuing further aggressive care in a futile endeavor is clearly unethical.

III) PALLIATIVE ALLEVIATIVE CARE

The palliative, alleviative, non-interventional decision's aim is total comfort of the patient. The interest of the average physician in the hospital setting as well as his deficient skill and low interest in hospice-type care are the result of a) inadequate medical education and training in hospice care and b) inbred philosophy of *doing something.*

EFFECTS OF REDUCED INTEREST IN PALLIATIVE CARE

The effects of the frequently occurring lack of interest and skills on the part of the physician regarding palliative care are as follows:

a) The physician may be in an uncomfortable role because it is foreign to his philosophy of doing something.

b) The situation is an unwelcome reminder of the limitations and failures of scientific medicine's treatment in end-stage care.

c) Medical frustration tends to lead to more aggressive care rather than to less aggressive care.

d) Discontent with the transfer of care from those intimate with the patient's complex problems to the hands of strangers and institutions unfamiliar with the patient during his prior independent function and good health.

e) The physician does not accept the thought that a good death may be the best outcome.

f) The physician may assume an adversarial and defensive position in his opposition as far as his relation with the family is concerned.

g) The physician may be in fear that the patient's eventual death will be scrutinized by peers at mortality conferences as demonstrating errors in management.

h) The physician may be alarmed that his patient's death may be reported to risk management with questions raised regarding liability.

i) The physician may be critiqued in mandated quality assurance reviews.

j) To the average physician, death is looked upon, not as a part of life, but the enemy of scientific medicine and the personal failure of the physician. "What else could I have done?" is a frequent question a physician asks colleagues at clinical conferences.

VIEW OF DYING AS A DIAGNOSTIC ENTITY

If the physician could see the process of dying as a diagnostic entity with definable features, he would be able to observe that:

a) Dying, unlike sudden death, is most often prolonged, always (by definition) incurable, irreversible, and inevitably directed toward a life-ending course.

b) It requires acceptance and accommodation.

c) One should focus on limitations of treatment.

d) Liability risks are clarified and minimized

e) It decreases the burden of difficult and painful decision-making.

f) It facilitates the offering of more humane forms of medical treatment with emphasis upon patient comfort.

g) It enables rejection of a narrow biomedical view of dying.

h) It enables the physician to relearn palliative skills (a popular form of medical care prior to modern scientific medicine, and a currently undervalued and underused concept).

i) It reduces medicalization and its impersonal, fragmented, overtesting, overtreating, prolonged, expensive, wasteful, questionably necessary hospitalization.

j) It emphasizes awareness that aggressive diagnostic and therapeutic measures (especially in the care of the elderly) are likely to slow and even harm the decline in the patient's quality of living. It generally fails to reverse the decline.

k) It enables the physician to devote more time with patients and listen to their concerns—a lost art in the patient-doctor relationship.

l) It helps reestablish other areas of thinking in the doctor-patient relationship.

m) It allows the physician to recognize that the inevitable decline of the dying elderly patient is not a failure of medical care, but rather a part of a normal process in aging with positive as well as negative dimensions; that dying bravely is heroic; and that death is a desirable relief from suffering.

GUIDING PRINCIPLES IN END-OF-LIFE
DECISION MAKING

There are three guiding principles in end-of-life decision making:

1) Respect for the patient's autonomy and self-determination based upon thorough disclosure (informed consent) on the part of the patient's physician. The chief concerns are the patient's rights, wishes, and freedom from outside influences.

2) Respect for non-maleficence and beneficences in the physician's and family's concern over the patient's a) best interests, b) quality living and c) quality of dying.

3) Aid in assessment of value of the patient's *quality of living* based upon the physician's ability to foresee the prognosis and the family's (as well as the patient's) ability to best judge the quality and value of the time remaining for the patient. In actuality, in a patient's recovery from serious illness, the patient is far better able to judge his new, possibly limited, quality of living for himself than is the physician.

THE FUTILITY FACTOR IN END-OF-LIFE CARE
BACKGROUND

More than ten percent of the population is over sixty-five years of age. People in their eighties comprise the fastest growing decade in numbers. The elderly are responsible for more than thirty percent of Medicare costs,especially in the last year of their lives, often in intensive care units at great expense in personnel in the prolongation of dying. Correspondingly, the costs are burgeoning. The important question is whether such investment of funds is sound ethically, economically, socially and medically.

In addition, there is inadequate health care coverage for patients requiring long-term care.

Although most patients elect to follow a quality of life ethic and seek dignity in dying in their end-of-life care, a sufficient number follow the quantitative or sanctity-of-life ethic with advanced, high-technological interventions in order to extend their length of life.

DEFINITION OF FUTILITY

The background leads to a point in health care reminiscent of the law of diminishing return—more and more input, less and less return. The ultimate is futility—a term signifying irreversibility and hopelessness. As a diagnostic entity, futility may be the most difficult concept a physician is called upon to consider. It is totally in conflict with his philosophic determination to improve a patient's ill health and at the same time acknowledging failure in the effort. Consequently, the physician's acceptance of futility may be challenged and his objectivity clouded. It is essential, however, that futility be finally recognized and appreciated so that appropriate action be established.

AIDS IN THE RECOGNITION OF FUTILE CARE

1) Futility may not be apparent until treatment has been implemented and observed to be failing.

2) Any treatment merely preserves unconsciousness or merely preserves the vegetating state.

3) Treatment fails to end the patient's total dependence on intensive medical care with constant monitoring, ventilatory support, and intensive nursing care.

4) Treatment fails to improve the prognosis, which is evidently poorer and poorer.

JUDGMENTS REGARDING FUTILITY

1) Once determined, a decision of futility permits the physician to withhold or withdraw the care that the physician deems inappropriate, with or without the family's approval.

2) The physician is not obligated to offer an option of futile care to the family.

3) The patient's family does not have the right to demand a decision of futile care or to deny the physician its consideration by him.

4) Futility pertains to failure of recovery and does not relate at all to quality living. It is ethically inappropriate for physicians to presume that their professional expertise qualifies them to know what kind of life is worth prolonging.

The patient and the family are best qualified to determine the patient's best interest. Example: In a seemingly irreversible coma, a patient might regain consciousness as a result of life-supportive measures only to be severely disabled with blindness, paralysis, etc. Some such disabled patients consider that they have sufficient quality of living and are grateful for their recovery. In these instances, the physician would be violating the patient's best interest if he had chosen to withdraw the patient's necessary means of treatment in the presumption of preventing survival with inadequate quality of living.

5) In view of the fact that patients are free to request life-sustaining treatment in a Living Will, physicians are not obliged to provide such treatment if the situation is regarded by him as "futile." A diagnosis of futility is a medical determination. In a dispute, the physician should seek medical corroboration and legal advice in his support. The issue can be a contentious one, however, pitting the patient's and family's autonomy against the physician's expertise with peer confirmation. The position of the patient and the family is purely an emotional one, whereas the physician's position is that further intervention prolongs the dying process in lieu of prolonging life. In his professional opinion, it would be a futile endeavor to offer aggressive therapy, such as surgery,

chemotherapy, hemodialysis, artificial ventilation, et al, for a patient with an advanced illness and in a near-moribund state with little expectation of cure or even palliation.

Once determined by the physician, futility takes precedence over the patient's or family's autonomy.

ETHICAL ISSUES REGARDING FUTILITY

1) An interesting ethical question has been raised regarding an arbitrary age cut-off, e.g., at ninety years for unrealistic, impractical intensive care. Elderly people oppose such arbitrary decision strongly, whereas younger patients are more inclined to favor it. Is not the goal of health care to improve quality living rather than extend the duration of life or prolong dying?

2) A troublesome question concerns the restriction and re-allocation of health care funds. Would such available funds be diverted to the health care needs of young patients, or would they be diverted to some non-medical purpose?

3) Is the philosophy of many to extend life a sane one?

4) Is it rational to seek a mystical fountain of youth or to make an imaginary effort to turn old age into an endless middle age? Should not dying and death be viewed more realistically and accepted as a part of life? No matter how much we spend, will we not still age and die?

5) In the absence of our ability to restore a patient to good health, is it not our aim to concentrate on relief of pain and suffering as with assisted suicide or with hospice care?

6) Is it not the preference of most people to experience social dignity and quality in their dying rather than to have torturous, life-extending technology?

FINAL THOUGHT

Despite its depressing content, the author deemed it essential to review the futility factor in a discussion regarding decision-making in end-of-life care. He wishes to redirect the reader's attention to the more pleasant theme of the text, namely that the true goal of medical science is to prevent premature death by 1) correcting all genetic mutations, inherited and acquired, and 2) improving or eliminating all adverse environmental influences on human beings in order to assure everyone of an encoded natural life span of 85-115 years.

Furthermore, it is our purpose to concentrate on the third and highest tier of *quality living* (compliance with the modern ethical principles) in developing an altruistic philosophy of societal compatibility and live in harmony with our neighbors, thereby attaining a perfect *semicircle of life*.

SECTION D

SUBJECT VII:

HEALTH CARE REFORM

Life is an end in itself, and the only question as to whether it is worth living is whether you have enough of it.

— Justice Oliver Wendell Holmes,
1841-1935

BACKGROUND

In the entire world, The United States ranks foremost in having the best educated professionals in health care, the highest and most advanced biotechnology, and the most and best in medical research. Despite this exalted and enviable position, it is ironic that the United States ranks among the lowest civilized societies in low birth weight percentages, neonatal and infant mortality, and life expectancy.

The reasons for the poor record are not primarily due to obvious causes such as smoking, alcohol consumption, auto accidents, guns, and violence.

More significant are 1) social factors such as income inequality with emphasis particularly on poverty, and 2) medical factors including medication errors and adverse drug reactions, hospital nosocomial infections, marginally necessary surgery, low ratio of primary care-preventive medicine to high specialty care, burgeoning costs of health care including the outrageous costs of vital drugs, inadequate health insurance coverage, maldistribution of costs and services, excessive aggressive terminal care, et al.

These issues will be considered in some detail in the ensuing pages of this chapter in order to establish a need for health care reform.

CHAPTER 26

HEALTH CARE REFORM

Do all the good you can,
By all the means you can,
In all the places you can,
At all the times you can,
To all the people you can,
As long as ever you can.

— John Wesley, 1703-1791

INTRODUCTION

The goal of quality living and the achievement of the perfect semicircle of life can never be realized without our immediate attention to the urgent need of health care reform, the last of our seven major subjects in health care with a multitude of serious ethical issues. Major revisions of the current status of health care are essential and are best described as reform.

The author has a naive understanding of the needs for health care reform based upon the fact that, like health care in other civilized societies, we in the United States desperately require, succinctly stated, a comprehensive, universal program that protects everyone, rich and poor, throughout everyone's entire life, and includes long-term care.

The fundamental issue is that millions of Americans lack adequate health insurance coverage. It is downright un-American not to have catastrophic care and long-term health care available for everyone, especially the poor, disabled, and mentally ill.

The author's position is best described by a simple anecdote. Shortly after the Clinton administration came to office in 1993, the President, in his First State of the Union Address, presented the first comprehensive, universal health care program in our history. It was bold and exciting, designed for the benefit of every American. Immediately after its presentation, it was attacked vigorously on television by an opponent of the Administration, not because it was too costly or too complex, but because, "we do not need health care reform because we have the best health care in the world." That may not be an exact quotation, but the point of it is close enough. The speaker, a prominent senator, really should have said, "I, a United States senator, enjoy the best health care in the world,"—a most egoistic comment, completely ignoring the fact that most people do not even come close to the senator's health care privileges. In the author's judgment, what would have been better suited to the responsibility of a senator would have been the statement that, "we have the best health care in the world, and every American citizen should enjoy the best and same care that is available to me." The author has no problem with the attack on the Clinton health care plan, which no major group supported, but raises the question: has any opponent come up with any other plan that would come near offering comprehensive, universal care, or even minimally adequate health care for all citizens?

No one can question that we have the best and most advanced health care in the world, and based upon the best biotechnology and the best trained personnel, the quality of care is consistently getting better and better. The major problem is that there is no equality of opportunity for the care. Hence, it must be universal (available to all equally) and comprehensive (inclusive of all ailments and circumstances).

The cost of health care currently is on the order of $1 trillion per year and rapidly burgeoning. In order to achieve cost control, resources must be reallocated and managed efficiently. Everyone must have freedom of choice of care within reason, and the integrity of the doctor-patient relationship must be preserved.

An appeal process must be available to every patient, who must have the legal right to recourse when maltreated.

WHAT IS COMPREHENSIVE, UNIVERSAL HEALTH CARE?

Comprehensive, universal care considers the delivery and availability of adequate, and at least minimal care, including acute and chronic illnesses, preventive care, hospitalization costs, long-term care, and home care for all, including the poor, children, elderly, disabled, mentally ill, all uninsured and many underinsured. The range of benefits must meet the basic needs with fair resource constraints and a fair distribution of costs and services. Every citizen must have the equal opportunity to pursue reasonable health goals without fear of bias.

Although the cost factor is of prime concern, it is not an issue per se. The cost relative to the benefit is the primary issue.

In order to accomplish ideal comprehensive care, there is need (as is already in operation) of a deliberate plan to reverse the number of medical specialists (seventy percent of physicians) to generalists (thirty percent of physicians). Only then could everyone be cared for with essential preventive medicine, nutritional guidance, immunizations, periodic health surveys, and total primary care for the entire family that is coordinated with specialty care. In order to support the increased need of primary physicians (family physicians and general internists) for the entire population, an increase in nurse practitioners, physician assistants, midwives, and other para-medical personnel would be needed.

THE ACCESS FACTOR IN HEALTH CARE

Many people are currently excluded from universal access to health care. The reason may not be deliberate, but it is surely not accidental. The barrier is predominantly a financial one, especially for the poor, unemployed, many children and elderly, underinsured, retired people, many disabled, mentally ill, homeless, and certain lifestyle abusers. It is not an exaggeration to state that more than twenty-five percent of the population is inadequately covered by insurance for lack of access to the care, regardless of the reason.

In late 2000, a number of managed care facilities made the shocking announcement that in the new year they were canceling the health insurance of under one million elderly and disabled patients, who would 1) be expected to seek their own health coverage with Medicare and elsewhere and 2) be without prescription benefits. The reason given was that government reimbursement for prescription costs was inadequate.

ETHICAL ISSUES REGARDING THE ACCESS FACTOR

1) Does equal access to health care for all mean equal health care for all?

2) Should not health care at least be minimally adequate for all?

3) Does ideal health care demand that everyone should not only be free from disease and infirmity but in a state of complete physical, mental, and social well being? (Remember the basic criteria in quality living—happiness, well-being, independence, and security for self and loved ones.)

4) Ethical barriers stand in the way of universal access:

  a) Limited ability to pay

  b) Bias against illegal aliens, poor, children and elderly, congenital and genetic disorders, disability due to decadent lifestyles:

alcohol, tobacco, and substance abuse, AIDS, teen pregnancy and criminality

c) Differences in cultural, racial, religious traditions

d) Employment status: full-time, part-time, or unemployed

e) Limited Medicaid and Medicare coverage (since 1965)

f) Forty million Americans are uninsured and forty million Americans are underinsured (no major medical coverage). Very few people can afford long-term care.

g) Thirty-three million elderly Americans (twelve percent of the population) utilize at least one-third of health care resources

h) To many patients, the hospital emergency department, which they cannot afford in the first place, is their family physician. Unless they represent a dire emergency situation, they are often denied care for lack of insurance coverage or available beds for admission.

THE POOR AND HEALTH CARE

The national costs of health care have been burgeoning for all segments of society, much more so than the costs for such vital areas as education and defense. The uninsured poor represent the largest group most severely affected in an ever increasing manner by the rising costs.

Prior to the 1960's, the poor as well as some other under-insured people were adequately or at least minimally attended by federal, state, and especially municipal hospitals and community clinics. Facilities and personnel were adequate for the needs. With the rapidly rising costs since the 1960's, however, most of the facilities were closed forever. The teaching hospitals, where young physicians as members of the house staff were pleased to receive on-the-job training with little or no compensation, were staffed by physicians, many from medical school faculties, all of whom enjoyed serving as educators. They too received little or no compensation.

Everyone was happy, most especially the patients, as long as the costs of service permitted the circumstances.

When these elysian facilities dried up, the poor had to seek health care elsewhere, or die in the effort.

Today, hospitals spend and lose close to fifteen billion dollars in uncompensated care for the poor, patients with AIDS, drug abusers, and sufferers of gun-shot wounds. Fifty percent of the costs are borne by tertiary care centers, who have available only twenty percent of hospital beds. By chance, the poor are concentrated in metropolitan areas of the larger cities in the environs of tertiary care centers (where by good fortune they receive the best medical care at no cost to the patients). Regrettably, the public and the medical profession are indifferent to the plight of the poor, as is evidenced by the fact that physicians are located in affluent areas in a ratio of 1: 300, whereas their location for practice in poor areas is 1: 15,000 people, despite the fact that many physicians are expected to return to poor areas whence they originate, but usually neglect to do so.

Physicians have a perfect right (legally but questionably morally) to avoid taking responsibility for care of the poor. The problem is not theirs, but society's. Their medical education was costly, not entirely repaid, and Medicaid pays a shockingly low rate of reimbursement for care.

The rates of morbidity, mortality, and hospitalization among the poor and uninsured is at least five times greater than among non-poor and the insured.

An outstanding point of irony in looking at these troublesome figures is that the poor and uninsured have the most to gain from reformed health care, but have the least opportunity to speak in their own behalf. The non-poor and insured have the most to say and the least to gain from reform. Veterans of our wars have the privilege of care at federally established hospitals for veterans, both for in-patient as well as out-patient services. Indeed, the poor take advantage of such available care if they qualify and if the distance is convenient. The primary problem is logistical in that the facilities are often not easily accessible, especially when urgently needed.

How do the poor attend to their health needs today in the absence of coverage? More would resort to Medicaid if physicians were more cooperative in attending to the poor, but the Medicaid rates of reimbursement offer very little inducement to the physician. Most poor then must wait until they need emergency care so that they can seek visits to nearby hospital emergency rooms, some dwindling outpatient facilities, and few, if any, community clinics. They rarely see the same physician at most facilities. The result is that the quality of the care is inferior to available superb care for paying and well-insured patients, who are able to select their own physicians.

RECENT TRENDS IN THE CLINIC CARE OF THE POOR
As though the poor are not sufficiently denigrated in their health care, a recent trend has emerged that adds to the degradation.

Since the origin of the general municipal hospital in the United States, with its roots in the Almhouse in Philadelphia, a physical facility known as the medical clinic has served as a major source of ambulatory care for the poor. It has been and still is operated without fee and staffed by physicians in providing their pro bono service as a payment for their hospital privileges. In hospitals with a house staff or residents, the trainees have been assigned to service in clinics as part of their education in the office care of ambulatory patients. The experience has been invaluable as a background for future private practice, even though their primary obligation was to the more exciting experience in hospital critical care of patients confined to bed with urgent problems. The residents are always presumably supervised in the clinics by members of the staff as part of the educational requirements, but supervision is too often absent. Besides, as a result of closures, the number of operative municipal hospitals for the poor and the number of clinics in private hospitals are greatly reduced.

The recent trend is that hospitals have been eliminating clinics because of their costs of operation. Although the process is legal, is it ethical and does it not have far-reaching adverse consequences upon the poor, whose only source of ambulatory care has been the clinics.

ETHICAL ISSUES

Clinic care of the poor can hardly be compared with the quality of private care of a paying (insured) patient.

How does one justify telling the clinic patient he is no longer welcome for care?

Where is he expected to go? Has anyone advised him where to go?

Does the firing institution arrange for transfer of the clinic patient in compliance with the ethical expectation to maintain continuing and uninterrupted health care? Such facilities may be available in metropolitan areas where there is an occasional veteran's hospital with clinics for qualified veterans. What about the absence of such facilities in the many communities all through the country with no special clinics for the uninsured?

What about the ethical issue of reducing the valuable office experience for the residents? Is not their education impaired?

The trend in reducing clinic care of the poor raises another serious issue reflecting the manner in which medicine may be practiced in the future. Whether one likes it or not, the advances in biotechnology demand finer and greater skills in the care of critically ill patients. Ergo, there is need of more and more skilled specialists in hospitals and who are newly named hospitalists. By the same token, more physicians are needed for the use of advances in drugs and procedures including surgery, for ambulatory and office care. These are known as generalists.

In order to satisfy this concept, the present breakdown of physicians who are specialists (seventy percent) and physicians who are generalists (thirty percent) needs to be reversed to thirty percent specialists (and hospitalists) and to seventy percent generalists (office practitioners). Lest there be any doubt about it, it takes as much education and skill to be a competent generalist as it takes to be a competent specialist.

The irony of such trend is that all medical school graduates are currently assigned as residents for training in hospitals as caretakers of critically ill patients in a succession of specialty services. There is little training in preventive, ambulatory, and family care. Thanks to the recent increase in residency training in Family Medicine and the return back to training in general Internal Medicine, there is some salvation in the perpetuation of office practice for cradle to grave care of the entire family.

The major question still remains: Where will the poor receive ambulatory care without required insurance? The least acceptable solution to the question is the current practice whereby the poor without on-going care wait for a critical moment and proceed to a hospital emergency department (where in some hospitals they may be turned away from care). Instead of on-going care, they are then attended from crisis to crisis. Medical care could hardly be more

inferior in quality—a sad commentary on care in the richest country in the world.

A rational suggestion to satisfy the medical needs of the poor in
inner city areas with too few physicians in too few community-
based health care facilities is to establish a National Health Service
Corps. It could serve as a revolving source and provision of young
physicians for assignment in underserved areas after their completion of hospital residency training as a repayment for their student
loans. Not only would the poor be served with quality health care,
but many patients with deteriorating illnesses due to illicit life-
styles could be salvaged and returned to normal society. Special
attention would be given to the needs of the disadvantaged and the
indigent.

In addition to quality health care, the poor would receive the
enormous psychological lift of realizing that their level of coverage
would be raised to the same level of coverage as for the insured and
the wealthy.

THE ELDERLY AND HEALTH CARE STATISTICS

The elderly comprise over twelve percent of the population and
utilize thirty-three percent of the health care resources. They are
responsible for the 700,000 new Medicare enrollees per year. The
group in the decade of the eighties is the fastest growing decade.
Eighteen percent of Medicare beneficiaries (over age sixty-five
years) receive eighty percent of the payment benefits.

Sixty five percent of health care expenditures go to five percent
of the elderly, often in the last year of their lives.

LIFE-STYLE ABUSERS AND HEALTH CARE

Some attention must be given to the high health care expenditures incurred by life-style abusers.

Their number, sad to say, is high, and includes abusers of alcohol, tobacco and illegal substances. Also considered are those responsible for drunk-driving accidents, violent crime, gun-shot wounds, and sexually transmitted diseases, especially AIDS. The entire group contributes to about 400,000 deaths per year in the United States.

An additional significant contributor to the costs of health care are the teenage pregnancies and the low birth-weight infants. The cost to save a premature infant weighing less than twenty ounces in a neo-natal intensive care unit is about $2,500 per day.

HIGH COST OF HEALTH CARE

The burgeoning, inflationary high cost of health care must be addressed as an emergency measure.

1) The United States expends increasingly more and more per capita than does any other industrialized nation: in 1950, five percent of the gross national product (GNP), and in 1992, fourteen percent of the GNP, and eighteen percent in 2000.

2) Our total cost of health care is close to $1 trillion per year and is continuing upward.

3) Approximately fifty percent of the costs are paid by public resources, especially Medicaid and Medicare since 1965.

4) The average insurance premium in 1993 for an individual was $2000 per year, and for a family, $5000 per year. These figures have been rising continuously.

5) The high cost of health care in the last year of a person's life is of particular concern and raises obvious ethical considerations. The average lifetime cost of health care is about $50,000 per person, about $10,000 (twenty percent) of which is in one's last year of life. Thirty percent of Medicaid and Medicare payments are for the last year of a patient's life.

6) In compliance with a quality of life ethic, ninety percent of people express a desire to prepare an advance directive usually excluding CPR and including do-not-resuscitate orders when ter-

minal and dying, but only ten percent actually prepare the necessary documents in writing.

Some reasonable recommendations by expert economists and health care experts have been made to control the rising costs:

1) Placement of a global budget or cap on costs with emphasis on improving efficiency, fairness, and equality of care

2) Payments based on ability to pay (like taxes)

3) Spread of costs wisely and arrival at a fair burden to all

4) Avoidance of a two-tier system

5) Supplementary out-of-pocket costs for amenities should be available to those who can afford them and wish to have them, but there should be limits.

6) Added costs in support of research and development of new technology to improve health care must be in the forefront of expenditures.

HEALTH CARE AS A COMMODITY

The utilitarian point of view that the greatest good be directed to the greatest number of people is the basis for the major ethical principle of beneficence, which includes equality and justice for all. The Jeffersonian declaration of "life, liberty. . . ." obviously refers to health care and well-being. Wellness is then a social good, a societal mandate, not a commodity in competition with all other concerns in our economy. Health care should not be delivered in accordance with one's ability to pay, but rather as a necessity. Paying more and getting more is a commercial philosophy, not a health care issue. It is a fact of life that physicians and hospitals are reimbursed on the basis of fee-for-service—the larger the service, the larger the fee.

Another fact of life is the litigious mentality of our society, as a result of which doctors practice a defensive medicine and order more testing than may be indicated in order to protect themselves against a charge of negligence. As a result, the services can be superfluous, inappropriate, unnecessary, and often marginal. The costs are thereby increased without justification.

Another factor in the commercialization of health care over its primary role as a social good is the application of high-tech procedures and studies in expensive specialty practices, hence a basis for the increase in specialization in recent years. Fortunately, the costs are met to some extent by third party payers. On the other hand, however, several thousand private insurers compete, not by reducing premiums and increasing benefits, but rather by insuring only the good risks, limiting coverage, excluding those who acquire costly illness, negating claims, and increasing deductibles. Third party administrative costs are reputedly high in the United States (twenty percent of health care costs compared with ten percent in Canada).

MALDISTRIBUTION OF RESOURCES AND SERVICES

An important factor that influences costs is the maldistribution of resources and services.

Available health care plans vary widely in their provision of health care services:

1) There are low cost plans that provide low quality benefits.

2) There are high cost plans that offer a high concentration of specialists (seventy percent of physicians) and tertiary care centers (five percent of hospitals) located in urban areas where the average income of the population is lower than normal. These centers have the best available advanced biotechnology and tend to practice an excess utilization of facilities which are often more than necessary.

3) Only five percent of expenditures go to the prevention of disease.

The result is an imbalance of health care with a lowering of delivery and efficiency. The obvious solution to the problem is a reallocation of resources.

4) Too many important needs in health care lack sufficient coverage. These include psychiatric and dental services, coverage for advanced cardiac surgery, bone marrow transplantation for leukemia, genetic testing, et al.

The reallocation of resources as a solution to the maldistribution factor in health care would primarily consider that monies should be rationed in accordance with the decision regarding where they would do the most good for most people (the utilitarian ethical principle).

ETHICAL QUESTIONS

1) Should age be a consideration, bearing in mind that the elderly consume a disproportionate share of the costs in the last year of their lives for care that often turns out to have been futile?

2) Should not the general rule apply that high-tech life-saving measures be reserved for those in early life, and that low-tech social services, pain control, and palliative care be reserved for those in their late years?

3) Will advancing years and their high-tech costs cause intergenerational conflict and discrimination?

4) Should not the policy be to forego heroic liver transplantation for an elderly patient with alcohol-related end-stage cirrhosis of the liver in favor of intensive neo-natal care?

5) Should rational allocation among health care needs be favored over other priorities, including education, housing, and defense?

6) Should there not be a more prudent spread of profits in managed care settings among physicians and their patients?

7) Should physicians in managed care settings be rewarded for ordering fewer tests than they deem necessary in order to provide a larger profit for the industry?

8) Should not patients in managed care insurance have recourse when they receive unfair treatment?

ROLE OF ACADEMIC HEALTH CENTERS
IN HEALTH CARE

There are about 120 university-based teaching hospitals plus many major affiliated teaching hospitals that comprise about twenty-five percent of the hospital beds needed for inpatient care. Their role in medical education is of paramount importance, but their provision of health care is equally vital. Many are in inner city locales where poor and uninsured reside. As a result, the tertiary care centers provide fifty percent of uncompensated hospital in-patient care. In addition, they must comply with their other function (besides teaching) of serving as a referral center for high-tech, advanced specialty care, the cost of which is generally above their means.

The focus of the tertiary care center is on the very sick patients with difficult problems. Consequently, their role lacks attention to much needed preventive care, which is left for the family physicians and community hospitals where medical education is greatly reduced in comparison with the tertiary care centers.

PROBLEMS IN MANAGEMENT

It has been demonstrated that a factor in the high costs of health care is the high administrative cost in the lack of efficient management. Administrative salaries in managed care facilities may be outrageously high. There is ample evidence of waste and inefficiency. An ancillary factor in the inefficient management is the shortage of primary physicians and the resultant deficiency in quality medicine.

To be sure, a reduction in administrative costs and waste would free up resources for a more efficient delivery of health care. Simplification of organizational complexity with minimal paperwork would improve service enormously. The physician should be allowed to practice medicine with minimal restraints and be relieved of tons of paper work. Minimal restraints would permit him to call upon needed specialists and special studies deemed necessary without the interference by non-medical administrative employees.

In managed care facilities, financial incentives to withhold treatments should be eliminated. They simply are in conflict with quality care.

The ability for every patient to choose a primary physician who is qualified and approved is fundamental in the preservation of the doctor-patient relationship.

There must be an effective and satisfactory grievance system where patients are able to register justifiable appeals and settlement of disputes.

FEDERAL ACTS FAVORING THE HEALTH OF THE CONSUMER

The federal government should not be blamed for our deficiencies in health care in view of the fact that some advances have been made by our Congress in the interest of health care:

1) Medicaid and Medicare (1965)

2) Employee Retirement and Income Security Act of 1974 (ERISA):

a) The federal government has authority to regulate employee benefit plans.

b) Employers have freedom to limit their health care coverage with regard to cancer therapy, organ transplantation, cardiac surgery, neonatal intensive care, psychiatric treatment and other expensive treatments.

c) Access to health care is everyone's right (but much more is needed in this area).

d) There should be no discrimination against employees based upon race, ethnicity, age, gender, or disability.

e) Employer-sponsored health plans are encouraged.

3) Patient Self-Determination Act of 1991

4) FDA, NIH, and Workers' Compensation Commission

5) Effort by the Clinton administration to establish a comprehensive universal health care program. Unfortunately, its acceptance failed. Blame for inadequacies in our health care cannot be laid entirely upon our government, even though our Congress has not led the way to a universal and comprehensive program.

BASIC ISSUES RELATING TO THE NEED FOR HEALTH CARE REFORM

It is worth reemphasizing that the United State is the most affluent of all industrialized countries, has the best possible health care, spends the most (as well as per capita) for health care. Despite all that, the United States rates among the lowest among the industrialized nations in life expectancy, infant mortality, level of immunizations, visits to a physician, and days per capita in a hospital. Above all, too many people lack adequate, or even minimal health care, and have no way of receiving needed care as the costs continue to rise and the problems continue to mount and become knottier and knottier.

Having addressed the health care issues of problems with access, plight of poor, children and elderly, high cost, treatment of health care as a business commodity rather than as a social necessity, faulty distribution of resources and services, problems with management, plight of our academic health centers, deficiencies in our governmental solution to the health care shortcomings, the question then arises: Is our health care in crisis?

What makes the matter especially critical are the three factors of 1) high cost, 2) decreased access, and 3) reduced quality, although the other deficiencies should not be ignored.

1) High cost: uncontrolled escalation, rising rapidly in expenditure to $1 trillion per year.

2) Decreased Access to care is caused by:

a) Our socio-economic status, called the mystique of privilege, allows the rich to obtain the best available health care, denies the best care to many, and little or no care to the poor.

b) Specialization in medicine is an expected happening in view of the explosion in medical knowledge and technology. Unfortunately, the much needed family physician correspondingly declined in numbers.

c) Insufficient and inadequate primary care has resulted in the loss of a desperately needed coordinator and monitor of care for an individual patient and for the entire family.

d) Availability of adequate health insurance has declined for millions of people, and to many, no insurance at all.

e) Shift of care for the poor and uninsured from the physician's office to the hospital emergency room, which has become over overutilized.

3) Reduced quality:

a) Care is often fragmented, inappropriate and inefficient

b) Resources have become maldistributed.

c) Concentration of care is predominantly urban.

d) Advanced biotechnology, although essential, has become overused, and often used as a replacement for the old-fashioned history and physical examination (which still ought to be the foundation of the doctor-patient relationship).

ETHICAL ISSUES

1) Whose problem is the crisis? It is obviously the consumer's (society), the provider's (doctor, hospital, and insurer), the government's (federal, state, and municipal), and the employer's (of the consumer); in fact, all of the above.

2) Do not responsibilities go with the numerous rights and privileges claimed by everyone? All participants in health care must be a part of, and share in the burden of, costs and responsibilities in all levels of care.

SURVEY OF THE PUBLIC REGARDING THE CRISIS IN HEALTH CARE

In surveying the public, blame is placed upon:

1) All within the system, except themselves, i.e., the doctors, hospitals, insurers, lawyers, pharmaceutical industry

2) Excess waste, abuse, greed, profiteering, overcharges in laboratory and other diagnostic facilities, drugs (especially new), procedures, surgical fees

3) Practice of defensive medicine to avoid law suits

4) Departure into alternative medicine as a result of high costs, in full awareness of their relatively dubious value

5) Fraudulent claims

6) Failure to emphasize increased care of the elderly who require an increase in attention

7) Neglect of the poor and underinsured (forty million in each group without insurance)

8) Failure to control urban problems of violence, drug abuse, gun-shot injuries, AIDS, car accidents

9) Failure to provide coverage for prescription drugs, eye-glasses, dental care, care of mentally ill, home health care, extended nursing care, preventive care

10) Obvious need for universal and comprehensive care

11) Costs and inablility to pay (as with taxes)

The consumer is entitled to the best technology without worry about costs (health insurance and government should cover all costs).

Return to health from illness or accident should be perfect. If imperfect, negligence may be responsible.

Solutions to the crisis are not the responsibility of the consumer of health care.

SURVEY OF THE MEDICAL PROFESSION REGARDING
THE CRISIS IN HEALTH CARE

1) Cost of health care has burgeoned by 1200 percent since origin of Medicaid and Medicare in 1965. The doctors' share in the costs has risen less than two percent. The doctors' responsibility in the rising costs has increased proportionately by very little since 1950.

2) Fifty percent of the income of physicians goes to administrative costs and overhead, malpractice insurance, and taxes.

3) The late start in acquiring income after medical school and hospital training as well as the large financial burden from educational loans have delayed significant income greatly.

4) The long work-week of about 60-70 hours is very stressful.

5) Uncompensated clinic duty is a community service.

6) Reduced fees for poor patients is a moral obligation.

7) Third party payers (private insurers and government) require enormous amounts of paper work resulting in large administrative costs and labor, and take valuable time away from patient care.

8) Over 1000 different claim forms amounting to a multitude of claims per year (for the entire profession) are enormous burdens.

9) There is a constant hassle from government intervention with coding procedures, demands of a resource-based relative value scale, Clinical Laboratory Improvement Act, Occupational Safety and Health Administration, Americans with Disability Act, etc.

10) Compliance with the reimbursement mechanism created by insurers limits the physician's time with patients.

11) There is a growing expectation of health care by consumers because of biotechnologic advances that is unaccompanied by an increased expectation in personal costs.

12) Too rapid advances in specialization have taken place at

the expense of the needed family physician (a missing entity for millions of patients).

13) An overworked hospital emergency room resulting from too many patients not requiring emergency care has developed.

14) The standard of care has moved from personal to impersonal, due to external influences.

15) The physician has been too limited in decision-making in life-sustaining situations by the insurer's judgment of futility rather than the physician's. The insurer allows no discussion or negotiation. The insurer alone decides reimbursements.

16) End-of-life decisions regarding care is decided, not by the physician, but by the third party payers, government regulators, and institutional policies.

17) Quality living standards are reduced to the limits set by third party payers who supercede physician decision-making, especially in the treatment of incurable diseases, congenital disorders, mental retardation, and profound disability.

18) There is too high a cost of dying and there is wastage in expenditure during the last year of the life of an ill patient.

19) There is a limited autonomy of the physician by standards of practice in managed care facilities.

20) The physician's increase in time, effort, and attention with reduced income is required by an aging population, all covered by insurance which is often poor or absent.

21) There is difficulty in attending patients in nursing homes, hospice centers and at home. Patients are often unable to visit the physician at his office.

22) There is too great an enormity of life-style abuses in the cost of health care, including violent crime, alcohol and substance abuse, high rate of accidents, excessive smoking, teenage pregnancies, low birth-weight of newborn infants.

23) The solution to the health care problem is not the responsibility of the physician.

24) Patients must be reminded that their expectation of rights

requires a corresponding assumption of responsibility—in fact, a responsibility for every right. Included in responsibility, patients should participate, in their own best interest, in being more thoroughly informed about the details of their health insurance coverage, participate in the concern for the poor and other uninsured, show a greater appreciation of their care, and acceptance of the best that medical care has to offer.

SURVEY OF ADMINISTRATORS REGARDING
THE CRISIS IN HEALTH CARE

1) The change from traditional professional ethos to entrepreneurial marketing orientation has gradually evolved as a definite trend.

2) The United States has the highest incidence of dissatisfaction with health care among the industrialized nations in the surveys of administrators, as well as doctors, patients, and insurers.

3) The health care system needs rebuilding

4) Americans are too demanding of special and expensive tests and procedures.

5) The third party payer system is inefficient.

6) The increase in the cost of health care to $1 trillion per year is more than in most industrialized countries added together.

7) The costs are due mostly to the explosion in biotechnology, which is quite ahead of the needs of most problems in health care.

8) Hospital costs in health care are due to increased severity of illness including cardiac and neonatal intensive care, organ transplantation, burn units, and high-tech care in all specialties.

The number of acute hospital beds has been reduced greatly in recent years in order to comply with rising costs. As a result, there is currently too often a shortage of beds throughout the country. Unfortunately, ambulances carrying the desperately ill patients are at times turned away, even though the patient may have been recently discharged from that hospital.

9) Lack of health insurance protection for forty million people

without coverage, forty million people with inadequate coverage, self-employed, employees of small businesses, part-time employees, dependents of employees, children, retirees, patients with pre-existing conditions, patients with high risk illnesses including AIDS, reductions in coverage after payment for large claims, decreased coverage after changing jobs, welfare patients who return to work and are no longer covered by Medicaid, out-of-pocket expenses for deductibles, etc.

10) Increase in aging and longevity are a growing concern.

11) Rise in managed care with increased restrictions on physician and consumers.

12) Trend toward a continued number of national chains with ownership of hospitals, ambulatory care centers, home health agencies, and physician-group practices.

13) Glut of specialists and sub-specialists, who are responsible for costly tests and procedures, and who perform an increased number of radical and marginally necessary operations and procedures with widely varying levels of skills.

14) Dearth of primary care physicians resulting in less than adequate preventive care, immunizations, inadequate child care, less than total care.

15) Malpractice litigation is excessive.

16) Administrators are not responsible for the crisis in health care.

SURVEY OF EXPERT ECONOMISTS REGARDING THE CRISIS IN HEALTH CARE

A variety of solutions to the health care crisis have emerged from many expert sources in recognition of the consumer's request for universal, comprehensive coverage and the provider's desire for independence and relief from restraints and bias:

1) Health care reform must not be any one interest-group's responsibility, but rather the responsibility of everyone concerned with health care, i.e., consumer, provider, administrator, and regulator (private and government) in return for which each must benefit.

2) Costs must be shared equitably among employers, employees, and government in a combination of private and public financing.

3) A global budget should be established by the federal government with an annual negotiated cap required for the total expenditures.

4) A trust fund (like Social Security) should be created.

5) A sliding scale of costs should be in place for part-time employees.

6) A surcharge for the public in a non-profit fund in each state should be established.

7) A public tax must be added to the health care system.

8) Cost containment via a two-track system must be regulated and competitive.

9) Managed care plans must be subject to price controls.

10) Consumers and providers may operate outside of the system with penalties for patients who purchase fee-for-service coverage.

11) A branch of a National Health Care Commission should be set up to address waste, fraud, and abuse of the system with submitted reports and recommendations to the National Health Care Commission, which oversees fifty state commissions, each with its own spending goal (paid by insurers for a set of benefits).

12) Rates are regulated and set by management-labor negotiations via the independent National Health Care Commission. Management is made up of representation from business, consumer groups, and federal or state government. Labor is made up of provider groups including organized medicine, hospitals, and the insurance industry.

13) Disagreements should be subject to binding arbitration.

14) Malpractice reform should have caps on pain and suffering, caps on actual damage, mandatory arbitration, pre-trial screening, recognition of the physicians' compliance with practice guidelines in the community they serve, and mandatory disclosure of insurance payments. The aim is to reduce the high cost of defensive

medicine, thereby reducing the impact of lawsuits upon medical costs.

15) Consumers must be free to choose among health plans consisting of groups of accountable providers that compete with each other for clients on the basis of quality of service and costs and the offer of a package of benefits with no less than a minimum standard of care.

16) Pre-paid group practices or group health plans may emerge to operate in lieu of fee-for-service care. The plans may be licensed within a community and patients are free to select the plan of their choice within some limitations. Their packages of standard benefits are offered with federal approval.

17) The plans must accept all enrollees including high-risk patients.

18) All physicians should be part of a plan.

19) All patients relate to primary care physicians who serve to coordinate health care.

20) Specialists and high-tech services are available and utilized by the primary physician, as needed. Overuse is discouraged and the consumer has limited personal access to specialty care.

21) Correction of problems with managed care programs:

    a) Reduce excessive emphasis on cost-containment,

    b) Reduce operation as a corporate structure for profit rather than as a societal structure for the common good,

    c) Emphasize quality care as the basic aim,

    d) Reduce restrictions, including freedom of choice in the selection of a physician,

    e) Improve the patient's ability to seek arbitration and redress in matters of dispute.

21) Promote Long-term Health Care: Long-term health care is an absolute necessity, although it is needed by a small percentage of the patient population. The costs are anticipated to be very high. The types of care include continuing care in a retirement community, assisted home care programs, daycare programs, skilled nurs-

ing care, assisted nursing care levels, sheltered-living programs, hospices, and nursing homes (mostly private, few governmental).

THE AUTHOR'S SOLUTION TO THE CRISIS IN
HEALTH CARE

The reader should be able to read the author's mind regarding his solution to the health care crisis: a) yes, health care is in crisis, b) health care should be universal and comprehensive c) no less than minimally adequate, d) cost controlled, e) a combination of details acceptable to the patient, the provider, the administrator, and insurer, and f) a solemn agreement by all participants to be compliant with the ethical principles set forth in Chapter 8. Essentially, these include honesty and respect for the law, non-maleficence, beneficence, and respect for the rights of all patients as well as those of health care providers.

CHAPTER 27

HEALTH INSURANCE

The highest proof of virtue
is to possess boundless power
without abusing it.

— Lord Thomas B. Macaulay,
1800-1859

INTRODUCTION

The major concern with private health insurance from the perspective of the patients and their doctors is that health care coverage is essentially identical with the operation of any business corporation. The aim of the private health insurance industry is the profit incentive. In its unique position in a close relationship with sick people and their impaired health, its highest priority ought to be that of a social good with a utilitarian viewpoint instead of a commercial enterprise. As a corporate entrepreneurship, however, its main concern is to offer the least possible coverage for the largest possible profit and income for its leaders and investors. Their best customer is the mythical healthy patient with no complaints. The logical conclusion, reductio and absurdum, is that the sicker the patient, the less likely, and certainly the more costly, will be his coverage. The health insurers demonstrate a constant drive toward reducing health coverage in favor of financial gain. As with any corporate structure, the virtues of competition demand as much coverage as possible for a competitive price.

The concerns that many people have leveled against their private insurers have emerged as sufficiently identifiable to constitute ethical issues The major ones are the following:

ETHICAL ISSUES

1) The health insurance industry is constantly alert to the avoidance of insuring or reinsuring high risk patients especially if they have had costly claims. The logical result of this philosophy reduction ad absurdum, is that the sicker the patient, the less likely is his coverage, the healthier the patient the more likely is his coverage.

2) The industry has no interest in, or recommendation for the health coverage of forty million poor and uninsured people or for another forty million people who are underinsured below minimal and less than adequate care.

3) Outstanding advances are made on a regular basis in biotechnology. The industry, however, often fails to recognize their usage and may refuse to cover new treatments urged by physicians by calling the innovations experimental. The innovations are a thorn in the side of the industry, mainly because of the enormous costs involved. The purpose is obviously intended to save costs without primary concern for the sick patient for whom no other treatment may be acceptable or available as far as the physician is concerned in desiring to apply the new technique for the patient. Examples are many.

4) One of the most egregious violations of good health care is the denial of the physician's request for a longer hospital stay for patients who do not fit the insurer's book regarding illness. The expert opinion of the patient's physician is denied—actually an insult to the judgment of the physician. It should not have to take a Congressional law, as has occurred, to convince the insurers of their injustice, especially when the word of a physician is countermand-

ed by a non-medical clerk in the insurance office. How frustrating to the physician!

5) A common issue of long duration, but only recently exposed, is that physicians are frequently plagued by insurance forms that require the wording of the physician's diagnosis and treatment to match exactly the wording of the insurer's reimbursement rules and regulations. Unsuccessful efforts by the physician to comply with the inflexible language expected by the insurer is frustrating to the physician, who is precise in his own findings and therapy. His management of the patient's problem is generally accurate and legitimate. He often fails, however, in his effort to convince the insurer representative that his patient should be covered insurance-wise. In desperation, the physician may (admittedly) reveal that, in the interest of his patient's expected and proper coverage, the physician may, as well as in the interest of his own reimbursement, manipulate the wording on the insurance form and fudge his execution of the form with the confidence that no one is suffering from the ethically dubious action. Is the physician committing a fraud? The insurer is likely to think so.

6) A major concern to most patients is the lack of adequate long-term coverage for long-term care at reasonable cost to the majority of insured patients, and total absence for the poor and underinsured. The problem is an ever-increasing one, considering the progressive aging of the population.

7) In addition, there are many health problems not usually available at all for coverage. These include mental illness, dental care, preventive care, prescription drugs, eye glasses, hearing aids, et al.

8) A troublesome and costly insurance carrier's use of the deductible is another example of an annoyance that is very common and disruptive of the relationship between patient, physician, and carrier.

9) A frequent problem has been the loss of health insurance when an employee changes jobs. Congressional aid has been given

that issue by the enactment of legal protection favoring continued insurability in the *Health Insurance Portability and Accountability Act of 1996*, which permits employees to take their health insurance with them when changing jobs. The mechanism was made possible through the introduction of the Comprehensive National Identification System (which resembles Social Security in its operation).

10) A patient on welfare is covered by Medicaid. When he has the good fortune to be able to become employed, often at a minimal wage in a small business, he may no longer qualify for any health insurance benefits.

SURVEY OF PHYSICIANS

In a state-wide survey of physicains, the following complaints have been levelled against several health maintenance organizations:

1) Unilateral and arbitrary decision-making in denials of coverage without mutual discussion or negotiation

2) Engaging in down-coding procedures

3) Delaying approval of care for sick patients

4) Breaching the terms of the contract with the physicians.

5) Arbitrary overruling a physician's determination of a medical necessity

6) Failure to reimburse physicians in a timely manner

7) Failure to provide a proper explanation of denial of payment for a claim

SUMMARY

In summary, the private insurance carrier could be, should be, and would be the best friend every patient ever had if only the industry operated on the altruistic ethical principle of social beneficence instead of egoistic corporate self-interest.

It is likely that all will not be well until we have universal and comprehensive health insurance with cost control as is common in other civilized societies. Otherwise, there is little relief in sight. The problems are endless, complex, frustrating for the doctor, the patient, and the insurer.

MY EVENING PRAYER

If I have wounded any soul today,
If I have caused one foot to go astray,
If I have walked in my own wilful way—
  good Lord, forgive!
If I have uttered idle words in vain,
If I have turned aside from want or pain,
Lest I should suffer through the strain—
  good Lord, forgive!

— Anonymous

EPILOGUE

Achieving one's natural life span requires the elimination of one's hereditary and acquired genetic imperfections and one's injurious environmental influences. One must also ascend a semicircular curve of quality living and satisfy three tiers:

1) basic, instinctual egoistic needs for happiness, well-being, independence, and security, 2) acquired egoistic desires for success, wealth, and power; and beyond these egocentric pursuits, one must also strive to achieve 3) an entirely altruistic tier of ethical principles: honesty of character, non-maleficence in conduct, beneficence in following The Golden Rule, and respect for the rights of all others.

The third tier occupies the summit of the curve and is mandatory for compatible existence in society. As a result of aging, quality living declines on the curve to the same point as the end of the life span.

The combination of a) the natural life span from birth to death and b) quality living may enable one to envision the semicircle of life modeled after the perfect semicircle. (See accompanying figure.)

Seven major medical subjects with ethical issues affecting quality living are addressed: 1) the doctor-patient relationship, 2) diet and nutrition, 3) medication, 4) advances in biotechnology, 5) medical research, 6) decision-making regarding late-life care, and 7) health care reform.

THE PERFECT SEMICIRCLE OF LIFE

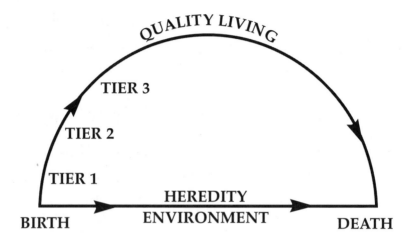

TIER 1: EGOISTIC, INSTINCTIVE:
   • **WELL-BEING, INDEPENDENCE,**
    SECURITY, HAPPINESS ('WISH')

TIER 2: EGOISTIC, ZEALOUS:
   • **SUCCESS, WEALTH, POWER**

TIER 3: ALTRUISTIC:
   • **HONESTY**
   • **NON-MALEFICENCE**
   • **BENEFICENCE**
   • **RESPECT FOR RIGHTS**

SUPPLEMENTAL READING

Ahronheim, JC, Moreno, J, and Zuckerman, C: *Ethics in Clinical Medicine*; New York, Little, Brown and Co, 1994

American College of Physicians: Ethics Manual, Third Ed; 1992

American Medical Association: Code of Medical Ethics, Council on Ethical and Judicial Affairs; Chicago, 1998

American Medical Association: Diagnostic and Treatment Guidelines on Elder Abuse and Neglect; Chicago, American Medical Association, 1993

American Medical Association: Opinions and Reports of the Judicial Council including the Principles of Medical Ethics; Chicago 1994

Annas, GJ and Elias, S, Eds; *Gene Mapping: Using Law and Ethics as Guides*; New York, Oxford University Press, 1992

Annas, GJ: Standards of Care: *The Law of American Bioethics*; New YorK,, Oxford University Press, 1993

Annas, GJ, and Grodin, M, Eds: *The Nazi Doctors and the Nuremberg Code: Human Rights in Human Experimentation*; New York, Oxford University Press, 1992

Annas, GJ: *The Law of American BioEthics*; New York, Oxford University Press, 1993

Appelbaum, PS, Lidz CW and Meisel, A: *Informed Consent: Legal Theory and Clinical Practice*, New York, Oxford University Press, 1987

Arras, JD, and Steinbock, B: *Ethical Issues in Modern Medicine*, 4th Ed; California, Mayfield Publishing Co, 1994

Beauchamp, TL and Childress, JF: *Principles of Biomedical Ethics*, 4th Ed; New York, Oxford University Press, 1994

Blank, RH: *Rationing Medicine*; New York, Columbia University Press, 1988

Blumstein, JF and Sloan, Eds: *Organ Transplantation Policy, Issues and Prospects*; Durham, Duke University Press, 1989

Brandl, RB: *Morality, Utilitarianism and Rights*; New York, Cambridge University Press, 1992

Brock, DW: *Life and Death: Philosophical Essays in Biomedical Ethics*; New York, Cambridge University Press, 1993

Brody, B: *Life and Death Decision Making*; New York, Oxford University Press, 1988

Callahan, D: *Abortion: Law, Choice and Morality*; New York, MacMillan Publishing Co, 1970

Callahan, D: *Setting Limits: Medical Goals in an Aging Society*, New York, Simon and Schuster, 1987

Callahan, D: *The Social Sciences and the Task of BioEthics*; Daedalus, 1999

Callahan, D: *What Kind of Life*; New York, Simon and Schuster, 1990

Cantor, N.: *Advance Directives and the Pursuit of Death with Dignity*; Bloomington, Indiana University Press, 1993

Cantor, N: *Legal Frontiers of Death and Dying*; Bloomington, Indiana University Press, 1987

Caplan, AL, Ed: *When Medicine Went Mad, BioEthics and the Holocaust*; Clifton, NJ, Humana Press, 1992

Daniels, C.R.: *At Women's Expense: State Power and the Politics of Fetal Rights*; Cambridge, Harvard University Press, 1993

Daniels, N: *Just Health Care*; New York, Cambridge University Press, 1985

Dedek, J: *Contemporary Medical Ethics*; New York, Sheed and Ward, 1975

Donagan, A: *The Theory of Morality*; Chicago, University of Chicago Press, 1977

Dworkin, G: *Theory and Practice of Autonomy*; New York, Cambridge University Press, 1988

Dworkin, R: *Life's Dominion: An Argument About Abortion, Euthanasia and Individual Freedom*; New York, Alfred A: Knopf, 1993

Eddy, DM: *Common Screening Tests*; Philadelphia, American College of Physicians, 1991

Edelstein, L: *Ancient Medicine*, Eds, Temkin, O. and Temkin, L.; Baltimore, Johns Hopkins University Press, 1967

Edelstein, L: *The Hippocratic Oath: Text, Translation and Interpretation*; Baltimore, The Johns Hopkins University Press, 1967

Engelhardt, HT: *The Foundations of Bioethics*; New York, Oxford University Press, 1986

Faden, RR and Beauchamp, TL: *A History and Theory of Informed Consent*; New York, Oxford University Press, 1986

Feinberg, J: *Social Philosophy*; NJ, Prentice-Hall, 1973

Field, MA: *Surrogate Motherhood: The Legal and Human Issues*; Cambridge, Harvard University Press, 1988

Fox, MA: *The Case for Animal Experimentation: An Evolutionary and Ethical Perspective*, Berkeley, University of Calilfornia Press, 1986

Fried, C: *Medical Experimentation: Personal Integrity and Social Policy*; New York, Americal Elsevier, 1974

Goldman, A I: *A Theory of Human Action*; Englewood Cliffs, NJ, Prentice-Hall, 1970

Gorovitz, S: *Doctors' Dilemmas: Moral Conflict and Medical Care*; New York, Oxford University Press, Inc, 1982

Harman, G: *The Nature of Morality: An Introduction to Ethics*, New York, Oxford University Press, 1977

Harrison's Principles of Internal Medicine, Eds; Isselbacher, Braunwald, Wilson, Martin, Fauci, and Kasper, 13th Ed, McGraw-Hill, Inc, 1994

His Holiness, *The Dalai Lama: Ethics for the New Millenium*; New York, Penguin Putnam Inc, 1999

Jonas, H: *Philosophical Reflections on Experimenting with Human Subjects: In Experimentation with Human Subjects*, Ed. P. Freund; New York, Braziller, 1970

Jonsen, AR, Siegler, M, and Winslade, WJ: *Clinical Ethics: A Practical Approach to Ethical Decisions in Clinical Medicine*; New York, MacMillan Publishing Co, Inc, 1982

Jonsen, AR: *The Old Ethics and the New Medicine*; Cambridge, Harvard University Press, 1990

Kant, I: *Foundations of the Metaphysics of Morals*; Transl, LW Beck, Indianapolis, IN, Bobbs-Merrill Co, 1959

Kass, L: *Toward A More Natural Science*; New York, Free Press, 1985

Katz, J: *The Silent World of Doctor and Patient*; New York, Free Press, 1984

Kevorkian, J: *Prescription Medicine: The Goodness of Planned Death*; Buffalo, Prometheus Books, 1991

Kuhse, H: *The Sanctity of Life Doctrine in Medicine: A Critique*; Oxford, Clarendon Press, 1987

Lamb, D: *Death, Brain Death and Ethics*; Albany State University of New York Press, 1985

Lauritzen, P: *Pursuing Parenthood: Ethical Issues in Assisted Reproduction*; Bloomington, Indiana University Press, 1993

Levine, RJ: *Ethics and Regulation of Clinical Research*; Baltimore; Urban and Schwartzenberg, 1981

Lifton, RJ: *The Nazi Doctors: Medical Killing and the Psychology of Genocide*; New York, Basic Books, 1986

Ludlam, JE: Informed Consent; American Hospital Association, Chicago, 1978

Mathieu, D, Ed; *Organ Substitution Technology. Ethical, Legal and Public Policy Issues*; Bolder, CO, Westview Press, 1988

McHugh, JT: *Death, Dying and the Law*, Ed; Our Sunday Visitor, Inc, 1976

Meisel, A: *The Right to Die*; New York, John Wiley and Sons, 1989

Menzel, PT, *Strong Medicine: The Ethical Rationing of Health Care*; New York, Oxford University Press, 1991

Mill, JS: Collected Works; Toronto, University of Toronto Press, 1969

Moody, HR: *Ethics in An Aging Society*; Baltimore, Johns Hopkins University Press, 1992

Moody, HR: *Ethics in an Aging Society*; Baltimore, Johns Hopkins University Press, 1992

Osler, W: *Aequanimitas*, Third Ed; Phila, P. Blakiston's Son and Co, 1932

Pellegrino, ED and Thomasma, DC: *A Philosophical Basis of Medical Practice*; New York, Oxford University Press, Inc, 1981

Pellegrino, ED and Thomasma, DC: *The Virtues in Medical Practice*; New York, Oxford University Press, 1993

Pellegrino, ED; and Thomasma DC: *For the Patient's Good: The Restoration of Beneficence in Health Care*; New York, Oxford University Press, 1988

Pence, G: *Ethical Opinions in Medicine*; Oradel, NJ, Medical Economics, 1980

Physicians' Desk Reference: 55th Ed, Medical Economics Co, NJ, 2001

President's Commission for Ethical Problems in Medicine. Defining Death; Washington, D.C., U.S. Government Printing Office, 1981

President's Commission for the Study of Ethical Problems in Medicine and BioMedical and Behavioral Research. Making Health Care Decisions; Vols 1-3; Washington, D.C.,

Quill, TE: *Death and Dignity*; New York, W.W. Norton and Co, 1993

Rachels, J: *The End of Life*; New York, Oxford University Press, 1986

Ramsey, P: *Ethics at the Edges of Life*; New Haven, Yale University Press, 1978

Rawls, J: *A Theory of Justice*; Cambridge, MA, Harvard University Press, 1971

Rodwin, MA.: *Medicine, Money and Morals: Physicians' Conflicts of Interest*; New York, Oxford University Press, 1993

Shenkin, HA: *Current Dilemmas in Medical-Care Rationing*; Lanham, MO, University Press of America, Inc, 1996

Sidgwick, H: *The Methods of Ethics*, Indianapolis, IN; Hackett Publishing Co, 1981

Singer, P: *Practical Ethics*, Second Ed; New York, Cambridge University Press, 1993

Snyder, L: Ed, Ethical Choices: Case Studies for Medical Practic; Phila, American College of Physicians, 1996

Sperry, WL: *The Ethical Basis of Medical Practice*; New York, Harper and Bros, 1950

Starr, P: *The Logic of Health Care Reform*; Knoxville, TN, Whittle Direct Books, 1993

Steinbock, B: *Life Before Birth: The Moral and Legal Status of Embryos and Fetuses*; New York, Oxford University Press, 1992

Suzuki, D and Knudtson, P: *Genetics; The Clash Between the New Genetics and Human Values*; Cambridge, Harvard University Press, 1990

Tooley, M: *Abortion and Infanticide*; New York, Oxford University Press, 1983

Tribe, L: *Abortion: The Clash of Absolutes*; New York, W.W.Norton, 1990

Veatch, RM, Ed: *Medical Ethics*, Second Ed; Boston, Jones and Bartlett Publishing, 1989

Veatch, RM: Case *Studies in Medical Ethics*; Cambridge, MA, Harvard University Press, 1977

Vibbert, S: *The Doctor Watchers—How the Pros Police Medicine*; Knoxville, TN, Whittle Direct Books, 1991

Walzer, M: *Spheres of Justice*; New York, Basic Books, 1983

Warner, R: *The Greek Philosopher*; The New American Library, 1962

Wertz, DC and Fletcher, JC, Eds: *Ethics and Human Genetics:* A Cross-Cultural Perspective; New York, Springer-Verlag, 1989

Williams, B: *Ethics and the Limits of Philosophy*; Cambridge, MA, Harvard University Press, 1985

INDEX